KT-363-600

Acknowledgements

We should like to thank the many experts who have provided information for this book and the freelance and self-employed people who have contributed to Part 2, particularly those who have answered questionnaires and allowed us to reproduce their comments.

We should be grateful for readers' comments and suggestions. There are as many ways of running small businesses as there are proprietors, and any advice on methods other than those we have indicated will be considered for inclusion in future editions of the book.

Comments or suggestions should be sent c/o the publishers.

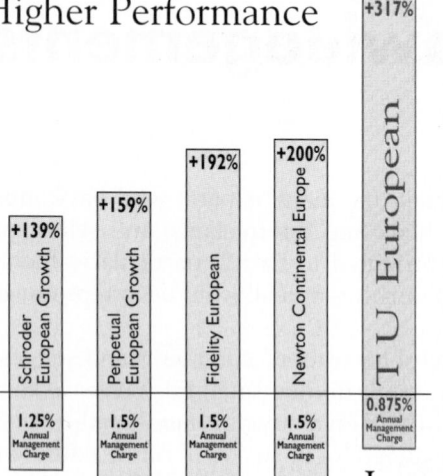

The Daily Telegraph

Guide to
Working
for
Yourself

TWENTIETH
EDITION

Godfrey Golzen
&
Helen Kogan

KOGAN
PAGE

First published in 1975
Sixteenth edition 1995
Seventeenth edition 1997
Eighteenth edition 1998
Nineteenth edition 1999
Twentieth edition 2000

Kogan Page Limited
120 Pentonville Road
London N1 9JN

© Godfrey Golzen, contributors and Kogan Page Ltd, 1995, 1997, 1998, 1999, 2000

British Library Cataloguing in Publication Data

A CIP record for this book is available from the British Library.

ISBN 0 7494 3309 4

Typeset by Jean Cussons Typesetting, Diss, Norfolk
Printed and bound in Great Britain by Thanet Press Ltd, Margate

Contents

Contents

Preface

The recession of the early 1990s showed that businesses which depend heavily on financial support from the banks and which are based on optimistic cash-flow forecasts are very vulnerable. That lesson still holds true. Those that do best are either service businesses with low overheads, those that have genuinely spotted a gap in the market (but are flexible about moving into other opportunities the moment they sense their business section going off the boil) or those that manage to plug into an enduring, recession-proof niche.

THE SCOPE OF THE BOOK

Those who become self-employed, whether full-time or part-time, are joining a trend which, whatever the state of the UK economy, remains on an upward curve. The Department for Education and Employment estimates that the total number of self-employed people is around 3.3 million – around 13 per cent of the workforce.

They are, however, a diverse group and not all will flourish equally or consistently. They include: sales and distribution, specialist consultancy, catering and tourism, technology and cleaning services, skilled crafts and techniques (especially where one person can offer more than one skill), and the professions. In this book the last-named group have been excluded because although there are certain sections of it that they would find helpful, there are nevertheless crucial differences between running a professional practice like that of an architect, doctor or lawyer, and an ordinary business. Otherwise we have identified the self-employed as falling into the following broad categories.

☐ People working part-time, often from home, in addition to a main job, perhaps as an interim stage to setting up a full-time business of their own.

- ☐ Freelances who provide a service and work full-time for several different principals.
- ☐ Those who provide goods and services as sole traders or partners, usually from premises other than their own home.
- ☐ Shareholders in small private companies who are also working directors. They are not strictly speaking self-employed, being employees of the companies they control, but in every practical sense the lessons of this book apply to them.

For any enterprise, Part 1, which covers the problems of raising capital, making financial projections and understanding commercial and employment law, will be useful. But it is particularly valuable as a crash course in basic business principles for those starting a small business. Yet the person (designer, typist, teacher, etc) who is simply supplementing his or her income by some freelance work will also find something of value in Part 1: how to assess yourself for tax purposes, the importance of proper invoicing, the part played by professional advisers, and the need to plan workload and meet schedules.

Though the reader should be aware of the several 'audiences' at which the book is aimed and should pay closest attention to the section which is of most direct concern, profit may also be gained from the other sections. And, who knows, today's freelance book designer may tomorrow have his or her own art studio, with staff to manage, creditors to satisfy and clients to cultivate. The section on business management will at least make you aware of the problems and pressures of expanding the scope of any business, and of the pleasures that come with success.

The second part of this book looks at some specific self-employment opportunities which are divided broadly between those that require capital investment – if on a small scale – and those where the level of investment is minimal or even non-existent. The range of activities described is obviously not comprehensive, but it covers, if briefly, some of the areas in which people thinking of self-employment have been found to be most interested. Certainly the principles that emerge are those that can be applied to any type of enterprise one cares to look at.

- ☐ Consider the drawbacks
- ☐ Be realistic about the risk you are taking
- ☐ Be aware of the competition to what you offer
- ☐ Be certain that your enterprise is financially sound
- ☐ Know and act within the law as it applies to you
- ☐ Use professional advice where necessary
- ☐ Fulfil commissions accurately and on time
- ☐ Commit yourself totally to a project.

These principles apply to the man or woman with a medium-sized business as much as to the retailer or restaurateur, the part-time editor, typist or translator. If a service is required and completion is guaranteed to a satisfactory standard, people are prepared to pay for it – a reputation is established and customers return. An established group of clients provide a basis on which to expand and perhaps diversify, and, if this is achieved without standards falling, the process will be repeated. Whatever your area of interest and size of operation, we hope that our advice aids that process and enables you to avoid the pitfalls and enjoy the profits of self-employment.

Age is no barrier to starting up a business. Indeed some recent research by Barclays Bank shows that around 50,000 small businesses are started by people over 50 every year. The average annual turnover of these third age businesses is £72,000 as compared to £113,000 for younger entrepreneurs, but start up costs are also lower, averaging £7000. In part this may reflect their more modest ambitions, but since over-50s businesses are mostly run from home, it also shows the advantages of not rushing into renting premises until you have to – a lesson that also emerges in later pages of this book: never buy unless you can't rent or lease, never rent or lease unless you can't borrow.

It is interesting to note, however, that although most third age entrepreneurs start their businesses with their own funds, a significant minority do get bank loans and in most cases they report that they have experienced no difficulty or age discrimination in this regard.

Since they mostly work from home, what do they need funding for? The surprising answer in many cases is that it is to buy computers and other technological aids. In spite of the fact that older workers are sometimes alleged to be less than comfortable with new technology, two thirds of older entrepreneurs use computers and a quarter are on e-mail.

These third age businesses are far from being a sideline. Though it is true that in most cases their owners have other sources of income and are working more to keep busy and interested than because they need the money, they work quite a long week: 35 hours on average. Where they do take things a bit easier is over the matter of holidays. Over one third report that they take three weeks holiday a year or more, whereas younger entrepreneurs often complain that their work barely leaves them any time off at all. That supports the claim that as people get older they are able to work smarter rather than harder.

Throughout this book, male and female pronouns have been used randomly. This implies no sexual discrimination; in most cases the opposite applies equally, and the reader's good sense will know when this is not so.

The text of this book was correct at the time of going to press. It incorporates the 2000 Budget, but readers should note the tendency to bring in further fiscal measures between Finance Acts.

Try this
at Home

EVERY ROOM SERVICE

Computer/Networking ✓
Internet ✓
Satellite & Cable TV ✓
Telephone & Fax ✓
Audio ✓
CCTV Monitoring ✓
Alarm System ✓

ORTRONICS

Whether you're running a business from home or you just want to monitor your childrens' activities, our *In-House* structured cabling system keeps you in control of all your communications needs - wherever you are in the building. Contact us today to find out how *In-House* can connect you to the lifestyle of the future.

Ortronics International Limited
Liberty House, New Greenham Park, Newbury RG19 6HW
Tel: +44 (0)1635 817 550   Fax: +44 (0)1635 817560

email: salesuk@ortronics.com.uk web: www.ortronics.com

Yes – but is the house ready for you?

By Martin Ashton

For anyone considering the option of working from home – an option which is becoming more and more viable today with the increasing choice of communication systems available down a telephone line – one of the most important but least obvious considerations is the house itself and its ability to cope with the ever-increasing range of modern communication systems.

There are usually two choices for someone approaching the decision to change their place of work to their home – conversion of an existing room, or construction of a totally new office.

If you intend to take over an existing room in your home for an office for the next few years, you must obviously give serious consideration to your communication needs during that time. The connection facilities you will need include:

1) Sufficient power points for computer, scanner, monitor, fax machines, VCR, mobile telephone charger, etc. It is not safe to use just one double socket with countless adaptors – preferable by far is to install upto 6 separate sockets for today's modern business needs. In addition, of course, the computer should be protected from current fluctuations by a surge protector – a relatively cheap device which simply interfaces between the computer and your mains power supply.

2) Sufficient telephone points for current and future needs. You may decide, on grounds of cost-saving, to start with just one business line for all external communication facilities – telephone, fax and Internet. However, you will soon find as the business grows that there is an increasing need to be on the phone and on the Internet at the same time – or maybe you want to send an urgent fax while reading some other vital e-mail. You can overcome this by ensuring in advance that the existing line to your home is upgraded to ISDN standards, enabling you to use the fax and Internet at the same time, or by adding an extra one or two additional lines. At the moment, many suppliers are providing quite large cost-saving deals on additional phone lines to domestic premises, and if you go down this route you will be assured of log-jam free external communications for the future.

If there is any chance of expanding your at-home business into other parts of the building, the problems of internal communication become as important as those of external communications outlined above. Consider, for instance, what would happen if, in a couple of years, you decide you need some part-time administrative help. Is there room in your existing office for another person? If not, where will they be located? Are there sufficient power and telephone points to support a second person? Will you have networking links between the two computers?

At this point, it would become an expensive and highly disruptive operation to upgrade the telephone, electric and communications systems within the structure of the building – so perhaps it would be more sensible to consider our second option – to design your new office building from scratch.

Construction from new

Whether you decide to go ahead with building a new office as an extension to your home or as a new stand-alone building, or whether you intend to move to a new home which is able to carry both your domestic and business needs, then all the principles outlined above must be considered.

In addition, the speed at which new advances in communication technology are coming on line makes it imperative that your future office is built to a sufficiently high standard that it will be able to accept modern technological improvements such as UMTS – Universal Mobile Telecommunications Systems. UMTS allows high-speed Internet access, video-conferencing, e-mail and a range of other information services to be transmitted to mobile phone handsets. This third-generation system will enable you to contact your home from your mobile telephone and operate appliances – turn on the central heating, check security by linking up with the security cameras, even draw the curtains and switch some lights on. Brilliant in concept, certainly – but what use is UMTS if your house cannot respond?

Ortronics International is a global organization based in Newbury, Berkshire, that has come up with the perfect answer to this and countless other similar internal and external communication needs. Developed in the USA, the Ortronics *In-House* system has been designed to provide an impressive range of benefits when it is incorporated into a home or small office – preferably at the build stage.

In-House is a complete structured cabling system that supports audio, video, data, voice, computer networking, Internet access and security monitoring systems throughout the whole of the building. The *In-House* system uses a central Control Cabinet as the hub of the communication system which can be equipped with any number of modules – comparable in some ways to building blocks – which in turn provide links to the audio, voice, data or video systems. The Cabinet itself can be located anywhere in the house – under the stairs, at the back of a built-in wardrobe – but not in areas of high humidity such as utility rooms housing washing machines, tumble driers, etc.

The Control Box, hub of the Ortronics In-House system

For a building equipped with a full structured cable system, the modules can be added as and when needed – initially, perhaps, to provide audio around the building so that you can be playing your favourite CD or keeping an eye on the kids playing in the garden while you work. You want coffee – so as you go into the kitchen you simply turn up the music in the kitchen speakers (and in the hall or any other rooms on the way) or switch the monitors over to the CCTV system. The flexibility in life-style that an *In-House* system can bring is almost unbelievable – the full range of computer, telephone and television services accessible in every room, the ability to see what your security or baby-monitoring cameras are seeing whenever you want, wherever you are, internal computer networking, and a lot, lot more.

And for someone considering working from home, the benefits are even greater – no more having to dedicate a family room or spare bedroom specially for an office. The Ortronics system allows you to work wherever you want in the building, with full and instant access to your computer and all external communication systems. So no more working from a cramped back bedroom or converted loft, you can work in whichever room you want, wherever you want with immediate and uninterrupted communication facilities to your family, colleagues and friends always available.

There is no doubt this is going to be the environment for the standard-setting home business of the future – but the future has already arrived, for Midas Homes are currently in the final stages of the development of over 50 new homes, every one of which incorporates an Ortronics *In-House*

system. Each home has been wired up to provide an average of 40 data outlets, 8 TV outlets, CCTV facilities at the front and rear, wall or ceiling speakers wherever required (yes, before you ask – even in the bathroom if required!) and sufficient integral wiring to cope with all immediate and long-term future needs.

A modern executive home which has been built to the highest IT standards, including the Ortronics In-House system.

(photograph courtesy of Midas Homes)

Even if it's not primarily used for work, the *In-House* system is perfect for today's modern family as it keeps pace with the benefits that technology can bring to their home – and the home in question can be anything from an apartment to a castle, for the *In-House* system is perfect for any building, no matter how big or small.

So the house of the future is now available in the UK – and if you don't want to move to keep up with the latest in-home technology, you must at least move on to consider the *In-House* concept – a building that is fully wired-up for the future, even if you're not.

*Martin Ashton,
UK Vice President,
Ortronics International Ltd*

 **AND**

TAKING HOME SECURITY AND HOMEBASED BUSINESSES INTO A NEW ERA

Trends

Perhaps the most important aspect of starting your own small business or working for yourself is timing. Finding the right product or service at the right time for the market place in a pioneering phase of a product or service's growth has propelled many start up businesses to enormous success. Identifying a growth trend or trends is critical to all business success. Trends are not short lived fads such as "Yo Yo's" that create short term wealth for a few, but waves that build up and up over decades like the plastics industry in the 1960's, the Electronics Industries in the seventies, and the IT industries in the eighties and nineties. Trends can also be socio-economic developments influenced by people's desires, concerns, dissatisfactions or age demographics of the population. A single trend can create millions of opportunities for new businesses, as well as existing corporations. It is, however, in pioneering new product's or services in new industries influenced by people's desires where the greatest opportunity lies in working for yourself. It is widely agreed that what happens in the U.S.A., in terms of growth trends, transfers to the UK, Europe and the rest of the World four to five years after it starts there.

ADT Fire and Security, part of the $22 Billion turnover Tyco International, and Homesafe Intelligent Systems offer any individual looking to start their own homebased business the unique opportunity of pioneering a product and service and a business system that is on track with multiple trends. It is also backed up by a track record of phenomenal growth rates and proven success in the USA.

On Trend

Perhaps the biggest socio-economic trend is people's desire for financial freedom and time freedom. Dissatisfaction working for someone else, due to longer hours, commuting nightmares and job insecurity make the UK workers, according to a recent survey, the most miserable in industrialised Europe with 70% of workers stressed and dissatisfied. This situation is fuelling an enormous wave of growth into homebased businesses. In the USA it is estimated that more than 20 million people are running their own part time (with aims of transferring to full time once the income is high enough) or full time homebased businesses.

Another major sociological trend is the acceptance and power of the personal recommendation from one satisfied customer to another, rather than the reliance on the seduction of multi-million pound advertising campaigns. Consumer power is here to stay. Look at the growth in consumer advocacy programmes and organisations. The people want quality, service, value and honesty from companies. This has led to a fast growing sector of distribution where a company takes it's products and services directly to the consumer based on recommendation and referral marketing, one satisfied customer to another.

But probably the most worrying trend in modern society today, (driven by huge media publicity), is the fear of crime and the fundamental desire for security of themselves, their families and their possessions.

The Market Place

Being burgled is everyone's nightmare come true. The intrusion into people's lives and their belongings being stolen or damaged can cause extreme physical and emotional distress. Over one million homes were burgled in the UK last year. It is widely believed that the market place for Intelligent Security is poised on the edge of an enormous growth curve. This enormous growth will be specifically in the demand and requirement for monitored and maintained intelligent alarm systems, which provide 24 hour, 365 days per year protection and qualify for police response.

In the UK, as in other countries, the market place for security products has been set back to day one by the recent directive from the Association of Chief Police Officers (ACPO), which stated that the police would no longer respond to any "unverified" alarm activations. Currently less than 1% of UK and European households have a protection system that qualifies for police response to an alarm activation. Experts are predicting that within ten years more than 5 million homes in the UK will have a recognised and approved intelligent monitored and maintained protection system that qualifies for a police issued unique reference number (URN) and therefore Level 1 Police response. In America over 100,000 monitored and maintained systems are being connected per month!!

The Ultimate Protection. The Ultimate Companies

ADT, part of Tyco International, is the biggest Security Company in the world and has been serving the UK for over 100 years. Now in conjunction with Homesafe Intelligent Systems, who have specialised in the UK Domestic market for twenty years, they are seeking a network of Associates to pioneer their state of the art Intelligent products throughout the UK and on into Europe. The product is professionally installed by security screened engineers. It is approved by NACOSS, BSIA or SSAIB (The Major Industry Associations) and recognised by ACPO (The Association of Chief Police Officers). When activated, the system, which costs from £299.00 fully installed and inclusive of VAT with moni-

toring and maintenance at less than 99 pence per day, communicates instantly via the telephone line all relevant details and what is happening in your home. The 24 hour alarm receiving centre and the 24 hour security staff directly linked to your home initiate a response procedure in seconds informing the Emergency Services utilising the police issued unique reference number.

The Ultimate Business Opportunity

No prior experience, nor investment is necessary to become a Homesafe Associate and a full and free training programme is provided in the initial stages and on an ongoing basis. The business is run from your own home on a part time or full time basis with no requirements for premises, employees, equipment or stock holding. There is both immediate money, rapid profits and monthly recurring revenue from every single customer creating a monthly residual income that could create financial freedom. The income stream is so flexible that the Homesafe business could be used to supplement your existing income by £200 to £300 per week or it could become a national or international business with no limit to the income potential.

As Homesafe's Chief Executive, Paul Dodds comments: "We have the right product at the right price at the right time. Using recommendation, the most ethical way of distributing products or services, and our unique proven customer generation system, you are able to offer to an untapped marketplace, 24 hour protection with police response 365 days a year. A service of tremendous value and something you can really feel proud of.

This is an opportunity where anyone, regardless of their background or experience, can achieve tremendous satisfaction coupled with the highest part time or full time incomes. All your success requires is a little vision, some commitment and effort and a good work ethic."

Homesafe Tel No: 0870 443 5000
Website: www.homesafeintelligent.com
EMail: info@homesafeintelligent.com

PITNEY BOWES LAUNCHES UNIQUE MAILING PRODUCT FOR HOMEWORKERS AND SOHO BUSINESSES

Pitney Bowes launched a new desktop digital mailing system aimed at SoHo businesses and homeworkers. The small device, called PersonalPost™, applies a postal frank impression to all sizes of envelope or parcel at a rate of up to ten items per minute. The product is currently the only one of its kind to be developed specifically for the mailing requirements of small businesses and home workers.

The PersonalPost? product automates many of the administrative processes associated with handling mail. Rather than having to make trips out of the home or office for stamps, PersonalPost? allows users to download postage over a telephone line within 30 seconds.

The system, which weighs just over 2.5 kilograms (under six pounds), comes with a set of postal scales to help users avoid overstamping (where excess postage is applied to individual mail items). The device also provides comprehensive accounting facilities for accurate postal record keeping.

Pitney Bowes' PersonalPost? includes a facility for automatic mail dating – usually only available on more expensive systems – to prevent improperly dated mail from being returned.

New MORI research for Pitney Bowes indicates that two-thirds (66%) of SoHo businesses feel franked mail looks more professional than stamped mail. The new product enables small businesses and home workers to frank even small volumes of mail and still post it into standard Royal Mail post boxes. Pitney Bowes has targeted the SoHo user with its new pricing. PersonalPost? is available for £595 (+VAT) to buy, or £19.95 (+VAT) per month to rent.

In addition to a frank postal mark, SoHo businesses can use any of the eight pre-loaded advertising slogans within PersonalPost? to improve the appearance of their mail. Alternatively, they can design and install their own company logo or special message.

"The SoHo sector encompasses the overwhelming majority of Britain's businesses and the sector's performance will continue to have a major impact on the country's economic well-being," commented Steve Hornsey, vice president Marketing & Office Direct, Pitney Bowes. "However, it's now clear that smaller organisations are failing to recognise the hidden financial impact of time spent on their own admin. Greater office automation has an obvious role to play in helping these companies grow."

He continued: "Pitney Bowes is the first supplier to produce a product for the SoHo market that has a significant role to play in improving the cost-effectiveness of SoHo business communications. Convenience has also been considered and as a result, PersonalPost? can be purchased on-line from the Pitney Bowes website."

About Pitney Bowes

Pitney Bowes is the world's leading provider of mailing and messaging products for organisations and businesses of all sizes. The company offers a full range of mailing equipment and related financial services and is actively developing new communications products and technologies.

The company is currently introducing a range of digital franking machines, all of which enjoy the advantages of being recredited on line. The 'third generation' in franking machines, these digital machines are software-driven. This means they can be easily upgraded, integrated with computer networks, and provide businesses with comprehensive management information about the mailing operation.

Pitney Bowes has a growing portfolio of Internet-enabled mail and messaging solutions, including internet-based metering technology. These systems, which will allow users to download postage from the Internet were invented by Pitney Bowes. Pitney Bowes also has the ability to manage the electronic delivery of documents from iSend which provides secure e-mail transmission over public networks, to Digital Document Delivery or D3, which allows firms to deliver employee and customer communications such as bill in either electronic or paper formats.

Pitney Bowes' vision is to draw upon its heritage in mailing systems by becoming a complete provider of messaging management services ? to add value to a company's total messaging throughput, encompassing both electronic and paper-based communications.

Since the establishment of the company in 1920, Pitney Bowes has grown to become a global business with a turnover of four billion euros (US$4.4 billion) and in 1999 achieved a significant climb in the FT500 survey of the world's leading companies. Pitney Bowes Inc. is listed on the New York Stock Exchange (NYSE: PBI) and can be seen on the Internet at www.pitney-bowes.co.uk

Run out of stamps? Again?

UK Postal Rates

Weight up to	1st Class	2nd Class
		19p
60g	26p	31p
100g	39p	41p
150g	52p	

PersonalPost™

The first franking machine for the smaller business.

You know the feeling. That urgent letter just has to go, now. But you've just used your last stamp. That's why Pitney Bowes has developed **PersonalPost**™. A desktop franking machine designed specifically for the smaller business that will revolutionise the way you do business.

Taking up an area of desk space only slightly bigger than a sheet of A4 paper, it neatly and efficiently franks any letter or parcel. It also prints your company logo or message, giving all your mail a professional image. A built-in modem allows you to purchase postage over the phone in just 90 seconds, so you'll never run out of stamps again. What could be simpler?

And with £10 of free postage when you order, it's frankly too good an offer to miss.

To find out more, call **0800 636 434**
Lines open Mon to Fri 8.30am - 6.00pm

Pitney Bowes

Keeping small offices posted
www.pitneybowes.co.uk

P119

Part One:

Running Your Own Business

1.1 Going it Alone

Between 1979 and 2000 the percentage of self-employed people in the total UK workforce rose from 7.4 to almost 13 per cent. That was a bigger jump than in any other European Union country, though it does no more than bring the UK up to around the European average, which is 15 per cent.

The important place of self-employment in the economy reflects the changing pattern of employment generally. Big employers in all sectors are cutting down their payrolls and buying in services from outside as and when they need them. Increasingly that may be true for some goods as well. A logical consequence of just-in-time manufacturing is that components as well as raw materials are sourced from the outside.

But the growth in self-employment is being driven by social as well as economic factors. Self-employment is sometimes seen as an alternative to unemployment. Certainly, this is true in some cases, but the evidence is that more people choose self-employment than are forced into it for lack of an alternative. A lot of people simply prefer it to working for someone else, particularly since the concept of a safe job no longer has any place in this age of mergers, acquisitions and rationalisations.

They are being encouraged in this course of action by the government, which has rationalised numerous initiatives to help small businesses by establishing a single initial point of contact, especially in start-up situations: Business Links (called Business Connect in Wales and Business Shop in Scotland).

The Business Link is the first place to go to for advice and information and co-ordinates the efforts of Training and Enterprise Councils (TECs), which are called Local Enterprise Companies in Scotland, Chambers of Commerce, local authorities and Local Enterprise Agencies. Depending on the nature of your request, they will or should direct you to the appropriate body, for example for advice on training, the availability of funding and consultancy services, premises and even business opportunities. For details of your local Business Link, ring 08457 567765.

WHO ARE THE SELF-EMPLOYED?

Research by the Institute of Employment Studies *(Self-Employment in the United Kingdom* by Nigel Meager) has come up with some interesting conclusions:

- ☐ Men are more likely to be self-employed than women, though the number of self-employed females has been going up rapidly.
- ☐ More older people are self-employed, which may be a reflection of the fact that the self-employed do not have to retire.
- ☐ More married than single people are self-employed, which points to the importance of the spouse (possibly as unpaid help?) in self-employment.
- ☐ More highly qualified women than men are self-employed, which may be a reflection of the difficulties women continue to experience in getting to senior positions in a great many firms.
- ☐ Self-employed people work considerably longer hours than their counterparts in the employed sector.

WHAT SELF-EMPLOYED PEOPLE DO

As might be expected, self-employment is stronger in the service sector than in manufacturing. The arts, building trades and management services feature prominently. Over the past decade entry into self-employment has been disproportionately high in financial, business and personal services such as catering and cleaning.

This also points to the nature of the market for self-employment. It is mistaken romanticism to think that we can go back to a society of individual craftspeople without an unacceptable drop in our standard of living. But maybe, it has been argued, we should leave to machines what machines do best, and get human beings to cater to the individual taste, the quirky needs, the one-off problems and the sudden emergencies and breakdowns that machines cannot handle.

This is certainly where the opportunities for the self-employed lie, and one of the objects of this preamble is to make an important practical point. The game the giants play has its limitations, but do not take them on direct. If, for instance, you are a skilled cabinet-maker, do not get into mass-produced furniture: you simply will not be able to get your prices down far enough to make a living, nor will you be able to handle distribution on the scale that mass production implies. Do something the giants do not do, such as making things to individual specification. If you have always wanted to own a grocery shop, do not do the same thing as the supermarket round the corner. Bake your own bread or make your delicatessen stay open round the clock – do something you can do better or differently.

HOW WELL PREPARED ARE YOU?

Having a sound idea is only part of the story. How prepared you are to take it further depends on the extent of your experience; not that it is absolutely essential at the 'thinking about it' stage to have all-round direct experience of the sort of self-employment opportunity you want to exploit. But you have to be aware of what you know and do not know about it. You may be a manager who is also a keen gardener and you want to set up a market gardening business. In that case you probably have a rather better knowledge of management essentials than that of a hypothetical competitor who is currently employed by a market gardener and wants to set up on his or her own. But on the finer points of growing techniques and hazards, and where to sell the products, your competitor is going to be much better equipped than you.

The first step, therefore, is to make a list of all the aspects you can think of about running the business: show it to someone who is already in the field to make sure nothing of importance has

Table 1.1   *Industry sectors for business starters*

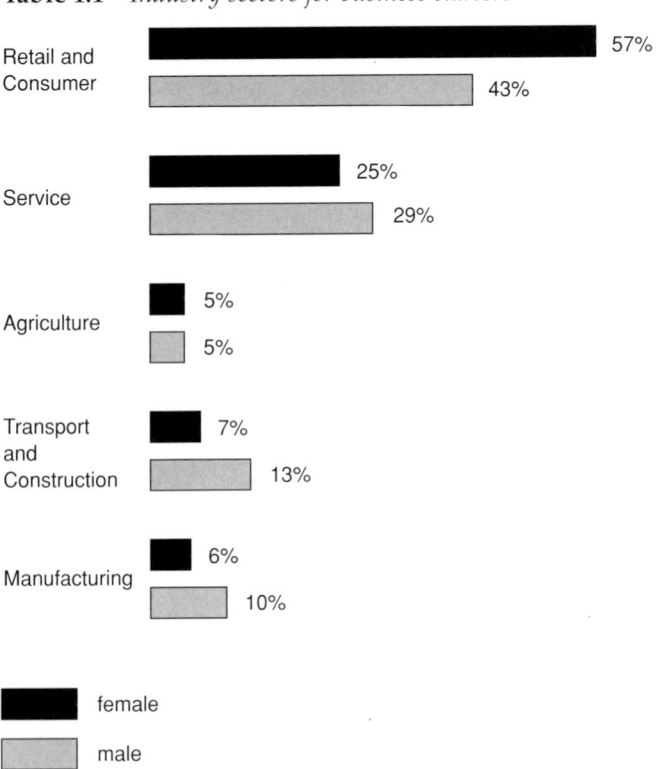

Source: Barclays Bank Small Business Characteristics

been missed out, and tick off the ones you think you can handle and consider how you are going to deal with the areas where your experience is limited. The best way may well be to gain practical first-hand experience. If you are thinking of buying a shop, for instance, working in one for a few weeks will teach you an amazing amount about the public's tastes – what sells and what does not – and you may save yourself hundreds of pounds in making the right buying decisions later on. As far as management principles are concerned, your library will provide you with lists for further reading.

You should also take advice from your local Training and Enterprise Council (Local Enterprise Company in Scotland). They fund the various Local Enterprise Agencies and are the prime source of information on training and other forms of support for local business. Information is free and counselling incurs only a modest charge. You should also ask about the business start-up courses that are being offered by business schools such as Cranfield School of Management. These courses are heavily

What was your employment status before starting up your new business?*	
Self-employed	16%
Employed full-time	52%
Employed part-time	6%
Student/full-time education	10%
Unemployed	9%
Other	6%

*Survey of small businesses with turnover of less than £1 million

Source: Barclays Bank Small Business Bulletin

subsidised by the government and are very good value for the modest fees they charge. By all accounts, attending such a course will dramatically increase your chances of small business success.

The small-business boom is attracting publishers in droves and it is already possible to spend quite a lot of money on books of advice of varying quality. It is worth mentioning, therefore, that several of the clearing banks have got into the act and are producing free books and pamphlets, some of which are very good. Ask your bank manager for any such material.

THE IMPORTANCE OF PLANNING

If you are going to borrow money to get your firm off the ground, the lender (if he has any sense!) will want to know how you plan to use his money and if the operation you have in mind is going to give him an adequate return on his investment. This means that you must have a clear idea of how your business is going to develop, at least for the next year, where you see work coming from and whether you are going to have the future resources, human and financial, to handle it (see Chapter 1.9 on the importance of cash flow and financial forecasting).

Even if you do not need to borrow money, planning is vital. Landing a big contract or assignment for a new business is a heartening beginning, but well before work on it is completed you should be looking around for the next job. The completion dates you have given should take this into account, unless the amount of money you are going to get from it is so much that you will have plenty of time to look for more work after this first job is done. But that, too, is a matter of planning.

IS SELF-EMPLOYMENT RIGHT FOR YOU?

Let us leave aside Samuel Smiles-like homilies about having to be your own hardest taskmaster. We will take it for granted that you are not considering working for yourself as a soft option. But apart from the question of whether your health can stand the fairly demanding regime that full-time self-employment implies, there are also other questions you have to ask yourself about your aptitude – as opposed to a mere hankering – for going it alone. First of all, there are severely practical considerations: whether you have enough money or the means of raising it. And remember you will need money not only to finance your business or practice, but also for your own personal needs, including sickness and holiday periods.

Self-employment may mean a drop in your standard of living, possibly a permanent one, if things do not go as planned. Are you prepared for that? Is your family going to like it? Have you seriously considered the full price to be paid for independence? Is your wife or husband able and willing to lend a hand?

Insecurity, a necessary condition of self-employment, is not everyone's cup of tea. Neither are some of the implications of being your own boss. One of the most important of them is the ability to make decisions and if you very much dislike doing this, self-employment is probably not the right channel for your abilities. You are constantly going to be called on to make decisions, some of them rather trivial, where it does not matter greatly what you do decide so long as you decide *something*; but some of them will be fundamental policy decisions that could make or break your business.

You are also going to be called on to make decisions about people, and these are often the hardest of all. It is extremely difficult to sack someone with whom you have worked in the intimacy of a small office, but sooner or later that kind of situation will land in your lap. So another quality that is called for is toughness. This does not mean overbearing nastiness, but it does mean the readiness, for instance, to part company with a supplier, even if she is a personal friend, if her service starts to fall consistently below standard.

We have touched on the question of your aptitude for self-employment as such, but there remains the matter of your aptitude for the sphere of activity you have chosen. A management consultant friend of mine uses a basic precept in advising companies on personnel problems: staff are best employed doing what they are best at. The same applies to self-employment and most people go into it with that in mind. The problem with self-employment, however, is that at least at the outset you cannot absolutely avoid all the aspects of the work, such as bookkeeping, that in a bigger organisation you might have delegated or passed on to another department because you yourself do not much enjoy doing them. What you have to do is to maximise the number of tasks you are good at and minimise the others. This may mean taking a partner to complement your skills or employing an outside agency to handle some things for you: selling, for instance, if you are good at making things but not so good at negotiating or dealing with people. That means less money for you, but at the risk of sounding moralistic, you are unlikely to succeed if making money is the only thing you have in mind and overrides considerations such as job satisfaction.

At the same time, the costs of doing anything in business must always be taken into account. For example, if you take a partner, is there going to be enough money coming in to make a living for both of you? Unless you constantly quantify your business decisions in this way, you are unlikely to stay in business very long. In fact, you should not even start on your career as a self-employed person without investigating very carefully whether there is a big and lasting enough demand for the product or service you are proposing to offer, and whether it can be sold at a competitive price that will enable you to earn a living after meeting all the expenses of running a business.

Barclays asked start-ups about the realities of running a small business and found that:

☐ 63% of new-business owners agree that running a new business is stressful;
☐ 90% do not regret setting up their business;
☐ new-small-business owners work an average of 51.5 hours a week and only take five days holiday in their first year.

It is said, of course, that business is a gamble and that there comes the point where you must take the plunge. However, there are certain times when the odds are better than at others. For instance, the closing down of a factory with heavy lay-offs would affect local business conditions, though it may also create opportunities if the demand for what the factory has been producing still continues. You have to weigh up such factors in arriving at the conclusion that your chances of success are better than 50:50. Unless you are reasonably sure you can beat those odds with whatever it is you are setting out to do, you ought to think again or get further advice on how you can either improve your chances or minimise your financial risk.

CHANCES OF SUCCESS

If you have faced the issues we have touched on in the last paragraphs and feel confident about dealing with them, your chances of success in self-employment, whether full-time or part-time, are good. As for the opportunities, they are legion and later we examine what is involved in some areas. The list obviously cannot be comprehensive (though it should serve as a stimulus to looking in other directions as well) and neither can the coverage of basic management techniques in Part 1. But one of the essentials of effective management is to pick out no more from any topic than you need to know to accomplish the task in hand. We hope that these chapters give you the kind of technical information that you will be concerned with at this early stage of your career as a self-employed person.

Table 1.2 *What do you consider to be the main strengths in helping you run your business?*

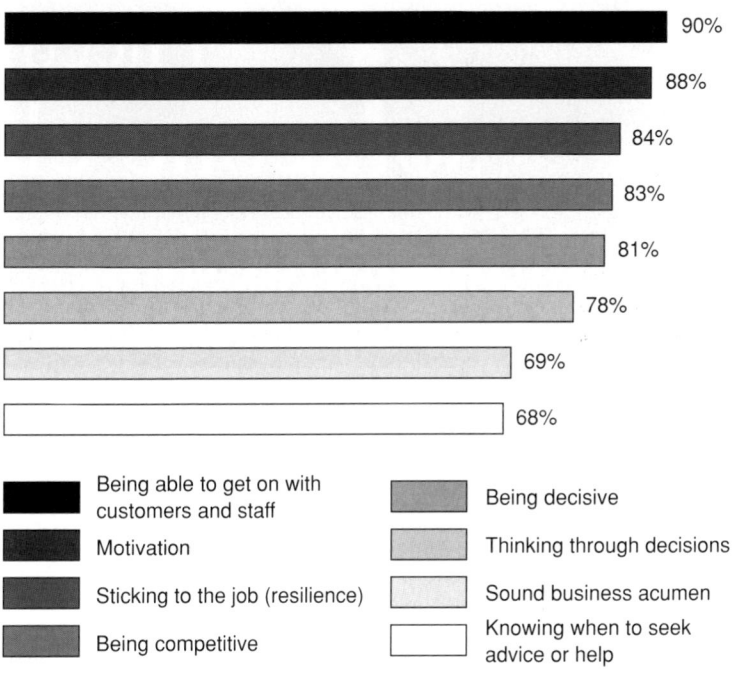

■ Being able to get on with customers and staff	▨ Being decisive	
■ Motivation	▨ Thinking through decisions	
■ Sticking to the job (resilience)	▨ Sound business acumen	
■ Being competitive	□ Knowing when to seek advice or help	

Source: Barclays Bank Small Business Characteristics

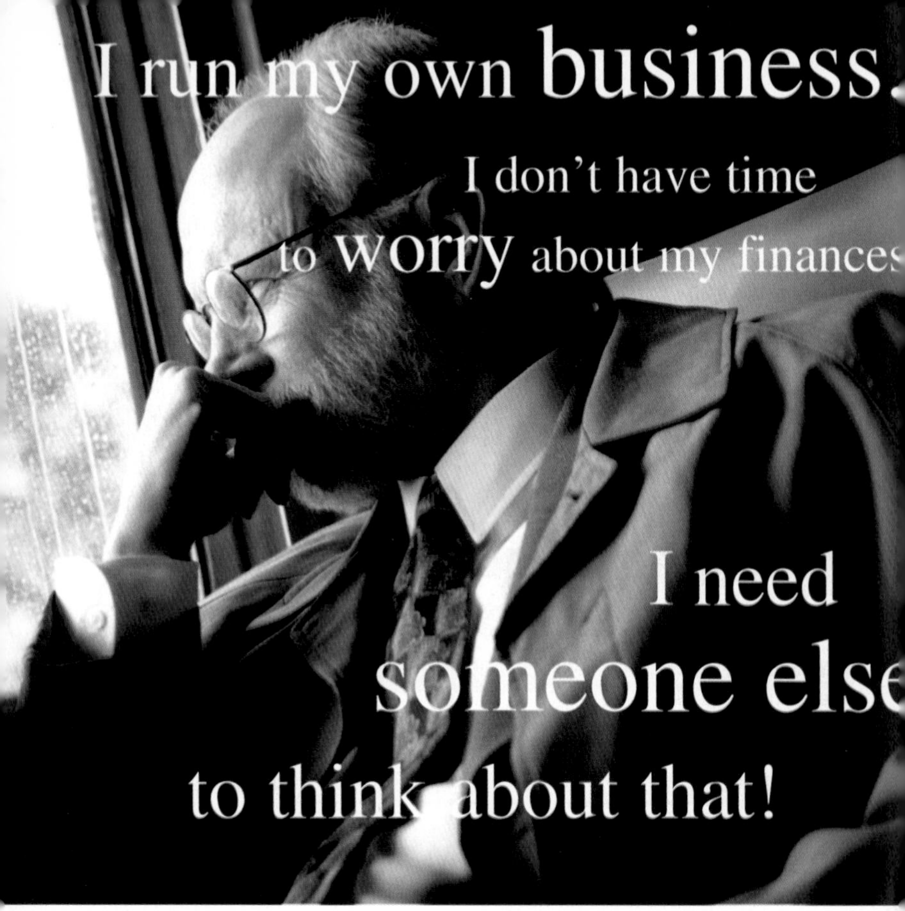

I run my own **business**.

I don't have time

to **worry** about my finances

I need

someone else

to think about that!

You run your own business because you value your independence. And independence means protecting your business. Especially its key asset – you!

At Lincoln, it's our job to make protecting you, your family and your business clear and understandable. You talk, we listen. Only then will we offer our advice. In a world that's complex enough, you'll be glad to know that it'll be simplicity itself.

For further information or to arrange an appointment, please telephone **free** on
0800 783 0222

Clear solutions in a complex world

Any advice offered relates only to the products of Lincoln Financial Group.
Lincoln is a marketing group regulated by the Personal Investment Authority,
providing life assurance, pensions, unit trusts and ISAs.
Registered office: Barnett Way, Barnwood, Gloucester GL4 3RZ.
Telephone 01452 374500, Fax 01452 374374. **www.lincoln-financialuk.com**

002057 - 5/00

Lincoln
Financial Group

Being self-employed
The real meaning of independence

According to the Oxford English Dictionary, independence is defined as: 'Not depending on another person for one's opinion or livelihood.'

For many, this underlies the attraction of being self-employed. And if you can offer expertise that's hard to find elsewhere, this may even present the opportunity to charge a premium for the service you provide. The increasing number of IT contractors provide a case in point. With increasing reliance on IT and use of the Internet, those with IT skills are sought by practically every company that has put its faith in the microchip.

But while the self-employed are able to reap the benefits of their efforts first hand, very few appreciate the other side to 'going it alone'. By definition, being self employed means forgoing the safety net of a sympathetic employer. And while you may have the support and understanding of your local bank manager, at the end of the day being self-employed really does mean having only yourself to rely on.

It goes without saying that being self-employed means working long hours. So it's unlikely that you will want to use the little spare time that you do have to think about your own financial affairs.

Yet time spent thinking about your own financial situation doesn't only have important benefits for your business, but should also go a long way to providing a more secure future for you and your family. Take the time to scratch beneath the surface, to reflect on your situation and why you are in business in the first place.

Among those questions that you should ask yourself, are:

✳ Do you have enough life cover? Your business may be on the up and up now, but will your family have enough to keep the business going should the worst happen?

✳ Have you made alternative plans for an income, if you were unable to work? And, as you are no longer a member of the state earnings related pension scheme or SERPS, where can you look for a pension in your retirement?

More often than not, investing in the right financial protection or investing for the future is considered to be a luxury – something that a business can only afford when the other overheads and liabilities have been met. So all too frequently, making the right financial plans will be sacrificed in the face of fluctuating earnings or increased pressure from rising costs.

But financial planning, whether it's for a replacement income during periods of long term illness or even your future retirement, is an important part of maintaining the independence that you already enjoy in being self-employed. So the cost must surely be treated like any other business expense.

Lincoln believes that it's important to get the right advice, to help protect the main asset of your business – you.

Wayne Taylor,
Marketing Projects Manager,
Lincoln Financial Group

Lincoln is a marketing group regulated by the Personal Investment Authority providing life assurance, pensions, unit trusts and ISAs. Any regulated advice offered will relate only to the products of Lincoln.

Checklist: going it alone

1. Can you measure the demand for your product or service in terms of money?
2. Who are your competitors and what can you offer that they cannot?
3. Is the market local or national and how can you reach it? Can you measure the cost of doing so in financial terms?
4. How much capital do you have and how easy is it to realise?
5. How much money do you need for start-up costs and if it is more than your capital, how can you make up the difference?
6. How long is it likely to be before your income meets your outgoings and how do you propose to manage until then?
7. Do you have any established contacts who can give you business?
8. Is your proposed activity a one-off opportunity or a line for which there is a continuing demand?
9. What aspects of your proposed activity do you have first-hand experience in and how do you propose to fill the gaps?
10. How good is your health?
11. What are you best at/worst at in your present job and how does this relate to your area of self-employment?
12. Is there any way you can combine your present job with self-employment for an experimental period while you see how it goes?
13. Have you made a realistic appraisal of your aptitude for going it alone, both generally and in the context of the line of work you have chosen?
14. Should you join up with someone else and, if so, is the net income you anticipate going to provide a livelihood for all the people involved?
15. Can you work from home or do you have to be in an office or other rented premises?

1.2 Starting a Business

Before you start talking to bank managers, solicitors, accountants or tax inspectors, you will have to start thinking about what sort of legal entity the business you are going to operate is to be. The kind of advice you seek from them will depend on this decision, and you have three choices. You can operate as a sole trader (ie a one-person business – it does not necessarily have to be a 'trade'), a partnership, or as a private limited company. Let us see what each of these options implies.

SOLE TRADER

There is nothing – or at least very little – to stop you from starting a business under your own name, operating from a back room of your own house.* But if the place you live in is owned by someone else, you should get the landlord's permission. If the business you are starting in your home is one that involves a change of use of the premises, you will have to get planning permission from the local authority's planning officer. In that case you may also find that you are re-rated on a commercial basis. If you own your house, you should also check that there are no restrictive covenants in the deeds governing its use. On the whole, a business conducted unobtrusively from a private residence is unlikely to attract attention from the local authority but, to be perfectly safe, it is as well to have a word with the authority's planning

---

*If your business is likely to disturb neighbours or cause a nuisance (noise, smells, clients taking up parking space) or if it necessitates your building an extension, converting an attic, etc, you must apply for planning permission. Your property may then be given a higher, commercial rateable value.

department since any change of use, even of part of your residence, requires planning permission.

The next step is to inform your local tax inspector or to get your accountant to do so (see Chapter 1.4 on choosing professional advisers). This is always advisable if the nature of your earnings is changing and imperative if you are moving from employee to full-time self-employed status, because it changes the basis on which you pay tax. The inspector will give you some indication of allowable business expenses to be set off against your earnings for tax purposes. These will not include entertainment of potential customers but will cover items 'wholly and exclusively incurred for the purposes of business'. These are spelt out in more detail in Chapter 1.14. Some things, of course, are used partly for private and partly for business purposes – your car or your telephone, for instance. In these cases only that proportion of expenditure that can definitely be attributed to business use is chargeable against tax. Careful records of such use must, therefore, be kept, and its extent must also be credible. If you are not exporting anything in the way of a product or service, you may be unable to convince the inspector that a weekend in Paris was in the course of business! But if you are, he is unlikely to quibble about a modest hotel bill.

The principal cautionary point to bear in mind about operating as a sole trader is that you are personally liable for the debts of your business. If you go bankrupt your creditors are entitled to seize and sell your *personal* possessions, not just equipment, cars and other items directly related to your business.

PARTNERSHIPS

Most of the above points are also true if you are setting up in partnership with other people. Once again, there are very few restrictions against setting up in partnership with someone to carry on a business, but because all the members of a partnership are personally liable for its debts, even if these are incurred by a piece of mismanagement by one partner which was not known to his colleagues, the choice of partners is a step that requires very careful thought. So should you have a partner at all? Certainly it is not advisable to do so just for the sake of having company, because unless the partner can really contribute something to the business, you are giving away a part of what could in time be a very valuable asset to little purpose. A partner should be able to make an important contribution to running the business in an area which you are unable to take care of. He may have some range of specialised expertise that is vital to the business; or he may have a range of contacts to bring in work; or the work may be of such a nature that the executive tasks and decisions cannot be handled by one person. He may even be a 'sleeping partner' who is doing little else apart from putting up some money in return for a share of the eventual profits.

But whatever the reason may be for establishing a partnership as opposed to going it alone and owning the whole business, you should be sure that your partner (of course, there may be more than one, but for the sake of simplicity we will assume that only one person is involved) is someone you know well in a business, not just a social, capacity. Because of this, before formally establishing a partnership it may be advisable to tackle, as an informal joint venture, one or two jobs with the person you are thinking of setting up with, carrying at the end of the day an agreed share of the costs and profits. That way you will learn about each other's strengths and weaknesses, and indeed whether you can work together harmoniously at all. It may turn out, for instance, that your prospective partner's expertise or contacts, while useful, do not justify giving him a share of the business and that in fact a consultancy fee is the right way of remunerating him.

Even if all goes well and you find that you can cooperate, it is vital that a formal partnership agreement should be drawn up by a solicitor. This is true even of husband-and-wife partnerships. The agreement should cover such points as the following:

1. Who is responsible for what aspects of the operation (eg production, marketing)?
2. What constitutes a policy decision (eg whether or not to take on a contract) and how is it taken? By a majority vote, if there is an uneven number of partners? By the partner

concerned with that aspect of things? Only if all partners agree?

3. How are the profits to be divided? According to the amount of capital put in? According to the amount of work done by each partner? Over the whole business done by the partnership over a year? On a job-by-job basis? How much money can be drawn, on what basis, and how often in the way of remuneration?

4. What items, such as cars, not exclusively used for business can be charged to the partnership? And is there any limitation to the amount of money involved?

5. If one of the partners retires or withdraws, how is his share of the business to be valued?

6. If work is done in office hours, outside the framework of the partnership, to whom does the income accrue?

7. What arbitration arrangements are there, in case of irreconcilable differences?

8. If one of the partners dies, what provisions should the other make for his dependants?

There are obviously many kinds of eventualities that have to be provided for, depending on the kind of business that is going to be carried on. Some professional partnerships, for instance, may consist of little more than an agreement to pool office expenses such as the services of typists and telephonists, with partners drawing their own fees quite independently of each other. The best way to prepare the ground for a solicitor to draw up an agreement is for each partner to make a list of possible points of dispute and to leave it to the legal adviser to produce a form of words to cover these and any other points he may come up with.

PRIVATE LIMITED COMPANIES

Legislation over recent years has made it less attractive to start out trading as a limited company unless you are in a form of business that might leave you at risk as a debtor – as might be the case, for instance, if you were a graphic designer commissioning processing on behalf of a client. The reason for this is that, in law, a limited company has an identity distinct from that of the shareholders who are its owners. Consequently, if a limited company goes bankrupt, the claims of the creditors are limited to the assets of the company. This includes any capital issued to shareholders which they have *either paid for in full or in part*. We shall return to the question of share capital in a moment, but the principle at work here is that when shares are issued, the shareholders need not necessarily pay for them in full, though they have a legal obligation to do so if the company goes bankrupt. Shareholders are not, however, liable as individuals, and their private assets outside the company may not be touched unless their company has been trading fraudulently. On the other hand, if creditors ask for personal guarantees, directors of limited companies are not protected and *personal* assets to the amount of the guarantee as well as business assets are at risk in the event of bankruptcy.

There is also another important area where the principle of limited liability does not apply. Company directors are liable, in law, for employees' National Insurance contributions. This is a personal liability which is being enforced by the DSS in the same way as bank guarantees. There have even been cases of non-executive directors of insolvent companies being pursued for non-payment of NI contributions by companies with which they were involved, though the Social Security Act of 1975 states that the directors are only responsible in such circumstances if they 'knew or reasonably could have known' that these were not being paid.

Company directors can also be held guilty of 'wrongful trading', which essentially means trading while they know their company is insolvent. In that case they may be obliged to contribute personally to the compensating of creditors.

Under EU legislation, a limited company can be formed by a single shareholder who must be a director. It must also have a company secretary, who can be an outside person such as your solicitor or accountant. Apart from this, the main requirements relate to documentation. Like sole traders or partnerships, a limited company must prepare a set of accounts annually for the inspector of taxes and it must make an annual return to the Registrar of Companies, showing all the shareholders and directors, any changes of ownership that have taken place, a profit and loss account over the year and a balance sheet.

Apart from the more exacting requirements regarding documentation, a significant disadvantage of setting up a limited company as compared to a partnership or sole trader is that sole traders and partnerships can set off any losses they incur in the first four years' trading retrospectively against the owners' income tax on earnings in the three preceding years. This may enable you to recover tax already paid in earlier years of ordinary employment. This concession does not, however, apply to investment in your own limited company, or to investments made in such a company by those closely connected with the shareholders. If it makes losses, those losses can only be set off against the _company's_ corporation tax in other years when it makes a profit. If it fails altogether, then the loss of your investment is a _capital_ loss which can only be set off against other capital gains you make – not against other earned income. Therefore, if the nature of your business is a service which does not involve exposure to liabilities that you need to protect – for instance, if you are a consultant, rather than a shopkeeper or a manufacturer incurring liabilities to suppliers – there may be a distinct advantage in opting for partnership or sole trader status rather than establishing a limited company; but see the recommendation to seek professional advice below. There may, for instance, be factors other than trading risks which need to be protected by limited liability. Highly profitable ventures can also benefit from limited company status because their profits are taxed at corporation tax rates rather than the much higher personal income tax ones.

The cost of forming a company, including the capital duty which is based on the issued capital (we shall come to the distinction between this and nominal capital shortly), is likely to be around £200, depending on what method you use to go about it. The cheapest way is to buy a ready-made ('off the shelf') company from one of the registration agents who advertise their services in specialist financial journals. Such a company will not actually have been trading, but will be properly registered by the agents. All that has to be done is for the existing 'shareholders' (who are probably the agent's nominees) to resign and for the purchasers to become the new shareholders and to appoint directors. Full details of the procedures are available from Companies House.

Alternatively you can start your own company from scratch, but whichever course you choose, professional advice is vital at this stage. The technicalities are trickier than they sound, though simple enough to those versed in such transactions.

Ultimately, the decision on whether or not to form a limited company depends on your long-term objectives. If you are planning to become an entrepreneur, and to build a business for significant capital growth, a limited company structure and the creation of shares has to be considered at an early stage. It will, for instance, be essential if you want to raise serious amounts of money from outside investors, as we will show in Chapter 1.5. But if you are thinking about what is essentially a salaried income replacement venture, a sole trader or partnership structure would usually be the better and simpler option.

REGISTRATION OF BUSINESS NAMES

One problem you may encounter with an 'off the shelf' company is when it has a name that does not relate meaningfully to the activity you are proposing to carry on. In that case you can change the company name by contacting the Companies Registrations Office on 029 2038 0801 and they will guide you through the procedure, which is straightforward and costs around £50. You can also contact the new companies section on the same number, and register a new company. This again is a straightforward procedure and costs £10. You can also write to the Registrar of Companies for information (The Registrar of Companies, Companies House, Crown Way, Cardiff CF4 3UZ). If your inquiry is about registering a new company, address it to The Registrar of Companies – New Companies Section.

The other option is to trade under a name which is different from the company's official one; for instance, your company may be called 'Period Investments Ltd', but you trade as 'Regency Antiques'. Until 1982 you had to register your business name with the Registrar of Business Names, but that office has since been abolished. Instead, if you trade under any name other than your own – in the case of a sole trader or partnership – or that of the name of the company carrying on the business in the case of a company, you have to disclose the name of the owner or owners and, for each owner, a business or other address within the UK.

The rules of disclosure are quite far-reaching and failure to comply with them is a criminal offence. You must show the information about owners and their addresses on all business letters, written orders for the supply of goods or services, invoices and receipts issued in the course of business and written demands for payment of business debts. Furthermore, you have to display this information prominently and readably in any premises where the business is carried on and to which customers and suppliers have access.

It is worth giving a good deal of thought to the choice of a business name. Clever names are all very well, but if they do not clearly establish the nature of the business you are in, prospective customers leafing through a telephone or business directory may have trouble in finding you; or, if they do find you, they may not readily match your name to their needs. For instance, if you are a furniture repairer, it is far better to describe yourself as such in your business name than to call yourself something like 'Chippendale Restorations'. However, if your name already has a big reputation in some specialised sector, stick with it.

Legislation makes it possible to protect a trading name by registering it with the Trade Marks Registry at the Patent Office. The advantage of that is that you can prevent other traders from using your name – or something very similar – and cashing in on your goodwill. You can also register a trade mark – the sign or logo that identifies your business on letterheads, packaging and so forth. The activities for which marks can be registered include service industries as well as manufacturing ones.

The rules governing the use of business names are like those for company names, except that the Registrar is less concerned about the fact that a similar trading name may already be in existence. Obviously, however, it is advisable in both cases to wait until the name you have put forward is accepted before having any stationery printed. There are, it should be said, certain words that the Registrar of Companies has proved likely to object to: those that could mislead the public by suggesting that an enterprise is larger or has a more prestigious status than circumstances indicate. Cases in point are the use of words such as Trust, University and Group. National adjectives ('British') are also unpopular. When you get to this stage the names of the proprietors (or, in the case of a limited company, the directors) have to be shown not only on letterheads, but also on catalogues and trade literature.

Limited companies, in addition, have to show their registration number and the address of their registered office on such stationery. This address may not necessarily be the same as the one at which business is normally transacted. Some firms use their accountant's or solicitor's premises as their registered office. You will probably see quite a number of registration certificates hanging in their office (they are required by law to be so displayed) when you go there. This is because it is to that address that all legal and official documents are sent. If you have placed complete responsibility for dealing with such matters in the hands of professional advisers, it is obviously convenient that the related correspondence should also be directed there. Bear in mind, though, that this does involve a certain loss of control on your part. Unless you see these documents yourself, you will have no idea, for instance, whether the important ones are being handled with due despatch.

LIMITED COMPANY DOCUMENTS

When you set up a limited company, your solicitor or accountant will be involved in drafting certain papers and documents which govern its structure and the way it is to be run. When this process has been completed you will receive copies of the company's Memorandum and Articles of Association, some share transfer forms, a minute book, the company seal and the Certificate of Incorporation. Let us explain briefly what these mean.

The Memorandum

This document sets out the main objects for which the company is formed and what it is allowed to do. There are standard clauses for this and your professional adviser will use these in drafting the document. The main thing to watch out for is that he should not be too specific in setting out the limits of the proposed operation, because if you change tack somewhere along the line – for instance, if you move from mail order to making goods for the customers you have built up – you may lose the protection of your limited liability unless the Memorandum provides for this. There are, however, catch-all clauses which allow you to trade in pretty much anything or any manner you like. Furthermore, the 'objects' clauses can be changed by a special resolution, passed by 75 per cent of the shareholders.

The Memorandum also sets out the company's nominal or authorised share capital and the par value per share. This is a point about which many newcomers to this aspect of business get very confused. The thing to remember is that in this context the value of share capital is a purely *nominal* value. You can have a company operating with thousands of pounds' worth of nominal share capital. This sounds very impressive, but what counts is the *issued* share capital, because this represents what the shareholders have actually put into the business or pledged themselves so to do. It is quite possible to have a company with a nominal capital of £1000, but with, say, only two issued shares of £1 each to the two shareholders that are required by law.

The issued share capital also determines the ownership of a company. In the case we have just quoted, then two shareholders would own the company jointly. But if they then issue a third £1 share to another person without issuing any more to themselves they would now own only two-thirds of the company. This is a vital point to remember when raising capital by means of selling shares.

Apart from determining proportions of ownership, issued share capital also signifies how much of their own money the shareholders have put into the company or are prepared to accept liability for. Therefore, in raising money from a bank or finance house, the manager there will look closely at the issued share capital. To the extent that he is not satisfied that the liability for the amount he is being asked to put up is adequately backed by issued share capital, he is likely to ask the shareholders to guarantee a loan or overdraft with their own personal assets – for instance, by depositing shares they privately hold in a public quoted company or unit trust – as security. In the case of a new company without a track record this would, in fact, be the usual procedure.

The nominal share capital of a new small-scale business is usually £100. It can be increased later, as business grows, on application to the Registrar of Companies. The point of such a move would be to increase the *issued* share capital, for instance if a new shareholder were to put money into the company. But, once again, it should be borne in mind that if the issued share capital was increased from £100 to £1000, and a backer were to buy £900-worth of shares at par value, the original shareholders would only own one-tenth of the business; the fact that they got the whole thing going is quite beside the point.

One last question about issued share capital which sometimes puzzles people: must you actually hand over money for the shares when you start your own company, as is the case when you buy shares on the stock market, and what happens to it? The answer is yes. You pay it into the company's bank account because, remember, it has a separate legal identity from the shareholders who own it. However, you need not pay for your shares in full. You can, for instance, pay 50p per share for a hundred £1 shares. The balance of £50 represents your liability if the company goes bankrupt, and you actually have to hand over the money only if that happens or if a majority at a shareholders' meeting requires you to do so. The fact that you have not paid in full for shares issued to you does not, however, diminish your entitlement to share in the profits, these being distributed as dividends according to the proportion of share capital issued. The same applies to outside shareholders, so if you are raising money by selling shares to people outside the firm, you should normally ensure that they pay in full for any capital that is issued to them.

The Articles of Association

These are coupled together with the Memorandum, and set out the rules under which the company is run. They govern matters such as issue of the share capital, appointment and powers of directors and proceedings at general meetings. As in the case of the Memorandum, the clauses are largely standard ones, but those relating to the issue of shares should be read carefully. It is most important that there should be a proviso under which any new shares that are issued should be offered first of all to the existing shareholders in the proportion in which they already hold shares. This is particularly so when three or more share-holders are involved, or when you are buying into a company; otherwise the other shareholders can vote to water down your holding in the company whenever they see fit by issuing further shares. For the same reason, there should be a clause under which any shareholder who wants to transfer shares should offer them first of all to the existing shareholders. The Articles of Association also state how the value of the shares is to be determined, the point here being that if the company is successful and makes large profits, the true value of the shares will be much greater than their par value of £1, 50p or whatever. It should be noted, though, that the market valuation of the shares does not increase the liability of shareholders accordingly. In other words, if your £1 par shares are actually valued at, say, £50, your liability still remains at £1.

Table A of the Companies Act of 1948, which can be purchased at any HMSO branch, sets out a specimen Memorandum and Articles.

The minute book

Company law requires that a record be kept of the proceedings at both shareholders' and directors' meetings. These proceedings are recorded in the minute book, which is held at the company's registered office. Decisions made at company meetings are signed by the Chair and are legally binding on the directors if they are agreed by a majority. Therefore, any points of procedure that are not covered by the Memorandum and Articles of Association can be written into the minutes and have the force of law, provided that they do not conflict with the former two documents. Thus, the various responsibilities of the directors can be defined and minuted at the first company meeting; so can important matters such as who signs the cheques. It is generally a good idea for these to carry two signatures to be valid.

The common seal

This used to be a stamp affixed with the authority of the directors, but nowadays documents can be executed by the signatures of two directors. That has the same legal effect as the seal used to have, but it may still be used in some special circumstances.

The Certificate of Incorporation

When the wording of the Memorandum and Articles of Association has been agreed and the names of the directors and the size of the nominal capital have been settled, your professional adviser will send the documents concerned to the Registrar of Companies. He will issue a Certificate of Incorporation which is, as it were, the birth certificate of your company.

COMPANY DIRECTORS

When your Certificate of Incorporation arrives, you and your fellow shareholders are the owners of a fully fledged private limited company. You will almost certainly also be the directors. This title in fact means very little. A director is merely an employee of the company, who is entrusted by the shareholders with the running of it. He need not himself be a shareholder at all, and he can be removed by a vote of the shareholders which, since each share normally carries one vote, is a good reason for not losing control of your company by issuing a majority share-holding to outsiders.

Another good reason is that since the ownership of the company is in proportion to the issued share capital, so also is the allocation of profits, when you come to make them. If you let control pass to an outsider for the sake of raising a few hundred pounds now – there are other means of raising capital than the sale of shares, as we shall show in Chapter 1.6 – you will have had all the problems of getting things going, while only receiving a small part of the rewards. Remember, furthermore, that without control you are only an employee, even if you are called 'managing director'.

Checklist: setting up in business

Sole trader
1. Do you need planning permission to operate from your own home?
2. Does your lease allow you to carry on a trade from the premises you intend to use?
3. If you own the premises, whether or not they are your home as well, are there any restrictive covenants which might prevent you from using them for the purpose intended?
4. Have you notified your tax inspector that the nature of your earnings is changing?
5. Are you aware of the implications of being a sole trader if your business fails?
6. Have you taken steps to register a business name?

Partnerships
1. Points 1 to 6 above also apply to partnerships. Have you taken care of them?
2. How well do you know your partners – personally and as people to work with?
3. If you do not know them well, what evidence do you have of their personal and business qualities?
4. What skills, contacts or other assets (such as capital) can they bring into the business?
5. Have you asked your solicitor to draw up a deed of partnership and does it cover all the eventualities you can think of?
6. Have you talked to anybody who is in, or has tried, partnership in the same line of business, to see what the snags are?

Private limited companies
1. Do you have the requisite minimum number of shareholders (two)?
2. Do you have a competent company secretary, who can carry out the legal duties required under the Companies Acts?

3. Are you yourself reasonably conversant with those duties?
4. Have you registered, if this is required, a company name and a business name?
5. Has permission been granted to use the names chosen?
6. Have the necessary documents been deposited with the Registrar of Companies? (Memorandum and Articles of Association, a statutory declaration of compliance with registration requirements, a statement of nominal share capital.)
7. Have you read and understood the Memorandum and Articles? Do they enable you to carry out all present and any possible future objects for which the company is formed?
8. Do your stationery, catalogues, letterheads, etc show all the details required by the Companies Acts?
9. Is the Registration Certificate displayed in the company's registered office, as required by law?
10. Do you understand the wide range of benefits – company cars, other business expenses, limited liability, self-administered pension schemes, etc – enjoyed by limited companies?
11. Clauses 1 to 3 of the 'Sole trader' checklist may also apply to you. If so, have you taken care of them?

1.3 Choices of Self-employment

Self-employment has traditionally taken the form of running a full-time business as either a limited company, partnership or sole trader as described in the last chapter. However, recent years have witnessed the rise in alternative forms of work. Not only can the number of hours that you work be a question of choice, but also who you supply and what form that relationship takes has become more flexible. For example, the rise in contract work has also opened up opportunities for the self-employed to work in a freelance capacity and this is the choice of a growing number of people. At the other end of the spectrum, taking up a franchise or participating in a management buy-out can provide opportunities for self-employment in national organisations with high turnovers. This chapter will examine the pros and cons of each of these opportunities.

PART-TIME WORK

Part-time work has become a significant part of the UK economy. Official figures show that one-third of the workforce are employed on this basis.

The range of ways in which people work part-time is also wide.

☐ 'Portfolio' part-time work – doing part-time jobs for several different employers on a regular basis.

☐ Working part-time for a single employer – for instance, the human resource strategy director for the employment agency, Reed Executive, works there only three days a week.
☐ Doing a part-time job as a spare-time activity, usually to earn extra money. Sometimes this takes the form of extending the job you do for your employer into private work in your spare time – a matter we will cover in a little more detail shortly.
☐ Casual work – occasionally taking on work to help out a friend or to augment one's income.

The Inland Revenue suspects that a significant part of the black economy, through which some £40 billion a year is lost to the Exchequer, flourishes through casual and spare-time work. Anecdotal evidence suggests they are probably right. A great many tradespeople express a strong preference to be paid in ready cash by private customers. Such payments are extremely difficult for tax inspectors to trace.

It is likely, however, that people who fail to declare their income from part-time work are more concerned to conceal their activities from the DSS than from the Inland Revenue. It is very easy to cease to be eligible for unemployment benefit by earning income of more than the basic unemployment benefit for any given six-day period. If this source of earned income does not continue and you wish to sign on again, there can be considerable delays before you receive unemployment benefit. There is a strong temptation, therefore, if you do something that brings in a few pounds a week while you are unemployed, not to declare it.

The government recognises the fact that income from a new business is usually less than the dole and the Business Start-Up scheme (see page 79) helps to bridge the gap.

TAX ADVANTAGES OF PART-TIME EMPLOYMENT

If you are married with another source of income, not declaring your earnings from part-time work might be a very unwise move – apart from being illegal. In the first place it is usually unlikely that you would have to pay tax on it at all because of the single person's earned income allowance of £4385. This means that the first £4385 of everyone's earnings is free of tax; so if you can arrange for your spouse to earn that amount of money from your source of extra income, you will not pay any tax on it – assuming he or she does not already have a job. Remember, it is the profit that is taxed, not the total earnings. If you cannot get that figure close to £4385 by setting off against gross earnings all the allowances described in Chapter 1.14, then you are either doing so well as to make it worth considering turning your spare-time occupation into a full-time activity, or you should get an accountant, or you should change the accountant you have. However, you do have to prove, to the satisfaction of the tax inspector, that your spouse really is working in the business – taking messages, typing invoices, book-keeping, or whatever. Holding the fort by looking after the kids and doing the shopping so that you can get on with it does not count.

All this is reinforced by the fact that even if you do not pay tax on them, there are definite advantages in earnings that are taxed under Schedule D. You will be able to claim allowances on services (gas, electricity and water) for the use of part of your house, plus a proportion of your bill for the telephone, stamps and stationery – whatever, in fact, can be shown to be reasonably related to the nature of the activity you are carrying on. Small is beautiful, provided you declare it.

PLANNING AND OTHER PERMISSIONS; INSURANCE

Strictly speaking, if you carry on a business from home you have to apply for planning permission, as indicated in Chapter 1.2. In practice, very few people bother when it comes to part-time work, though if what you are intending to do creates a noise, a nuisance or a smell (and some crafts and home repair activities do some or all of these things even when carried on in quite a small way) you should inform the local authority of your intentions. Complaints from neighbours not only cause embarrassment but can also result in your being required to find proper premises, the cost of which may invalidate your whole idea. Applying for planning permission will highlight such potential problems, and fore-warned is forearmed. By the same token, if planning permission has been granted you will be able to face most complaints with equanimity.

If you are doing anything with food – making pâtés for your local delicatessen, for instance – you should inform the environ-mental health inspector. Here again, very few people bother and, in fact, the health officials are more concerned with commercial kitchens than domestic ones, which are generally cleaner; on the other hand, you could be liable for prosecution if it turns out, for instance, that the cause of someone being made ill by your pâté was a breach of the health regulations.

One important precaution you should not neglect if you are planning to work from home, whatever that work is, is to tell your insurance company. This is because your normal house and contents policy covers domestic use only and if you change the circumstances without telling the insurers they could fail to pay you in the event of a claim – and would probably do so if the loss was caused by the undeclared activity. Additional insurance cover will not normally cost you much, which is often more than could be said for any loss that occurs.

ASSESSING THE MARKET

From the point of view of anyone contemplating full-time self-employment, the principal advantage of part-time work is not really that it is a source of extra income, however valuable an incidental that may be, but that it serves as a trial run for the real thing. Opinions may differ as to what the prime factors here are in order of priority, but few would disagree that the most important thing is to assess whether there is a market for the goods or services you are proposing to offer, at a price that will bring you a worthwhile profit. Working part-time at something will give you an idea whether the demand and the competition will enable you to do that.

For instance, if working 12 hours a week, evenings and week-ends, produces a gross £100 a week – £4800 a year, allowing for four weeks' holiday – and your present income is, say, £22,000, there is a marginal case for considering full-time self-employment. By working 48 hours a week you could, on that evidence, gross about £19,000 in a 48-week year. Of course, it would depend on what your costs were, but some of the fixed ones – tools, for instance – would not change if you expanded your activities. If there was evidence of a very strong demand, you might even consider raising your prices, especially if the experience you have gained about the market indicates that you are appreciably cheaper than the competition. Alternatively, you might discover that by making one or two modifications you could either charge more than the competition or create a stronger demand for your original concept. It is much easier to make these adaptations to market conditions while still operating at a modest level and with a main income from another source.

OBJECTIVES

Whether the person in a £22,000-a-year secure job throws her hand in for £19,000-worth of insecurity depends not only on financial factors but on personal objectives. Here again, working part-time before making the commitment to full-time self-employment will help you to shape your thinking about what those objectives are and what they are worth to you. If independence is the overriding factor, you might feel that even a sizeable financial sacrifice is worth making. On the other hand, if money is the main objective and you are secure in your main job, then clearly, in the instance we have given you, you are much better off earning an extra £4800 a year from your part-time job, plus £22,000 a year from your main one, than giving up the latter altogether – unless you could see a way of doing better than £4800 _pro rata_ over a 48-hour week.

Another objective that could be tried out is whether you can work with an intended partner. Some very successful businesses are run by people who have little in common except a respect for each other's abilities, but it is usually difficult to test such

35

qualities unless you have actually worked closely with someone. Trying out a partnership arrangement on a part-time basis is a good way of doing this.

ASSESSING YOURSELF

There is also the question of assessing your own suitability because there is a big gap between pipe dreams of independence and the reality, even when it comes to working full-time at something you have previously enjoyed doing as a hobby. Apart from the fact that what is fun as a hobby can sometimes be quite another proposition done hour after hour and day after day, there is often a huge difference between amateur and professional standards. For instance, it may take you all day to turn out a widget – that mythical, all-purpose British unit of manufacture – whereas a professional can do it in a couple of hours. That is fine when you are doing it more or less for fun, but fatal if you are trying to earn a living, unless you are confident you can get to professional standards fairly quickly.

Whether you can actually do so usually depends on how good you are at working for very long hours, initially for not much money and spending a great deal of your 'spare time' on administration: keeping records, writing letters and preparing quotes. You will not know your capacities in this respect until you try, but working part-time will give you an inkling.

It will also give you some indication of your family's attitudes to your work. If you are working part-time on top of a full-time job, you are probably reasonably close to putting in the sort of hours that are needed to make a success of self-employment at least for an initial – and usually prolonged – period of time. In other words, your family will not see a great deal of you unless they are able and willing to pitch in as well. They may view this prospect with equanimity; on the other hand, workaholism can be as great a source of family tension as alcoholism. When working part-time, it is quite easy to cut down the hours you are putting in, or even to stop altogether. If your living depends on it, the case is altered completely.

FINANCIAL COMMITMENT

One of the advantages of part-time work is that you are keeping your overheads, or fixed costs, low. You can work from home instead of renting premises or offices. You can hire equipment instead of buying it. You may even be able to use facilities available at your place of work – photocopying, for instance – though to what extent that is a wise move depends on the attitude of your employer. Some take it as a sign of initiative, provided that it does not interfere with your regular job. Others hate it, in which case you will have to be very careful how you go about it, and at least account for everything you use. The point is, though, that for part-time work you will not have to 'tool up' expensively and, indeed, you should avoid irreversible financial commitments as much as possible. Do not, for instance, buy a van until you are sure you are going to get profitable use out of it, or unless you want one anyway. Do not, to take another case, buy a knitting machine – hire it and see whether you really can make knitting pay.

The principle can be extended to any given activity. You should never buy anything unless you have to and until you have established an ongoing need for it. This is so with full-time activities, and it is even more the case with part-time work, because by definition the number of hours you have in which to amortise the cost – to make a profit and get your money back – are far fewer.

OPPORTUNITIES

Extension of full-time employment

In the previous section I referred to the situation where someone is carrying on into evenings and weekends private work normally done for an employer in the daytime: typical examples might be repair and building work, some forms of design, and teaching extended into exam coaching. The great advantage of this type of work is that it can give you a direct access to the market. Everybody who walks through the door at your place of employment is a potential private customer, whereas in other forms of part-time work, finding the market is an important but difficult part of the total concept. Furthermore, private, part-time clients can later be turned into sources of work on a larger scale, either directly or as leads to other work. Even suppliers can be useful people to get to know, both in terms of establishing your credibility when it comes to asking for credit and in the matter of sorting out good and reliable suppliers from the many other varieties.

The principal disadvantage of this type of work is that it can lead to a conflict of interests. The temptation to steer work your way rather than towards your employer can be very strong. It need not be anything as blatant as buttonholing your employer's customers at the door. There are subtler ways of bending the rules. The best way to avoid such temptations is to develop your own clients and contacts as soon as possible.

Turning a hobby into a source of income

This is usually the most satisfying form of part-time work because people generally perform best at what they most enjoy doing. Furthermore, many people, especially the over-30s, find that they have gone or been pushed into careers that do not reflect their real interests or skills, or that they have simply developed new ones that they find more satisfying than what they do for a living. Practising crafts of various kinds is a case in point.

The trap here is the one that we have referred to earlier – that there is a world of difference between doing something for fun and working at it full-time. Professional craftspeople have years of experience which enable them to turn out work quickly and economically. They also know the market: who buys what, at which price; what sells and what does not. In the case of photography, to take another instance, the good amateur turned professional is competing in a field where contacts are all-important and where high standards of work depend not only on individual skill, but on having the latest equipment.

Learning a new skill

Sometimes people learn a new skill, perhaps at an evening class, which is capable of being turned to commercial use – particularly these days when the range of services available from shops and manufacturers has become increasingly scarce and expensive. Popular examples are picture framing and upholstery.

There are also non-manual skills which can be turned to good account, such as selling; quite a number of people are engaged in party plan or catalogue selling. The problem there, however, is that it is difficult to go into a higher, full-time gear to make a living from that type of work, because commissions are fixed percentages and, in the case of catalogue selling, quite small ones.

Reviving an unused skill

This is also very popular, especially with women thinking of returning to work. The most frequently cited example is typing, but, as it happens, this one neatly illustrates the importance of observing the laws of supply and demand in choosing even a part-time source of income. Because there are many women available for such work, the rates are not particularly good. The only way you can lift yourself into a higher bracket is by identifying a service which few other typists offer and for which there is also a demand: in a university town, for instance, there might be a call for someone who can type theses quickly and accurately. An exporter, to take another example, might have a demand for someone who can type accurately in another language.

The same supply-and-demand principle also applies to translating. There are many graduates around who can translate from one of the main European languages into English, but rather fewer who can do the more difficult, reverse kind of translation: from English into idiomatic French, German or Spanish. Even rarer, and therefore more marketable, is fluency in another language *plus* a qualification in a specialist subject such as law or science.

USING AN EXISTING ASSET AS A SOURCE OF INCOME: ACCOMMODATION

By far the biggest asset that most people own is their house. When there is a need for more money, or as members of the family grow up or move away, that asset can be a source of income: rooms can be let, the house can be subdivided into flats or even – ultimately – the whole place can be turned into a guest house. The advantage of these courses of action is that little skill or training is required to turn them into money-making activities. The disadvantage is that they are full of legal pitfalls which deter a great many people. The common option is to circumvent the law by moving into a cash only, black economy relationship with tenants, but by that token you also lose much legal protection that would be available if there was a dispute. By getting a tenancy agreement drawn up you can protect yourself to a large degree, especially if you are also the kind of student of human nature who can spot a potential troublemaker before she crosses your threshold.

The best kind of asset to have is a country house grand enough to attract paying sightseers rather than tenants. But in that case you would have an army of legal and financial advisers at your elbow and perhaps would not be reading a book like this!

Letting rooms

In recent years, and especially since the 1980 Housing Act, there have been many horror stories about the difficulty of getting rid of unwanted tenants, even, on occasion, when they have been well behind with the rent. For this reason it is very unwise to let rooms without having an agreement drawn up by a solicitor; even the Citizens' Advice Bureau staffed, in general, by people whose natural sympathies lie with the tenant, recommend this. It is usually unwise, incidentally, to have a room-letting agreement which runs much longer than on a month-to-month basis because, except in extreme circumstances, the courts are likely to take the view that an agreement will have to run its full course before being terminated.

The other piece of legislation to beware of is the Rent Act of 1977 which gives the tenant the right to go to a tribunal and ask for a 'reasonable' rent to be applied if he thinks you are asking too much. A register of reasonable rents is kept at your local authority's Rent Assessment Panel office, if you want to check what these are, but you will often find that these do not allow for subtle shades of amenity – the social difference between nearby streets, for instance.

The best way to get good tenants is to select them – not by race or sex, which is illegal – but by asking for references from their previous landlord.

FREELANCING

There are obviously overlaps between working part-time and working as a freelance. A person contributing regular articles to journals and newspapers could be doing so part-time and still be described as a freelance. In general, though, a freelance is regarded as someone who is self-employed full-time, providing a service to a range of different principals as the demand occurs, or as she can persuade them to buy the service that is being offered.

Some occupations have a very high freelance content because of the unpredictability of the flow of work. The prime example is the world of films and television. Over a third of the members of BECTU (Broadcasting, Entertainment, Cinematograph and Theatre Union), the principal trade union in this sphere, are freelancers, employed by a variety of different companies for anything from a day to six months, according to the duration of a particular project. Performing artists, too, tend almost exclusively to be freelancers, even though they may have spells when they are attached to a particular orchestra or a repertory company.

In the media and even in certain parts of industry, the tendency to put work out to freelancers and other suppliers of *ad hoc* labour is growing rapidly. When trading conditions are uncertain, employers are reluctant to commit themselves to taking on people full-time. It makes more sense to bring them in as and when they are needed or to commission them – even to the point of subcontracting whole jobs to them.

There are also many tasks in many firms which need to be done but where the in-house demand is neither large nor constant enough to justify the employment of a full-time member of staff. It is people in such occupations, which can range from manual jobs like that of the firm's carpenter to services like public relations, who often find themselves at risk when times get hard.

Yet, operating as freelancers for their own firm, plus other clients, they often have a highly profitable new lease of working life.

HOW FREELANCERS FIND WORK

The circumstances just described bring out a number of points about freelance work. It is often very difficult, for instance, simply to decide to 'go freelance', as many redundant executives have found to their cost when they wanted to set up as consultants. You need to have contacts, reliable sources of work and a known track record in your chosen area. Many freelancers report, in fact, that their first client was their previous employer or someone whom they got to know through their former workplace.

Even so, freelance work is patchy and unpredictable. The elements of self-marketing and constant self-motivation are vital. Freelance management consultants, for instance, reckon to spend at least 40 per cent of their time hunting for work: identifying opportunities from reports in the business, trade or professional press, and following them up with letters, phone calls or proposals. The same pattern can be seen in other freelance occupations: photographers and entertainers check in with their agents; writers prepare material 'on spec' for book and magazine publishers. It is a fairly insecure life until you get established and clients start ringing you, rather than the other way round. Indeed, many freelancers are of the opinion that to make a success of it, you need at least one reliable source of regular work – someone who brings you in for one day a week, for instance.

CHARACTERISTICS OF FREELANCE WORK

The reason why a lot of practising freelancers recommend getting this kind of underlay is not purely financial. There are also psychological factors involved, especially for those who have previously worked alongside others. Freelancing is a lonely way to earn a living. With some kinds of job – writing for instance – you can spend weeks on end without seeing anyone.

It is also unpredictable. There can be long periods, particularly when you first start, when little or no work comes in and your bank balance sinks as low as your spirits. As a self-employed person, you cannot claim unemployment benefit either, even though no work is coming through. On the other hand, you still have to pay your National Insurance stamp.

Periods of inactivity may be broken up by spells when the workload is almost too much. Very few freelancers ever turn work away, though. Once you lose a potential customer – even though you may not need him at that juncture – he is very difficult to get back when circumstances change. If, however, you can't do the job because it coincides with something else, it is essential to say so rather than to make promises that cannot be kept. This applies to delivery dates as well.

COSTING AND PRICING

Broadly, the rules set out in Chapter 1.10 apply, but there are additional factors to consider. As we have said, you often have to spend a considerable amount of time just looking for work; it varies, obviously, according to your status and occupation. On the other hand, whether you can reflect this fact in full in your scale of charges depends on our old friends – supply and demand. As against that, you have the advantage, in the case of many types of freelance work, that you are working from home. Usually your equipment costs are low too, though that would not be true of photography. The employer, in engaging you, should consider that it is generally reckoned that the cost of having a person on the staff full-time is twice their annual salary, taking into account NI contributions, holidays, pensions and so forth.

INCOME TAX AND FREELANCE WORK

Freelancers are normally taxed under Schedule D. However, as we will point out at the end of Chapter 1.14, the Inland Revenue are challenging Schedule D status where a substantial amount of

work is done for one particular employer, as that in effect constitutes a master-and-servant relationship. This is a particular
danger when people work through an agency and are paid by the
agency, not by the client.

FRANCHISING

The risky nature of freelancing might not be suitable for everyone.
However, another form of self-employment that *is* regarded as
providing reasonable security is running a franchise. The best-
known UK franchises are Body Shop and McDonald's, though in
fact quite a number of familiar high street shops, restaurant
chains and a great many kinds of home and business services are
operated as franchises. This means that the person operating the
franchise – the franchisee – has bought from the franchisor the
right to trade under an established name, rather than establishing
his or her credentials from scratch.

That in itself can be a great advantage, but taking up a franchise
goes further than that. The franchisee is buying a working business blueprint that has previously been tried, tested and de-
bugged by the franchise owner – the franchisor – and by his other
franchisees. With it he buys training, start-up support, an operating manual and a helpdesk for day-to-day problems, at least in
the early stages. He also buys the exclusive right to operate that
franchise in a given territory.

The format for operating the business is laid down very
precisely, down to the stationery headings, the uniform you wear
when on duty, the layout of your premises and how much you
charge your customer for goods or services. The idea is that if you
follow the format, you cannot fail because it has been tested and
found to work. If you put in the hours, you will generate a
predicted level of turnover and predicted net profit margins.
These will enable you to recoup your initial investment – the start-
up costs and the upfront fee you pay for the right to operate the
franchise and to be trained in running it as a business – within two
to three years.

The net margin is calculated to allow not only the usual overheads, but also a royalty to the franchisor. That varies between 5

and 10 per cent, depending on whether or not the franchisee involved is buying goods from the franchisor on which the franchisor himself makes a profit as a supplier or wholesaler. It sounds like a wonderful idea. Where's the catch? First of all let us say that franchising has proved itself to be a very good way of starting a business of your own. Failure rates are low and because of this the banks have been more ready to lend money to franchisees than for many other forms of small business, especially in the start-up phase. In fact the franchising department of your bank is the best place to start investigating a franchise proposition, because there are quite a number of snags to watch out for.

CHOOSING A FRANCHISE

One unscrupulous operator confessed to me in an expansive post-lunch mood, 'There's two born every minute – in case one of them dies.' There is very little legislation in the franchising field and there have been plenty of instances where franchisees have been induced into parting with their upfront fee and have seen very little in return for their money. The bank may not say outright that this or that franchise proposition should not be touched with a bargepole, but if several banks refuse to lend you money on it, don't go further. Either you are wrong for the business or the business is wrong for you. Or it is just plain wrong, full stop, probably because the pilot stage when the format is tested has not been carried out properly, or not at all, or because the upfront fee and/or royalties are regarded as too high or because the thing is simply known to be badly run.

There are also businesses that call themselves franchises but are really variants of pyramid selling, where you get paid for recruiting other members to a chain of people, each one selling stuff, often of very little intrinsic value, to the next link down. Strictly speaking, this form of trading is illegal, but there are ways around it which sail very close to the borders of the law without actually breaking it.

Even if you don't actually need the money, a check with the bank is worth making. It will cost you nothing and it could save you a great deal of money. Indeed, if the franchisor tries to pressurise you out of taking sensible precautions, walk away immediately.

In addition to the bank check, you should always ask to talk to existing franchisees, even of a reputable franchise, chosen by you at random, not ones nominated by the franchisor. Things can change. Ask whether they are achieving the income levels and profit margins forecast and how many hours a week it takes to do that; whether, given the chance, they would make the decision to take up that franchise again; and if there is anything they would like to change. That could be a negotiating point if and when you come to signing a contract.

A final check is to ask whether the franchisor is a member of the British Franchise Association (BFA). Not all of them are, but many of the goods ones have membership. The BFA is a franchisor body but it lays down standards and conditions which also protect franchisees.

One of the problems in franchising is that not all good ideas work well everywhere. That is certainly true of franchises that have been a great success in other countries, notably the US, but it is also true within the UK. In the 1980s there was a household-name health food franchise which did extremely well in the south-east of England, but turned out to be a terrible flop in the meat and two veg belt north of the Wash. A tremendous amount depends on the area, even within the same town.

Franchisors make great play with the notion of an 'exclusive territory' but it doesn't mean all that much. There is nothing to stop a franchisee from a different franchisor opening up a similar business in your exclusive territory, or indeed a similar, non-franchised business doing this. Think how many fast-print shops and fast-food outlets there are around, for instance.

At the same time, there is no doubt that those who get into a good franchise at an early stage, before all the plum territories are assigned, can make a lot of money. Some of the early Body Shop franchisees are now very wealthy. It shows that franchising, format though it is, still calls for the exercise of some commercial judgement.

The average length of a franchise agreement is seven to ten years, but these days very few products or services hold their competitive advantage for as long as that. You need to be sure that the franchisor is sufficiently resourceful to keep coming up with new ideas and sufficiently resourced to develop them. In the recession of the 1990s it was noticed that some franchisees got into difficulties because the franchisors were themselves under pressure. They could not give the franchisees enough support.

Not everyone is temperamentally suited to being a franchisee. Though to a large extent it is your own business, you are still tied to the franchisor in regard to what you can and cannot do – for instance, you may be limited as to the range of services you can offer or the goods you stock. That condition may become very irksome if you think you see business opportunities that your contract prevents you from exploiting.

The franchise agreement is a long and complicated document which sets out what your obligations are to the franchisor, and vice versa, during the term of the contract. Only sign it after making sure that you understand it fully and that it neither omits nor adds anything different from that which you agreed or assumed verbally. In fact, you should also show it to a lawyer who knows about franchising. That may not necessarily be your usual lawyer. If he is not confident of his knowledge in this field ask him, or the bank, to recommend someone that is.

A fuller account of this topic is given in _Taking Up a Franchise: the Daily Telegraph Guide_ by Colin Barrow and Godfrey Golzen, also published annually by Kogan Page.

MANAGEMENT BUY-OUTS

Management buy-outs are at the more expensive end of the spectrum of self-employment opportunities discussed in this book, but they are becoming more common and, at the lower end of the cost range, are comparable to setting-up costs of franchises in the medium to upper price field: £100,000 to £250,000.

The opportunity for a buy-out occurs when the owners of a business decide to dispose of all or a part of it. That may give the existing management the chance to become bidders for it themselves. Indeed, there have been cases where the entire workforce became bidders, with the existing management becoming their spearhead. A notable example was the management buy-out of the National Freight Corporation, which received a great deal of publicity when, on a subsequent flotation, large capital gains were made by those members of the workforce who had participated in the buy-out.

The NFC buy-out was a large one which occurred in consequence of a privatisation measure. More commonly, buy-out opportunities occur because the owners:

□ want to sell out to raise cash;
□ decide that the business is not a core activity;
□ feel the business is not sufficiently profitable;
□ feel the business needs investment which they are unable or unwilling to make.

Another cause can be the business going into receivership.

In recent years finance for buy-outs that look as though they stand a chance has been readily available from sources of venture capital, though the bidders are expected to shoulder a considerable part of the risk. As with other kinds of business loan, the providers of finance expect to see a business plan. Where larger sums are required, it has to go into a lot of detail. Among the points to be covered are:

□ descriptions of the assets and liabilities of the company;
□ the nature and value of work in progress;
□ detailed cash-flow projections;
□ the background and qualifications of the buy-out team, which must include a good finance director.

However, there is another equally important set of conditions that have to be fulfilled. By law the owners have to satisfy their shareholders that the buy-out represents the best deal for them, though that need not necessarily mean that they are the ones that have come up with the best offer financially. But if that is not the case, they do have to demonstrate that a sale to them is the best solution, either because it is the quickest or because, if the buy-out participants left the company, its saleability would be diminished. The latter is often particularly true of service-based companies with few tangible assets.

Buy-out negotiations are complex and can be fairly protracted: four to six months is about the minimum. Good (and therefore expensive) legal and financial advice is essential and should be costed into the total financial requirements.

The question is, though, whether the owners should be approached with an offer or be asked to name a price. Some financial institutions like to have a clear idea from the start about how much money they are being asked to put up – in other words, they prefer the owners to name a price. On the other hand, a cash bid can sometimes surprise the owners into parting with the business for a modest price. This is where commercial judgement about how to structure the bid is called for.

It also requires a lot of preparation in assessing the value of what the buy-out team is acquiring. That should be clearly specified in the bid document; otherwise you may find that the owners are excluding a particularly promising development or valuable asset. However, the advice given by the experts is that having fixed a maximum price for the buy-out related to a sum that will enable you to repay the loan and its interest charges (and also make a living) within a reasonable period of time, you should not go beyond that figure.

Checklist: further self-employment opportunities

Part-time work

1. Have you informed your local authority if your employment creates a noise, nuisance or a smell and you intend to use your home for part-time work?
2. If you are involved in preparing food, have you informed the environmental health inspector?
3. If you are planning to work from home, have you informed your insurance company to arrange additional cover?

4. Have you assessed whether there is a market for your goods or services at a price that will bring you a worthwhile profit?
5. Have you identified your objective for working part-time and, if it is to reduce the hours worked, is the financial sacrifice worth making?
6. Are you able to fulfil the administrative demands as well as your core product/service?
7. Can you hire equipment instead of buying it?
8. If you are developing a hobby as part-time work, are you able to upgrade your work, to meet professional standards and to produce it quickly and economically?

Freelancing
1. Have you a good source of contacts? Could your current employer provide you with freelance work?
2. Are you self-motivated and have you identified further areas and media where you can investigate future freelance opportunities?
3. Are you able to work by yourself?
4. Have you identified the going rate for your work and, after taking into account periods without work, are you able to survive financially?

Franchising
1. Have you approached your bank to see if they support your franchise application?
2. Have you talked to other franchisees to see their financial outlook and hours of work?
3. Have you contacted the British Franchise Association for good guidelines and advice?
4. Does your location suit the franchise product?
5. Is the franchisor well enough established to support you through economic downturns?
6. Are you prepared to follow a business structure prepared by someone else?
7. Ask your bank to recommend a lawyer who specialises in franchising.

Management buy-outs

1. Have you prepared a business plan including the assets and liability of the company, the nature and value of the work in progress, detailed cash-flow projections and the qualifications and skills of the buy-out team?

2. Check the bid document to see that important assets are included.

1.4 Professional and Other Outside Advisers

We have already touched on the importance of the role that professional advisers, particularly accountants and solicitors, are going to play in the formation of your business, whether it is to be a limited company or some other form of entity. You are going to be using their advice quite frequently, not only at the beginning but also later, in matters such as acquiring premises, suing a customer for payment, preparing a set of accounts or finding out what items are allowable against you or your company's tax bill. Obviously, therefore, how you choose and use these advisers is a matter for careful thought.

MAKING THE RIGHT CHOICE

Many people think that there is some kind of special mystique attached to membership of a profession and that any lawyer or accountant is going to do a good job for them. The fact is, though, that while they do have useful specialist knowledge, the competence with which they apply it can be very variable. A high proportion of people who have bought a house, for instance, can tell you of errors and delays in the conveyancing process, and some accountants entrusted with their clients' tax affairs have been known to send in large bills for their services while overlooking claims for legitimate expenses that were the object of employing them in the first place.

So do not just go to the solicitor or accountant who happens to be nearest; nor should you go to someone you only know in a social capacity. Ask friends who are already in business on a similar scale and, if possible, of a similar nature to your own, for recommendations. (If you already have a bank manager you know well, he may also be able to offer useful advice.) The kind of professional adviser you should be looking for at this stage is not in a big office in a central location. They will have bigger fish to fry and after the initial interview you may well be fobbed off with an articled clerk. Apart from that they will be expensive, for they have big office overheads to meet. On the other hand, a solo operation can create a problem if that person is ill or on holiday. The ideal office will be a suburban one, preferably close to where you intend to set up business, because knowledge of local conditions and personalities can be invaluable, with two or three partners. Apart from that, personal impressions do count. You will probably not want to take on an adviser who immediately exudes gloomy caution, or one who appears to be a wide boy, or somebody with whom you have no rapport. Some people recommend that you should make a shortlist of two or three possibles and go and talk to them before making your choice. Stoy Hayward are particularly interested in the small business area and franchising; they have offices in London and the regions.

Professional associations will also have details of members in your area. The Law Society runs a scheme, Lawyers for Your Business (LFYB), to help small companies assess their legal needs by offering a free consultation with a local member. The LFYB telephone hotline is 020 7405 9075. Details can also be found on the Law Society's Web site at www.lawsoc.org.uk. The Institute of Chartered Accountants in England and Wales (ICAEW) also provides details of local practitioners to members of the public. Its Practitioner Bureau can be contacted direct on 01908 248090 and its Web site address is www.icaew.co.uk/. The Institute of Chartered Accountants Scotland also publishes a list of members and can be ordered on 0131 247 4883, with details shown on the Web site www.icas.org.uk.

WHAT QUESTIONS DO YOU ASK?

Obviously, later on you will be approaching your adviser about specific problems, but at the outset you and he will be exploring potential help he can give you. Begin by outlining the kind of business or service you intend to set up, how much money you have available, what you think your financial needs are going to be over the first year of operation, how many people are going to be involved as partners or shareholders and what your plans are for the future. An accountant will want to know the range of your experience in handling accounting problems and how much help you are going to need in writing up the books, and he will advise you on the basic records you should set up. Remember to ask his advice on your year end/year start; this does not have to be 6 April to 5 April, and there may be sound tax reasons for choosing other dates. He may even be able to recommend the services of a part-time bookkeeper to handle the mechanics but, as we shall show in Chapter 1.7, this does not absolve you from keeping a close watch on what money is coming in and going out. It should be stressed at this point that, certainly in the case of a private limited company, the accountant you are talking to should be qualified, either through membership of the Institute of Chartered Accountants or the Chartered Association of Certified Accountants. Someone who advertises his services as a book-keeper or merely as an 'accountant' is not qualified to give professional advice in the true meaning of that term, though someone good if unqualified can do a very adequate job in preparing tax returns for something like a small freelance business.

A solicitor will also want to know the kind of business you are in and your plans for the future. But she will concentrate, obviously, on legal rather than financial aspects (so do not go on about money – she is a busy person and this is only an exploratory visit). She is interested in what structure the operation is going to have and, in the case of a partnership or limited company, whether you and your colleagues have made any tentative agreements between yourselves regarding the running of the firm and the division of profits. She will want to get some idea of what kind of property you want to buy or lease and whether any planning permissions have to be sought.

HOW MUCH ARE ADVISERS GOING TO CHARGE?

This is rather like asking how long is a piece of string. It depends on how often you have to consult your advisers, so it is no use asking them to quote a price at the outset, though if you are lucky enough to have a very clear idea of what you want done – say, in the case of an accountant, a monthly or weekly supervision of your books, plus the preparation and auditing of your accounts – they may give you a rough idea of what the charges will be. Alternatively, they may suggest an annual retainer for these services and any advice directly concerned with them, plus extra charges for anything that falls outside them such as a complicated wrangle with the inspector of taxes about allowable items. When calculating the likely cost of using an accountant remember that his fees are tax-deductible.

An annual retainer is a less suitable way of dealing with your solicitor because your problems are likely to be less predictable than those connected with accounting and bookkeeping. A lot of your queries may be raised, and settled, on the telephone: the 'Can I do this?' type. Explaining that kind of problem on the telephone is usually quicker and points can be more readily clarified than by writing a letter setting out the facts of the case (though you should ask for confirmation in writing in matters where you could be legally liable in acting on the advice you have been given!). However, asking advice on the telephone can be embarrassing for both parties. You will be wondering whether your solicitor is charging you for it and either way it could inhibit you from discussing the matter fully. You should therefore check at the outset what the procedure is for telephone inquiries and how these are accounted for on your bill.

A GUIDE – NOT A CRUTCH

For someone starting in business on their own, facing for the first time 'the loneliness of thought and the agony of decision', there is a temptation to lean on professional advisers too much. Apart from the fact that this can be very expensive, it is a bad way to run a business. Before you lift the telephone or write a letter, think. Is this clause in a contract something you could figure out for yourself if you sat down and concentrated on reading it carefully? Would it not be better to check through the ledger yourself to find out where to put some item of expenditure that is not immediately classifiable? Only get in touch with your advisers when you are genuinely stumped for an answer, not just because you cannot be bothered to think it out for yourself. Remember, too, that nobody can make up your mind for you on matters of policy. If you feel, for example, that you cannot work with your partner, the only thing your solicitor can or should do for you is to tell you how to dissolve the partnership, not whether it should be done at all.

YOUR BANK MANAGER

The other person with whom you should make contact when you start up in business is your bank manager. The importance of picking a unit of the right size which we have mentioned in connection with professional advice also holds true in this case. A smaller local branch is more likely to be helpful towards the problems of a small business than one in a central urban location with a lot of big accounts among its customers. You might also discuss, with your accountant, the possibility of going outside the 'big four'. It is necessary to be careful here because there have been some notorious failures of 'fringe banks', but there are a number of solid smaller banking houses which are more accommodating about charges on handling your account and loans. If you are changing banks, as opposed to merely switching branches, it will be difficult for you to get a sizeable overdraft until the manager has seen something of your track record.

You must inform your bank manager of your intention to set up in business, providing her with much the same information as you gave to your accountant. Indeed, it is quite a good idea to ask your accountant to come along to this first meeting, so that he can explain any technicalities.

You may be operating a small-scale freelance business that does not call for bank finance. It is very important, in that case, to keep your personal and business accounts separate, with separate cheque and paying-in books for each one. Mixing up private and business transactions can only lead to confusion, for you as well as your accountant. Even if you are simply, say, a one-person freelance consultancy, it is worth keeping your bank manager well informed about your business. Your cashflow as a freelance might well be highly erratic and unless he knows you and your business well he will be firing off letters about your unauthorised overdraft.

INSURANCE

If you are setting up a photographic studio and an electrical fault on the first day destroys some of your equipment, you are in trouble before you have really begun. If you are a decorator and a pot of paint falling from a window sill causes injury to someone passing below you could face a suit for damages that will clean you out of the funds you have accumulated to start your business. Insurance coverage is, therefore, essential from the start for almost all kinds of business.

Insurance companies vary a good deal in the premiums they charge for different kinds of cover, and in the promptness with which they pay out on claims. The best plan is not to go direct to a company, even if you already transact your car or life insurance with them, but to an insurance broker. Brokers receive their income from commissions from the insurance companies they represent, but they are generally independent of individual companies and thus reasonably impartial. Here again, your accountant or solicitor can advise you of a suitable choice, which would be a firm that is big enough to have contacts in all the fields for which you need cover (and big enough to exert pressure on your behalf when it comes to making a claim), but not so big that the relatively modest amounts of commission they will earn from you initially are not worth their while taking too much trouble over, for instance when it comes to reminding you about renewals. Apart from these general points you will have to consider what kinds of cover you need and this will vary some-what with the kind of business you are in. The main kinds are:

1. Insurance of your premises.
2. Insurance of the contents of your premises.
3. Insurance of your stock.
   (The above three kinds of cover should also extend to 'consequential loss'. For instance, you may lose in a fire a list of all your customers. This list has no value in itself but the 'consequent' loss of business could be disastrous. The same is true of stock losses. If a publisher loses all his books in a fire it is not only their value that affects him, but also the consequent loss of business while they are being reprinted, by which time the demand for them may have diminished.)
4. Employer's liability is compulsory if you employ staff on the premises, even on a part-time basis.
5. Public liability in case you cause injury to a member of the public or their premises in the course of business. You will also need third-party public liability if you employ staff or work with partners.
6. Legal insurance policies, which cover you against prosecution under Acts of Parliament which relate to your business (eg those covering unfair dismissal and fair trading).
7. Insurance against losing your driving licence – important if your business depends on your being able to drive.
8. Insurance of machinery, especially mechanical failure of computers, the consequences of which can be disastrous for most kinds of business.
9. Professional indemnity insurance. If you are offering a service, such as consultancy, many clients will demand that you are covered for loss that they might incur as a result of your advice.
10. Product liability insurance. The same principle as the above applies if you are manufacturing or supplying goods. Your customers will expect you to be covered against claims from faulty products.

Your broker will advise you on other items of cover you will need. You should check, for instance, that your existing policies, such as home and vehicle insurance, cover commercial use if that is what you envisage, but do not leave the whole business of insurance in his hands. Read your policies carefully when you get them and make sure that the small print does not exclude any essential item.

Insurance is expensive (though the premiums are allowable against tax inasmuch as they are incurred wholly in respect of your business), and you may find that in the course of time you have paid out thousands of pounds without ever making a claim. However, it is a vital precaution, because one fire or legal action against you can wipe out the work of years if you are not insured. For this reason you must check each year that items like contents insurance represent current replacement values and that your premiums are paid on the due date. Your broker should remind you about this, but if he overlooks it, it is you who carries the can.

Membership of the Federation of Small Businesses (see Appendix 1) includes automatic free legal insurance which covers legal and professional insurance of up to £1,000,000 to protect your business against various legal actions including: Inland Revenue investigations, VAT Tribunals, employment disputes, Health and Safety at Work prosecutions, Consumer Protection Act prosecutions and claims against your business for personal injury. This service also includes a free legal help line open 24 hours a day, 365 days of the year.

Another interesting scheme is Allianz Legal Protection. Its Lawplan enables policyholders to pursue business-to-business debts. It also covers a wide variety of legal costs related to business activities, such as contract disputes. Obviously the need to get cover for such eventualities would depend on the kind of enterprise you are engaged in.

OTHER ADVISERS AND SUPPLIERS

In the course of transacting your business, you will probably need the services of other types of people: builders, to maintain and perhaps refurbish your premises; printers, to produce letterheads, advertising material, etc; surveyors and valuers to assess your property; and so on. You should apply the same criteria to these as to your professional advisers. The services should be reasonably priced, and the service performed to the required standard. If the service is of a professional nature, the consultant should be a member of the relevant professional body. If this does not apply, it may be worth asking for recommendations from the local Chamber of Commerce, or via your nearest Business Link.

Local Enterprise Agencies

There are LEAs throughout the country – a complete list is available from Business in the Community (see address in Appendix 1). LEAs are sponsored by local firms or local branches of national companies, banks, accountancy practices and various public sector bodies. Apart from underwriting the running costs, sponsors often second members of their staff to them. Sometimes these are experienced managers on the eve of retirement, but quite often they are young high-flyers on the way up, being exposed, as part of a career development plan, to a wider variety of business problems than they would get in their own offices.

The quality of advice and their general helpfulness is high – for instance, they will help you to prepare a business plan and advise you on methods of obtaining finance. LEAs also run courses on basic topics like marketing and finance. They are less able to advise on the conduct of specific types of business activity, unless it is one that a seconded member of the LEA's staff happens to know about. Many do, however, operate 'marriage bureaux', putting small businesses in touch with potential customers or investors. Some also maintain registers of suitable properties for small businesses.

Calling in to your Local Enterprise Agency in the early stages of setting up business increasingly ranks with visiting your bank manager as one of the vital first steps of working for yourself.

The Department of Trade and Industry

The Department of Trade and Industry runs a number of programmes, many at regional level, to help small businesses. They fall into three main groups:

1. Consultancy help, ranging from initial advice on the telephone to troubleshooting visits by approved independent consultants.
2. Information and technology transfer, which covers issues like specialised advice on how to protect intellectual property.
3. Grants for research and development.

The Small Business Service has also been set up to help start-ups. The SBS offers guidance on compliance with regulations and provides a new automated payroll service to all new small employers.

The initial contact in all these cases is the DTI itself (1 Victoria Street, London SW1H 0ET; 020 7215 5000) but it is as well to be able to describe, before you ring them, exactly what the nature of your problem or request is. Useful information is also available on the DTI Web site with information fact-sheets on employment and other issues; see www.dti.gov.uk.

Checklist: professional advisers

Solicitors
1. How well do you know the firm concerned?
2. What do you know of their ability to handle the kind of transactions you have in mind?
3. Is their office convenient to the place of work you intend to establish?
4. Do they know local conditions and personalities?
5. Are they the right size to handle your business affairs over the foreseeable future?
6. Have you prepared an exhaustive list of the points on which you want legal advice at the setting-up stage?

Accountants
1. Have they been recommended by someone whose judgement you trust and who has actually used their services?
2. Are the partners members of one of the official accountants' bodies? If not, are you satisfied that they can handle business on the scale envisaged?

---

3. Is their office reasonably close by?
4. Does it create a good and organised impression?
5. Can they guarantee that a member of the firm will give you personal and reasonably prompt attention when required?
6. Have you thought out what sort of help you are going to need?
7. Have you prepared an outline of your present financial position and future needs?
8. Have you considered, in consultation with your solicitor, whether you want to set up as a sole trader, a partnership or a limited company?

Bank manager
1. Is your present bank likely to be the right one for you to deal with in this context?
2. Have you informed your bank manager of your intention to set up a business?
3. Have you established a separate bank account for your business?
4. Have you discussed with your bank manager the possibility of switching your account to a local, smaller branch?

Insurance
1. Do you have a reliable reference on the broker you intend to use?
2. Is he efficient, according to the reports you receive, about reminding you when policies come up for renewal?
3. Has he any track record of paying promptly on claims?
4. Have you prepared a list of the aspects of your proposed business which require insurance cover?
5. Are you fully insured for replacement value and consequential loss?
6. Have you read the small print on your policies or checked them out with your solicitors?

1.5 Presenting Your Case for Raising Capital

Banks make money by lending out the funds deposited with them at rates of interest which vary according to government policy. During periods of economic expansion that rate will be lower – and money easier to get – than during the 'stop' parts of the 'stop and go cycle' that seems to be endemic in the British economy since the war. But banks, like everybody else, have to continue to trade even through less prosperous times. You will find, therefore, that the bank manager will be willing to discuss making money available to you, because potentially you are a source of income to him. How much that will be depends somewhat on the size of the branch you are approaching. This is an argument in favour of going to a large branch if you need a sizeable sum; on the other hand, in a smaller community, where personal contacts still matter, your professional adviser may well have a shrewd idea of what the bank manager's lending limits are.

EXISTING BUSINESS

Whether you can convince the bank manager your business is a good risk depends on how well you have thought out your approach. To some extent he will go on personal impressions and on what he can gather of your previous business experience. If you have already been running your own firm for a year or two he will have some hard evidence to go on in the shape of your profit and loss account and your balance sheet. He will look at the financial position of your firm, particularly the relationship of current assets to current liabilities of debtors to creditors (see Chapter 1.7). He will want to be satisfied that you are valuing your stock realistically and he will want to know how much money you (and your partners, if you have any) have put into the business from your own resources. In the case of a limited company he will want to know what the issued share capital is.

If a business has been operating for three years, a bank will want to look at its historic cash flow in order to see if it has been able to meet the repayments of future loans. Michael Brand in *A Guide to Sources of Finance for SMEs* (Kogan Page) describes this approach as 'driving by looking in the rear view mirror'. However, this does have the advantage over start-ups in providing hard facts for banks to base their decisions on, rather than projections of future earnings.

NEW BUSINESS

While businesses that are able to show evidence of previous trading are advantaged, the banks do still lend to start-ups even though the amount tends to be less and a number of other factors will need to be taken into account. Proposals for lending to a new business will need to be fully worked out and have realistic and thorough cash-flow projections.

The bank will be looking to see whether your business satisfies three criteria:

1. That its money is secure, and in the case of a new business it will probably ask for security to be in the shape of tangible items like fixed assets within the business, or shares and other assets belonging to the owners in their private capacity in a ratio which may be as high as 1:1.
2. That your firm is likely to have inflow of enough liquid assets to enable the bank to recall its money, if necessary.
3. That you will be able to make profitable use of the business and pay the interest without difficulty.

There is a saying that banks will only lend you money if you do not need it, and reading these requirements you may be coming to the conclusion that there is an element of truth in this. But what it really means is that there is no use going to a bank to bail you out of trouble. A business in trouble generally requires assistance on the management side at the very least and banks are just not in a position to provide such assistance, no matter how glowing the prospects might be if the firm could be brought back on track. So the bank manager is only going to be looking at present and quantifiable situations. He will not be very interested in often vague assets such as goodwill and will be even less interested in your hopes for the future.

If you have only just set up in business you may not have much more than hopes for the future to offer; the bank manager will obviously be cautious in such cases. But can these hopes be quantified and have you outlined a thorough cash-flow budget? If you are opening, say, a new restaurant, facts such as that you and your spouse are excellent cooks, have attended courses in catering and have established that there would be a demand for a good place to eat in a particular locality, are relevant. But what the bank also wants to know is:

☐ what your start-up costs are going to be;
☐ whether you have fully worked out what your overheads and direct costs are (ie items like rent, rates, gas and electricity, depreciation on equipment, staff wages and the cost of food);
☐ what relation these are going to have to your charges for meals;
☐ what levels of seat occupancy you need to achieve to make a profit.

This might take quite a lot of working out and it is advisable that you consult closely with your accountant in preparing your case for the bank. Indeed it may be a good idea to take your accountant along with you when you are approaching the bank for financial help.

It is, however, not impossible to do this by yourself. What you need is a 'business plan' and all the banks actually have kits which show you how to prepare them – the one produced by NatWest is particularly good. Even if you do not need finance, it is a good idea to prepare a business plan because it will focus your mind on the main issues that are likely to determine the success of your venture. The salient points are as follows:

- [ ] your business experience;
- [ ] your existing assets and liabilities;
- [ ] the product or service you are proposing to offer, the geographical market for it and how you propose to reach it;
- [ ] the likely demand for it – ie whether it is continuing and to what extent it is seasonal or susceptible to technological obsolescence;
- [ ] competition: where it is and how you propose to counter it by means of price, service, etc;
- [ ] requirements for and likely costs of premises and/or equipment;
- [ ] how much of your own money you are proposing to put in;
- [ ] the amount of finance required and what it is going to be used for;
- [ ] what security you are able to offer;
- [ ] cash flow and profit and loss forecasts for the first 12 months.

A business plan should always be kept as clear as possible and the information should be structured in a way that enables the reader to follow it easily. Lenders and investors who are looking for hard facts and figures need to be included to back up your case. A lender will want to see projections that include the worst-case scenario as well as the best and you will need to show that you have anticipated some of the pitfalls that might occur, and that you have an idea of how you might deal with them.

It is always worth bearing in mind that you might not be present when your business plan is being read and will not have the luxury of being able to explain complex details. There is also the likelihood that the reader's attention will wander off after four pages. It is perhaps wise then to follow a simple structure which allows the reader to find their way around the proposal and which follows a logical sequence.

Edward Blackwell in *How to Prepare a Business Plan* (Kogan Page) has produced a useful guide to this structure:

1. A brief statement of your objectives.
2. Your assessment of the market you plan to enter.
3. The skill, experience and finance you will bring to it.
4. The particular benefits of the product or service to your customers.
5. How you will set up the business.
6. The longer term view.
7. Your financial targets.
8. The money you are asking for and how it will be used.
9. Appendices to back up previous statements, including, especially, the cash flow and other financial projects.
10. History of the business (where applicable).

You need to be able to demonstrate that you have a good grasp of your business and understand the nature of the industry into which you are proposing to enter. Your professional adviser should be able to provide an objective view before submitting the business plan to the bank and should help point out any areas where the detail is unclear. On the basis of this information the bank manager will decide what form of help he is able to offer.

Checklist: presenting your case

1. Have you prepared a written description of your firm?
2. Have you described what skills the key people in your firm have to offer?
3. Have you identified your objectives?
4. Have you described how your product or service compares with the competition's?

5. Have you included what firm orders you have secured?
6. Have you identified what your realistic expectations, opportunities and goals are?
7. Do you have supporting evidence on orders you have obtained or are likely to obtain?
8. Have you (and your associates if any) made as full a commitment to your enterprise in terms of time and money as can reasonably be expected of you?
9. Have you previously obtained financial help for this or any other business? Have you repaid it within the period due?
10. If you have any loans outstanding on the business, how much are they for, for what purpose and how are they secured?
11. Can you produce an up-to-date balance sheet showing the present financial state of your company?
12. Do you have a detailed cash-flow projection, monthly over the first two years and quarterly thereafter, showing cash flow over the period of the loan?

1.6 Different Sources of Capital

There are many methods of raising money. Some of these are direct forms of borrowing or obtaining loans; others are ways in which you can spin out your cash resources. But for most small businesses, and many large ones, bank borrowing is the one most widely used.

OVERDRAFTS

The commonest form of help, as far as the small business is concerned, is an overdraft rather than a bank loan. You will be given facilities to overdraw up to a certain amount, but the advantage of an overdraft, as opposed to a loan, is that interest (usually 2 to 3 per cent above base lending rate) is paid only on the actual amount by which you are overdrawn. Overdrafts are particularly useful, therefore, for the firm whose pattern of business fluctuates, such as the market gardener whose income is higher in spring than in winter, or a business which needs money to finance a large contract until the first progress payments are received. The disadvantage of an overdraft is that it can be called in. Though in practice this rarely happens, it is unwise to use money raised in this way to finance medium- and long-term requirements, particularly those which make no immediate contribution to profits, such as having your office done up! A more likely peril than the overdraft being called in, however, is the fluctuation of interest rates. If these go up sharply because of some economic crisis, you want to be in a position where you are keeping the facility you are using down to a minimum.

Overdrafts are not a suitable way to finance longer-term needs, such as plant, business equipment and premises. For them it is best to take out a bank loan. The duration can be as long as 20 years, though 5 to 10 years is more usual. The longer the period of the loan and the larger the amount – size and duration usually being connected – the more detailed the business plan will have to be.

During the period of the loan, the borrower pays interest and repays the capital sum. As with overdrafts, interest rates are usually 2 to 3 per cent above base rate – sometimes more – but there is some minor scope for negotiation about that. This is worth some investigatory shopping around, because over a long period of time even a fraction of a percentage point can add up to a lot of money when larger sums have been borrowed.

Some schemes also offer the option between a rate of interest fixed at the time of borrowing and a variable one. The former type is advantageous if interest rates are low at this point, though the reverse is true if they are not. There are also schemes which give the option to switch between fixed and variable rates during the term of the loan.

For larger sums you might consider, with the help of your trusty financial adviser, an approach to the Investors in Industry (3i) Group. Its London office is at 91 Waterloo Road, London SE1 8XP, but it also has local offices in other cities. The advantage of 3i is that although it is a commercial body (it was in fact founded by the clearing banks and the Bank of England), it is rather less aggressive than some of its competitors in its approach to participation in the equity and management of the companies to which it lends money; but it is not, on the whole, interested in getting involved in businesses that are not yet established, especially small ones.

In the case of a limited company, the bank is likely to call on individual directors to guarantee any overdrafts or loans against their personal resources. There are certain pitfalls about some forms of guarantee and it is vital that you check with your solicitor when entering into such an arrangement. The most common cause of problems comes when you form a business with partners or shareholders outside your family. The bank will ask that your guarantee will be on a 'joint and several' basis. This harmless-sounding phrase means that if things go wrong and the bank calls in its guarantee, they will collect the money not from the individual guarantors but from the one or ones whom they have identified as being most able to pay. Those who have met their obligations are then left to make their own arrangements to collect from those who have not – the banks will not take action to pursue the defaulter. The enormous costs of litigation then mean that unless the sums involved are very large it is not worth taking legal action. For instance, one group of 'joint and several' guarantors among whom such a problem arose were told by their bank manager that it would probably not be worth taking action over a default of under £3000. Legal costs would swallow up such a sum and even if they won their case they might not get costs.

If you find unacceptable the terms under which your bank is offering finance, it is worth shopping around to see if you can get a better deal elsewhere. The banks are now much more competitive with each other than they used to be and have become very well aware that the government is keeping a sharp eye on evidence of interest rate cartels between them.

You might also try one of the growing number of foreign banks now located in London. The American ones are reported to combine the highest degree of reputability with adventurousness in advancing risk capital.

MONEY FROM LOCAL AUTHORITIES

Local authorities are empowered to spend a certain percentage of the rates in the general interest of the area, including business development. That means that grants may be available for such purposes as start-ups, job creation, rent or improvement subsidies.

The existence of grants for such purposes is not usually well publicised, but Local Enterprise Agencies (details of local agencies are available from the National Federation of Enterprise Agencies on 01234 354 0555 as well as the Department of Trade and Industry on 0207 215 5000) should have information on grants in their areas and who to contact about them at the local authority offices. Business in the Community on 0207 224 1600 can also give lists of any regional schemes designed to help small businesses.

It is worth bearing in mind that these grants are not necessarily restricted to existing ratepayers. The object is to attract businesses and create employment, so if the local authority where you live refuses you a grant, a neighbouring one might take a different view – assuming, of course, that you agree to locate your business there.

In some cases local authorities will make loans even if they are unwilling or unable to offer a grant. The important thing is to find out what their criteria and objectives are in framing your application. In some London boroughs, for instance, special consideration is given to businesses which undertake to employ members of ethnic minority groups. Again, the Local Enterprise Agency should be able to shed some light on this. But whatever approach you decide to use, it will have to be based on a business plan similar to the one you use to borrow money from the bank which is described in Chapter 1.5.

PRIVATE LOANS

You may have friends or relatives who are prepared to lend you money, but private loans are a rich source of misunderstanding and so you should be clear about all the implications of such an arrangement. The best plan is to get a solicitor to draw up the terms of the loan, covering the rate of interest, the period over which the loan is repayable and the circumstances under which it can be withdrawn. It must also be made clear to what extent, if any, the lender has any say in the running of the business and what the nature of this control is. Normally, however, the lender should not be entitled to participation in management matters; nor does the existence of his loan entitle him to a share of the profits, no matter how strong a moral claim he thinks he might have once your business starts making real money. In the case of a limited company, you must explain to the lender that a loan is not the same thing as a shareholding, though of course the offer of a loan might be conditional on acquiring shares or the option to acquire them. You should be clear about the implications of this: it entitles the shareholder to a percentage of profits in proportion to his holdings, and though loans can be repaid it is virtually impossible to dismantle issued share capital in this way.

Often private loans are not offered directly but in the form of guaranteeing an overdraft, on the basis that if the recipient of the overdraft is unable to repay it, the guarantor is liable for that amount. Losses incurred by the guarantor of a capital loan can be treated as a capital loss, to be set off against capital gains.

GOVERNMENT INITIATIVES

Over the last few years there have been various government initiatives to encourage investment in small enterprises and these have been developed into two main strands.

The Enterprise Investment Scheme. This scheme replaces the Business Expansion Scheme which was discontinued in 1993. Investors can still qualify for tax relief on funds invested in small, unquoted companies but the level of relief has been reduced from 40 to 20 per cent. However, the amount an individual can invest and get tax relief on is now £150,000 per annum, and he or she gets capital gains tax relief on the sale of shares in an investment of this kind. There is no limit on the amount that qualifying companies can raise by this method.

The Loan Guarantee Scheme. The idea of the scheme, which was launched in 1981, is that the government guarantees the bank for a large proportion of a business loan when it feels the idea behind a proposition is basically sound but where the bank is unable to take the risk for other reasons.

There are two tiers to the scheme. Established businesses that have been trading for at least two years can borrow up to £250,000, with the government guaranteeing 85 per cent of that. A sum of that size requires DTI approval, but there is a small loan facility of up to £100,000 (the minimum is £5000) for less ambitious enterprises which can be processed much more quickly. That carries a 70 per cent guarantee.

In both cases there is a small premium of 0.5 per cent on fixed-rate loans and 1.5 per cent on variable rate loans.

The government has millions of pounds available to foster the development of new and/or small businesses, the money being offered in the form of cash grants and special rate loans. In particular, it is trying to promote industrial development in the so-called special development areas, which in the main are those areas where traditional industries, such as shipbuilding, are on the decline and where unemployment is therefore apt to be high. The minimum project values go as low as £10,000 to £50,000 and though the authorities tend to look more favourably at established businesses which are relocating in development areas, the prospects are certainly worth investigating if you are in or are thinking of moving to such an area. Development areas offer the further advantage of usually having a large pool of local labour, and though the spectre of unemployment is no longer a guarantee for getting a cooperative labour force together, unions in such areas are often fairly realistic in their demands. Application forms for assistance in moving to a development area can be obtained from the Department of Trade and Industry, 1 Victoria Street, London SW1 0ET.

If your proposed enterprise is in a small town, a run-down part of a large one, or a rural area in England, you should contact your Local Enterprise Agency (addresses obtainable from Business in the Community), local Training and Enterprise Council, or Business Link.

A number of similar regional bodies also exist. These include the Welsh Development Agency, the Scottish Enterprise, Highlands and Islands Enterprise, and the Northern Ireland Development Unit. Your nearest Business Link should be able to advise you on whether you have a case for approaching them.

Further help for small and new businesses include:

- ☐ The SMART scheme which provides grants to individuals and small/medium sized businesses to review, research or develop technologies leading to commercial products.
- ☐ Export Awards to help exploit niche markets.
- ☐ Regional Selective Assistance which provides grants of up to 15 per cent of the eligible project costs. Administered through Government Offices in England or from the National Assembly for Wales, Scottish Executive and Northern Ireland Office.

☐ LINK supports collaborative research partnerships between UK industry and the research base.
☐ Research and development tax credit for smaller firms. Information supplied by the Inland Revenue.

Information on all of these schemes can be found on the DTI's Web site www.dti.gov.uk as can details for the help provided to particular industries such as tourism and design.

Business Start-Up Scheme

To help people set up in business, the Government has run several schemes over the years. First there was the Enterprise Allowance Scheme and then the Business Start-Up Scheme. This no longer runs on a national basis but your local Training and Enterprise Council (TEC) or Job Centre should be able to tell you if there is a scheme to help fund your new venture. Generally, you have to be unemployed for six weeks (although schemes vary from region to region) and must prove that you have a sound business proposition.

You will generally be required to invest some of your own money – around £1,000 – and in return will be given cash to help start your business. This can be payable for anything between 26 and 66 weeks and vary from £20 to £90 per week. As each region has its own rules and regulations, find out as much as possible about these to ensure your application is not rejected.

Free literature

A number of useful free guides on government schemes to help small business have been issued by banks and major accountancy practices. Check with your bank to see what it has to offer in the way of loans or other schemes to assist new businesses.

MONEY THROUGH THE EU

The bank, or possibly your Local Enterprise Agency, should be able to tell you whether you could be eligible for a loan from the

European Investment Bank. These loans are administered through UK banks and though they are mostly for larger sums and bigger projects than the average start-up, they also have medium-term loans for which the minimum amount is as low as £16,000, with a very competitive rate of interest.

Your best chance for an EU loan would be if you were located in an iron and steel closure area and were creating jobs for workers who have been made redundant from those industries. In fact with these European Coal and Steel Community loans there are special interest discount incentives for job creation. For more information on the banks which participate in arranging European loans for business contact the Department of Trade and Industry on 020 7215 5000 and ask for the Regional European Funds Directorate. Or you can contact The European Investment Bank, London Offices, 68 Pall Mall, London SW1 5KS or call 020 7343 1200.

INFORMAL EQUITY CAPITAL

Contrary to popular impressions, most venture capital companies are not interested in business start-ups, unless they are looking for an investment of upwards of £250,000 or so. That generally means enterprises which are already up and running. Management buy-outs and buy-ins are typical examples.

For start-up ventures of the kind we are mostly talking about in this book, a more likely source is what is called informal equity capital: 'business angels' to give them their more colloquial name. They are individual private investors, operating either singly or as syndicates, who are prepared to finance entrepreneurial businesses at an earlier stage and on a smaller scale than venture capitalists are likely to consider.

But where do you find your angel? The answer is through a Business Introduction Service. A directory of these is published by the British Venture Capital Association (Essex House, 12–13 Essex Street, London WC2R 3AA; 020 7240 3846). Firms listed there put together information about enterprises looking for capital – the usual minimum is £10,000. These are circulated to potential investors who usually pay an annual subscription to receive this information. When a deal is made, the enterprise receiving the investment pays a fee to the provider of the introduction.

In many ways, business angels operate like venture capital firms – indeed, the BVCA says that raising informal equity capital may well be the first stage on the way to approaching the venture capital market for bigger sums at a later stage. Business angels provide equity finance in return for a share in the business. They may want to play an active part in running it, which is why some prefer local firms. Business angels taking part in the Enterprise Investment Scheme introduced in the autumn 1993 Budget are allowed to be paid directors of the companies into which they have put money. This was not the case with the Business Enterprise Scheme (BES) which it has replaced.

Participation can be a good or bad thing, depending on personal chemistry, whether the angels can make a genuine contribution, and whether the terms of participation have been clearly set out. The BVCA booklet notes that angels have no desire to take control of the businesses in which they invest, but obviously the potential for friction with an outside shareholder actively involved in running the show should not be discounted: getting the right angel is quite as difficult as it is for angels to find the right investment.

What angels look for is much the same as with venture capital providers: a thorough business plan, which covers not only the business itself, but also full details of the management team, when the investor can expect to get his or her money back and with what return. It follows, therefore, that a great deal depends on the introduction service's ability to find the right match. On the one hand, it should help firms looking for finance to present their case in a way which is likely to attract investors. On the other hand, it should be proactive in recruiting them. Venture Capital Report (tel 01865 784411), the market leader in this field, produces a monthly summary of opportunities and mails it to 750 subscribers, ranging from wealthy individuals to financial institutions. The Local Investor Network on 020 7332 0877 also produces a monthly list of companies looking for investors which is mailed to 350 subscribers.

The BVCA says that one of the big advantages of raising money via the informal equity capital market route is that business angels are quicker to make decisions and also less fixated on short-term gains. It may be that recognition of this situation has encouraged the government to give more scope to business angels under its Enterprise Investment Scheme. A recent change to capital gains tax has also been introduced in order to encourage venture capital companies to sponsor SMEs: for companies who invest for three years the tax is cut from 40 per cent to 22 per cent, and for companies investing for five years the tax is cut to 10 per cent. The introduction of the Corporate Venturing Scheme in the 2000 budget is further intended to encourage investment in SMEs.

Consider, however, the consequences of giving away an equity stake as opposed to raising a loan if you possibly can. The great success story, from the point of view of investing in a start-up, was that of the man who got 50 per cent of Body Shop for an investment of £4000 after Anita Roddick had been turned down by the banks. But if your business grows into the kind of mega-success achieved by Body Shop, having parted with a large chunk of it for a modest investment might be a decision you will look back on with regret.

HIRE PURCHASE ARRANGEMENTS

Hire purchase arrangements can also be made with the help of a finance company. This is a useful way of financing medium- to longer-term commitments, such as the purchase of machinery, equipment and vehicles. The arrangements are basically similar to a private hire purchase contract, in that the buyer asks the finance company to buy the asset. She then hires it for a specific period, paying hiring charges and interest as she goes along, and can then exercise an option to buy goods at the end of an agreed period. Until that point they remain the property of the finance company, and there is thus no need, as a rule, for the hirer to provide security as is the case with a loan. On the other hand, the finance company will require her to maintain the asset in good order, to insure it and possibly to fulfil other special conditions such as providing satisfactory evidence that the money earned from it will at least cover the high interest charges involved.

_____

The periods over which a hire purchase agreement may run vary with the nature of the asset, but in general terms the Finance Houses Association lays down that 'the goods should have a useful life greater than the period of the hire purchase agreement'. This, however, raises the question of what is a 'useful life'? It may be that the item in question, while still technically useful, will become hopelessly antiquated during the period of the agreement. In these days of rapid technological change, it is unwise to enter into unduly long-term commitments.

It is worth calculating the true rate of interest reflected in leasing or hire purchase charges over the given period of time. As in every other form of business, there are sharks around who turn out to charge astronomical rates of interest. It is worth getting more than one quote if there are several possible sources from which to obtain equipment on lease or hire purchase.

OTHER SOURCES OF FINANCE

Investors who buy shares in small unquoted companies will be able to offset losses incurred in the disposal of such shares against taxable income, not just against capital gains. The problem, of course, is how do you find private individuals with risk capital? Surprisingly enough they do exist and, equally surprisingly, one way of getting at them is through stockbrokers. Stockbrokers have, in the past, been very coy about recommending investments of this kind, but the new legislation might, as it is intended to do, make them change their policy.

One is reluctant to suggest names of brokers because, as in the case of finance houses, there are horses for courses; but here again discreet inquiries by your accountant or bank manager might bear fruit.

Another source of information on private individuals with money to invest are solicitors and accountants in rural areas and small towns. They are often much more in touch with the situation on the availability of such funds than their colleagues in larger, more imposing metropolitan offices.

USING YOUR OWN MONEY

Inevitably you will have to put up at least some money of your own. Even if your form of business involves selling an intangible skill, as in the case of consultancy, you are going to need some basic equipment, not to mention the fact that you need to have enough money to live on until your business income builds up. You should bear in mind that any money of your own that you put into your firm should be earning a rate of interest comparable to what you could get outside (ie greater than its opportunity cost), and this must be reflected in your costing and estimating. This topic is dealt with in more detail in Chapter 1.9.

Apart from ready cash in the form of savings, jewellery and other liquid and saleable personal assets, you will also have other, less immediate resources to turn to. The most obvious is your house if you own it or the value far exceeds the mortgage still outstanding. Investigate taking a mortgage on another house and selling the one you are in.

Life insurance policies are also worth bearing in mind because companies will generally be prepared to lend money against up to 90 per cent of their surrender value. Interest rates on these loans are generally lower than on bank overdrafts.

It is possible in the case of a limited company for the share-holders to lend money to the company. This does not increase their liability in the same way as taking up issued share capital. However, outside lenders like banks do not take kindly to such arrangements because it indicates a certain reluctance by the shareholders to put their money where their mouths are!

RAISING MONEY BY EFFECTIVE CASH MANAGEMENT

Any method of raising money from the outside costs money. In a period of high interest rates, borrowing can be so costly as to swallow up the entire profits of a business that is overreliant on it. There are instances where borrowing huge amounts of money has made sense, for instance in the property market, where the value of assets in the early 1970s increased much faster than the value of the money borrowed to acquire them. But subsequent events showed that this is dependent on the assumption that the asset does go on appreciating in value at a very rapid rate, and certainly, from the point of view of the smaller business, one could state as golden rules the following: never borrow more than you have to; never buy until you need to. And when you need to, consider whether hire purchase or even leasing might not make more sense for you than committing cash to an outright purchase. Remember it is cash that pays the bills, not assets or paper profits.

A surprising amount of borrowing can be avoided by effective cash management. It is not dishonest to take the maximum period of payment allowed by your suppliers, and though you do not want to get the reputation of being a slow payer, once you have established a reputation of being a reliable account your suppliers may give you quite a bit of leeway before they start pressing you for payment even on an overdue sum. Nor is it dishonest to take note that some suppliers press for payment fairly quickly, whereas others are more lax. The former get paid first.

The reverse is true in the case of the customers you supply. Send out invoices as soon as the work is done. You are more likely to get paid at that point than some weeks later when the novelty has worn off and maybe quibbles have arisen. Send out statements punctually and make sure that your terms of payment are observed.

Take one simple example of how money can work for your business. If your VAT quarter is January to March you have to pay over the VAT you have billed to your customers minus the VAT you have been billed by your suppliers by the end of April. Thus, if you can send a lot of invoices out to customers on 1 January and get the money in quickly, all your VAT can sit in a deposit account for nearly four months. Equally, if you are planning to buy a large piece of equipment (say, a van) on which there are many hundreds of pounds in VAT for you to claim back, juggling with the precise date on which you make the purchase can minimise the damage to your cash flow.

PROGRESS PAYMENTS

In the case of work done on contract – say, a design or consultancy job involving sizeable sums of money over a longer period of time such as three or four months – it is worth trying to persuade your customer to make advance and/or progress payments. After all, you are going to be involved in considerable expenditure before the final sum becomes due. Whether an approach of this kind should be made depends, of course, on how well you know the customer and how badly you think he needs you. If you need his work more than he needs your services, you should consider a bank overdraft, though the cost of this should be reflected in your charges.

CREDIT FACTORING

Credit management is a tricky business which has sunk more than one promising new enterprise which, hungry for business, too inexperienced or simply too busy to pay attention to time-consuming detail, has let its credit index – the length of time money is outstanding – get out of control. A possible solution is to have a credit factor to look after this aspect for you. The firm using such services continues to send out its own invoices but the factor, who, of course, gets copies of the invoices, takes over the whole business of collecting the receivables. He will also generally give advice on credit limits and, if required to do so, may be able to discount the invoices, ie allow you to draw cash from him against a percentage of the amounts he is due to collect. Naturally a fairly substantial fee is charged for this service, varying with turnover, and on the whole factors are not interested in firms whose annual turnover is less than £100,000, nor in those invoicing too many small amounts to small customers. Your bank should be able to advise you on the choice of a factor. Indeed a number of banks have subsidiaries which offer a factoring service. There is also now an Association of British Factors, made up of some of the largest firms in the business.

COPING WITH EXPANSION

Edward Heath, when Prime Minister, came in for some derisive criticism when he described the dire state of the British ecomony at that time as 'suffering from the problems of success'. It is, nevertheless, a phrase which would ring true for many a businessperson caught unprepared on a tide of expansion, even though at the level of the small firm the symptoms are somewhat different. They may emerge as problems with people, when the staff who were in at the beginning find it difficult to handle a larger-scale operation; or as mistakes made in interviewing and selecting people for new jobs in an expanding company; or simply when the owners are stretched in too many different directions to look at individual trouble spots in enough detail.

Most frequently these trouble spots turn out to be connected, directly or indirectly, with finance. You are producing something for which there is a demand; the world starts beating a path to your door; you appear to be selling your product profitably, and suddenly, in the midst of apparent plenty, you start running out of cash. What has probably happened is that you have forgotten that in general you do not get paid until you have delivered the goods, but your suppliers and the additional staff you have taken on have to be paid out of cash flow generated by a previous and smaller scale of operation.

The way to avoid this situation is to make complete budgeting and cash-flow forecasts (see Chapter 1.9) because you will then be able to select the financial package that is appropriate: short-term loans and overdrafts to meet seasonal or fluctuating demands, such as the materials to supply a big contract; long-term finance for plant, machinery or vehicles, or to make a tempting acquisition; finance from within by tighter controls and better cash management to keep the ordinary course of expansion on an even keel. In other words the trick is to find the right mixture, not just to grab the first jar of financial medicine on the shelf. It may not contain anything like the cure you need.

Checklist: raising capital

1. How much do you need? Have you made an initial cash-flow projection?
2. Is it to finance short- or long-term financial facilities?
3. Should you be looking to your bank for overdraft facilities? If so, to what limit?
4. Should you be looking for a loan from your bank or some other commercial or official body? If so, how much and over what period?
5. Have you considered leasing or hire purchase as an alternative to raising a lump sum? If this option is open to you, have you worked out the cost of leasing and credit finance as compared to interest charges on loans?
6. If your need for cash is related to difficulties with credit control, have you considered invoice factoring?
7. Have you considered turning personal assets into cash?
8. Assuming options 5, 6, and 7 have been considered and rejected, have you worked out how to repay the loan and interest charges?
9. What security can you offer a lender, and has it been independently valued?
10. Exactly how do you propose to use the money?
11. If you are approaching a merchant bank or private individual for venture capital, how much of the equity in and control of your company are you prepared to let go?
12. If you are raising money to enable you to fulfil a large contract, have you talked to your customer about the possibility of them paying you in stages?

1.7 Simple Accounting Systems and Their Uses

Any bank manager will tell you that at least 80 per cent of all business failures are caused by inadequate record keeping. Unfortunately, this fault is by no means uncommon in small businesses because the entrepreneurial person who tends to set up on their own is often temperamentally different from the patient administrative type who enjoys paperwork and charting information in the form of business records. He or she is apt to feel that what really keeps the show on the road is obtaining and doing the work, or being in the shop to look after customers. However, unless you record money coming in and going out, owed and owing, you will never have more than the haziest idea of how much to charge for your products or services, where your most profitable areas of activity are (and indeed whether you are making a profit at all), how much you can afford to pay yourself and whether there is enough coming in to cover immediate commitments in the way of wages, trade debts, tax or professional fees, rent, rates, etc.

It used to be the case that only a limited company was obliged to keep proper books of account: the definition is that they have to do so 'with respect to all receipts and expenses, sales and purchases, assets and liabilities and they must be sufficient to give a true and fair picture of the state of the company's affairs and to explain its transactions'. Under the 1994 Finance Act this provision has effectively been extended to apply to all kinds of business. You are now required to:

> ☐ Set up adequate records of all business transactions, including personal drawings and personal money put into the business. Retailers will have to keep separate records of goods taken for personal use.
> ☐ Maintain those records throughout the year and keep them up to date.
> ☐ Retain the documentation for a recommended six years.

As a rule of thumb, if your scale of operations is big enough to come within the orbit of VAT (that is, if your turnover is, or is likely to be, over £51,000 a year) we suggest you get qualified help with the bookkeeping that will be required. But first of all, let us look at the very basic records you ought to keep if you are in business for yourself at all, even as a part-time freelance.

TWO STARTING POINTS

At the small-scale sole trader end, one reason why you need to keep records is to justify your expenditure claims to the tax inspector. For this purpose you may find that your most useful investment is a spike on which incoming receipts, invoices, statements and delivery notes can be placed. This ensures that essential documentary evidence of expenditure is retained and kept together, not used to put cups on or carried around in your wallet for making odd notes on the back. As your business grows you may find that the spike should be supplemented by a spring-loaded box file in which all such items should be placed in date order.

However, not all expenditure can be accounted for in this way. Fares, for instance, are not generally receipted, nor is postage, or you may be buying items for personal use at the same time as others that are directly connected with your business. Thus it is a good idea to carry a notebook around with you and enter up any expenses that you have incurred that are not documented. You will find that the tax office will accept a certain level of claims of this kind provided they bear a credible relationship to the business you are in. For example, if you are earning income from travelling round the country giving lectures, they will accept a fairly high level of claims for fares, but not if the nature of your business is carrying out a local building repair service.

For larger outlays you may find credit cards a useful record-keeping aid. Apart from the fact that when card companies render their account for payment they provide a breakdown of where, when and how items were purchased, they also, in effect, give you six weeks' credit. During periods of high inflation this is a real consideration.

KEEPING A CASH BOOK

The next stage is to keep a cash book. It does not have to be anything elaborate. The object of the exercise is to provide a record from which an accountant or bookkeeper can write up a proper set of books and to save their time and trouble (which you have to pay for) in slogging through dozens or possibly hundreds of pieces of paper in order to do this. Since your professional adviser will have to work from your records it is a good idea to ask him what is the most convenient way of setting them out. He may suggest that you buy one of the ready-made books of account, though such books are not suitable for every kind of self-employment. If you find it difficult to follow his instructions, or you are using a ready-made book and are having trouble with it, here is something very simple you can do (see Table 7.1).

Buy a large (A4) ruled notebook and open it up at the first double page. Allocate the left-hand page to sales and the right-hand page to expenditure. If sales and expenditure fall into further categories which you want to keep track of, say, if you want to keep travel costs separate from the cost of materials, or if you are registered for VAT, divide up the page accordingly. You should also rule up columns for the date, the invoice number and

Table 7.1 Sample entries from the cash book of a cabinet-maker

INCOME

Date	Invoice No	Date paid	Details	Amount (£)	VAT (£)
2.5.00	8061		Six tables	224	39.20
6.5.00	cash		Desk	400	70.00
10.5.00	8062		Dining table	300	52.50
12.5.00	cash		Repair of wooden chest	160	28.00

EXPENDITURE

Date	Invoice No	Cheque/ Credit card	Details	Amount (£)	VAT (£)
3.5.99	–	911112	Wooden Top timber yard	850	148.75
4.5.99	Petty cash voucher 23	cash	Stamps	6	–
5.5.99	Petty cash voucher 24	cash	Expenses: trip to Harwich to inspect timber	40	7
13.5.99	–	911113	Electricity bill	80	14.00

the details of the invoice. Enter up these details at the end of each day's trading and you will find that it works both as a discipline in checking that all your sales and purchases are logged and that you now have a further record in addition to the documents on your spike or in your box file.

MORE ELABORATE SYSTEMS

This sort of record is fine as far as it goes and in a small business engaged mainly in cash transactions your accountant may not need very much more than this to produce a set of accounts. In a larger concern, or one that operates extensively on taking and giving credit, it has some obvious limitations. For example, keeping track of when payments are made or received can become rather messy and difficult, and you will need to have a separate record, called a ledger, of the customers and suppliers with whom you do business so that you can see at a glance how much you owe or are owed in the case of individual accounts. Such details will be taken from further books – purchases and sales daybooks and a more elaborate kind of cash book than the simplified one we have described above. Though we have recommended that you leave the details of this kind of book-keeping to a qualified person, let us look briefly at what is involved.

1. _Cash book._ Shows all payments received and made, with separate columns for cash transactions and those made through the bank (ie payments by cheque). Amounts received from customers are credited to their account in the ledger (see below). Payments made to suppliers are debited to their account in the ledger.
2. _Petty cash book._ Shows expenditure on minor items – postage, fares, entertainment and so forth, with a column for VAT.
3. _Sales daybook._ Records invoices sent out to customers in date order, with some analysis of the goods or service supplied and a column for VAT.
4. _Purchases daybook._ Records similar information about purchases.

5. *Ledger.* Sets out details, taken from sales and purchases daybooks, of individual customers' and suppliers' accounts and serves as a record of amounts owed and owing. Details from the analysis columns of the sales and purchases daybooks are also transcribed, usually monthly, under corresponding headings in the ledger. This enables you to see at a glance where your sales are coming from and where your money is going.

6. *Capital goods ledger.* If you own expensive capital equipment – cars, lorries, machine tools, high-class film or photographic equipment, etc – you should have separate accounts for them in the ledger because the method of accounting for them is somewhat different. Capital items depreciate over a period of time (as you will know if you have ever sold a car) and this fact must be reflected both in your balance sheet and profit and loss account, and in the way you price your goods and services.

   Writing down capital goods affects your tax liability. With some items you can write down the full advantage of this concession. How you deal with depreciation is very much an area where you are dependent on your accountant's expert advice.

ELECTRONIC BOOKKEEPING

There are many different reasons for putting your accounts system on to a computer. Routine tasks become much quicker, statements and other regular correspondence can be mail-merged and personalized and up-to-date balances included. Correcting any mistakes can be done at the touch of a button and if your business is growing, a computerized accounting system will make life much easier when you take on new staff, increase your spending or have more invoices to chase.

Perhaps the most useful aspect of a computerized accounts system is the fact that once the information is recorded, it can be used to give you a snapshot of the business performance at any time, which is ideal when preparing your end-of-year accounts.

The following are a few points to bear in mind when looking to purchase a bookkeeping package:

☐ Don't walk into a shop or dealership and buy the cheapest thing on offer. Remember, it is not the PC that does the real work, it is the software and if you buy a system that is not suited to your business it could cost you a lot of time, effort and money later on.

☐ Define what it is that you need your accounting software package to do. Do you want to run your whole system on it or just do some sales invoicing? Will you need to automate just the main ledgers or would you like to put sales-order processing, purchase-order processing and stock control onto the computer? Do you have any special procedures or requirements specific to your business that you must stick to, whatever the system? It is important that you answer these questions before you start shopping around.

☐ Collect some information on accounting software products and PCs and read some of the reviews published in computer magazines.

☐ Talk to your accountant, who may be able to advise you about some packages. Information may also be available from authorized software dealers, large retail stores such as PC World and professional bodies such as the Institute of Chartered Accountants.

It is also worth remembering that computers do crash and if you have failed to make copies of your accounts on disk on a regular basis you could land yourself in deep water. Back-up stationery, such as invoices, are worth having as well in such a situation so that a technical problem shouldn't turn into an income-threatening crisis.

TRADING AND PROFIT AND LOSS ACCOUNT

From the books described above, your accountant can draw together the information needed to compile the trading and profit and loss account (see Table 7.2). The function of the account is to tell you whether you have been making a gross profit and a net profit on your trading. It must be compiled annually and preferably more often than that, quarterly for instance, to enable you to measure your progress and make your VAT return.

To put together the account he begins by identifying the period you want to cover. He then totals up the value of all sales, whether paid for or not. Then he takes your opening stock and adds it to the purchases (but not expenditure such as rent or repayment of interest on loans). From this he takes the value of your stock (based on cost or market value, whichever is lower) at the end of the period you want to cover. Deducting the value of opening stock plus purchases from the value of sales will give him your gross trading profit (or loss) over the period.

Table 7.2   *Example of a trading and profit and loss account*

Trading and Profit and Loss Account for year ended 31.12.00

	£	£
Sales		65,000
Purchases	30,000	
Opening Stock	5,000	
	35,000	
Less Closing Stock	6,000	29,000
Gross Profit		36,000
Rent and Rates	3,000	
Salaries	9,000	
Heat, Light	600	
Phone	350	
Travel	800	
Repairs	500	
Depreciation	1,800	
Professional Advice	450	
		16,500
Net Profit		19,500

Using this information he can work out the net profit and loss over the same period. The gross profit figure from your trading account appears at the top and against it he sets all the items from the various expenditure accounts in the ledger. He also includes in this figure the depreciation on capital equipment, but not its actual cost (even if you purchased it during the period in question) because that crops up later, in the balance sheet.

Deducting these from the gross profit gives you your profit over the period. If the total expenditure exceeds the gross profit you have obviously incurred a loss.

THE BALANCE SHEET

We have mentioned in the previous section that capital equipment does not figure in the profit and loss account, but goes into the balance sheet. The balance sheet is a picture, taken at a particular point in the year (usually at the end of a company's financial year), of what the firm _owes_ and what it _owns_ (see Table 7.3). (This is not the same as a profit and loss account, which covers a period of time.)

In a balance sheet the assets of the firm used to be set out on the right and the liabilities on the left, but it is modern practice to display them as below. However, all the assets and all the liabilities are generally not lumped together, but distinguished qualitatively by the words 'fixed' and 'current'.

'Fixed assets' are items which are permanently necessary for the business to function, such as machinery, cars, fixtures and fittings, your premises or the lease on them. 'Current assets', on the other hand, are things from which cash will be realised in the course of your trading activities. These include the amount owed to you by your debtors (from the customers' accounts in the ledger), and the value of your stock (from the trading account). It also, of course, includes cash at the bank (from the cash book).

With liabilities, the position is reversed. 'Fixed liabilities' are those which you do not have to repay immediately, like a long-term loan from a kindly relative. What you do have to repay promptly, however, is the interest on that loan and this goes under

Table 7.3 *An example of a balance sheet*

Balance Sheet as at 31.12.00

	£	£
Fixed Assets		
Vehicles	3,200	
less depreciation	800	2,400
Fixtures and fittings	2,000	
less depreciation	500	1,500
		3,900
Current Assets		
Stock	6,000	
Debtors	1,800	
Cash	150	
	7,950	
Less Current Liabilities		
Trade Creditors	1,590	
Net Current Assets		6,360
Total Assets		10,260

Represented by	Authorised	Issued
Capital (2,000 shares at £1 each)	1,000	1,000
Loan repayable 2000		2,000
Profit		7,260
		10,260

'current liabilities' if it is due, but has not been paid at the time the balance sheet has been prepared. The same is true of any amounts you owe to your suppliers' accounts in the ledger. Another item that goes on the 'liabilities' side is the share capital in the business and the profit from the trading account, because both these amounts are ultimately owed by the company to the shareholders. Where, on the other hand, the company has been making a loss, the amount is deducted either from profits retained from earlier periods or from the shareholders' capital.

WHAT SHOULD YOU BE LOOKING FOR IN YOUR RECORDS?

You will want to know whether you are making or losing money, but there are many other useful bits of information to be gleaned as well. If you are making a profit, what relationship does it bear to the capital employed in the business? You can calculate this by subtracting total liabilities from total assets. If you are making less than a 15 per cent return on capital, you are not, on the face of things, making much progress, though, of course, you could be paying yourself a very handsome salary before the profit figure was arrived at.

The percentage return on capital can be calculated by the following sum:

$$\frac{\text{profit}}{\text{capital employed}} \times 100$$

Another thing you can work out from your balance sheet is whether you are maintaining sufficient working capital to meet your requirements for new stock or materials or to pay for wages and rent. Here you look at current assets and current liabilities. The calculation:

$$\frac{\text{current assets}}{\text{current liabilities}}$$

gives you your _current_ ratio. If you have, say, £1000 of each you are said to have a current ratio of 1:1. Clearly, in that case you would be in trouble if a major debtor were to go bankrupt. So it may be that you should cut back on some item of expenditure you were planning on. Furthermore, the current ratio includes certain items, like stocks, which may not be immediately realisable. If your current ratio is low, and you are still in two minds whether or not to buy that new machine, you might apply what is known as the _acid test ratio_, which shows your ability to meet liabilities quickly if the need arises. Here you simply deduct stock from your figure for current assets to give you a figure for liquid assets, ie debtors and cash. If the ratio of liquid assets to current liabilities is too low, you may have more money tied up in stock than you should have.

Even the acid test ratio assumes that your debtors are going to pay you in a reasonable period of time: most likely within the terms of trade you are allowing. But is this assumption really correct? Look at the annual sum:

$$\frac{\text{debtors}}{\text{sales}} \times 365$$

If your sales are £10,000 and your debtors owe £1000, they are near enough to meeting net monthly terms for you not to worry about it. But if your debtors, on the same sales turnover, are running to £3000, there is something wrong with your credit control and you are probably heading for serious trouble.

Another important ratio is profit to sales. What this should be depends on the sort of business you are in. Your accountant should be able to advise you here on the basis of her knowledge of similar traders. If your percentage is on the low side you may be buying badly, failing to pass on cost increases, or possibly incurring losses from pilferage.

There are other ratios to look out for, but we hope that you will now be clear that the balance and trading and profit and loss accounts are not just a financial rigmarole you have to go through, but very valuable indicators of the way your business is going, or the financial state of some other business you are thinking of buying. They are also useful for:

1. Assisting the bank manager to determine the terms of an overdraft.
2. Selling your business to a proposed purchaser.
3. Agreeing tax liabilities with the inspector of taxes.

Checklist: simple accounting systems

1. Do you carry a notebook to record smaller items of business expenditure, such as taxi fares, as soon as they are incurred?
2. Have you considered using credit cards for larger outlays?
3. Do you have a system for filing incoming invoices as soon as they are received?
4. Have you asked your accountant what books and records she advises you to keep?
5. Do you know and understand the procedures involved? If not, have you asked your accountant to recommend someone who can help you on a regular basis – at least once a week or once a month, depending on your scale of operations?
6. Do you have any idea of the ratios current in your type of business, so that you can measure your performance against the norm?

1.8 Invoicing and Credit Control

Time is money, as the old saying goes. It ought to be written large in the minds of anyone giving credit, that is, any business that supplies goods and services which are not on a strictly cash-on-the-nail basis.

In these days of tight money there is a tendency for many customers, including large and reputable firms, to delay payment as long as possible because, as noted in Chapter 1.6, taking credit long – and preferably giving it short – is one way to maintain a flow of cash in the business. The supplier who does not demonstrate that he is in a hurry for payment, therefore, is the one who comes last in the queue. However, help to improve the payment culture has come in the form of the Statutory Right to Interest (SRI) which was introduced in November 1998. Under the SRI any business with under 50 employees – including sole traders – can charge interest on late payment. While the DTI hopes that the parties involved can work out a payment time between themselves, the SRI can enforce a payment schedule of 30 days after which interested can be charged. The right will eventually be rolled out to all businesses regardless of size.

SENDING OUT INVOICES AND STATEMENTS

The first step towards ensuring that you are not in this position is to issue an invoice for work done or goods supplied as soon as possible after you deliver. On the invoice you should give the customer's order number. If it was a telephone order and you forgot to get an order number, you should at least give the date of the order. You should also state when you expect to receive payment. The usual period is between seven and 30 days after delivery. Many private individuals, in fact, pay on receipt of an invoice. Business firms, on the other hand, expect to receive a statement of their account at the end of the month, setting out invoices due or sent during this period: their dates, invoice number, the nature of the goods and the amount. You can have statement forms printed, but if you are not a limited company you can use your letterheads for this purpose, simply typing the word STATEMENT at the top. Every customer who has received an invoice and not paid at the end of the month when it is due should get a statement, which should repeat your payment terms.

The particulars of the invoice(s) are drawn from your customer's ledger, though it is essential to keep copies of the actual invoices as well, filed in date order. You are going to need them for VAT purposes, or to check queries. When you receive payment, check that it tallies with the amount due on the customer's ledger entry, mark off the details against each individual item as shown in the previous chapter and enter the amount in the cash book. If the customer requires a receipt, ask her to return the statement (or the invoice if she has paid on that) with her remittance – otherwise you will be involved in time-consuming typing – tick off the items paid, and attach a receipt form or bang on a rubber stamp, 'Paid'. Be uniform about your systems. If you have two different ones for the same part of your operation you are going to waste a lot of time looking in the wrong place when you come to check a document.

Do not neglect the process of checking payments, because any amounts unpaid must go into next month's statement. Some invoices which have appeared on your statement will not be paid because they are not yet due for payment. For example, if your terms are 30 days and you have invoiced an item on the 20th of the month, a business customer is unlikely to pay until the month following. Quite often he only activates payments at the end of the month, unless he is unusually punctilious, efficient or being offered extra discount for quick settlement.

As already mentioned, the Statutory Right to Interest does allow interest to be charged on late payment. At the time of its introduction in November 1998, according to Barclays Small Business Bulletin only 24 per cent of small business owners said that they were planning to use the legislation because they did not want to upset customers and create additional administration. However, there is some indication that the introduction of SRI has already improved the payment culture even when so few people are planning to use it.

Even with the additional threat of being able to add interest, there will still be times when a client can't or won't pay. What, then, happens when the payment becomes overdue? This is extremely annoying, because at best it is going to involve you in extra correspondence. You must be tactful and patient if you want more business from your clients, and remember that some large organisations are slow in paying, not by choice but because they are dictated to by their computer accounting systems. But if your patience is exhausted, there are usually three stages. The first is a polite reminder of the amount due, how long it has been due and of your terms of supply. This should be coupled with asking the customer whether she has any queries on any of the invoices which might explain the delay. If there is no reply by the end of that month, write again, referring to your first reminder and setting a deadline for payment with additional payment. A telephone call to the customer is often opportune at this stage. If that deadline is not met, you will have to write again, referring to your previous reminders and threatening legal action unless a new and final deadline is met. (If you have a large number of credit accounts, it may pay you to have sets of blank letters for each stage prepared in advance.)

In most cases the threat of legal action will do the trick, but how you proceed after that depends on the amount of money involved. Fortunately the Court and Legal Services Act of 1990 has simplified procedures. Debts of any amount can be recovered in the County Court, without involving solicitors – though, of course, their services may ultimately be necessary if the claim is disputed by the debtor.

Then there are three important points to establish before starting legal action:

1. Can the defendant actually pay? Wringing blood from a stone is a notoriously fruitless exercise.
2. Can you prove the claim by producing documentation about what was actually agreed, such as a confirming letter? Bounced cheques, reminders to pay, etc are also relevant.
3. Are you sure you have got hold of the right person? You may have been dealing with an individual acting on behalf of a company. In that case the claim is against the company.

The next stage is to issue a default summons in the County Court. It does not have to be in the area where the defendant lives, which could be in your favour if the case is undefended. If it is defended, the matter will automatically be heard in the defendant's County Court, though here again there is an option to full-scale proceedings. If the amount involved is less than £1000 the matter automatically goes to arbitration. This means both parties are obliged to accept the arbitrator's judgment.

The default summons involves a certain amount of paperwork. The court officials will brief you if you choose to do this yourself rather than getting your solicitor to do so. Remember, he may charge you anything from £50 to £200 per hour, depending on how high-powered a firm you choose.

In the first place the summons is sent by post. The defendant then has 21 days in which to reply and if he fails to do so or to announce his intention to defend the action, then you as the plaintiff are entitled to judgment, which will include the amount claimed, plus court costs: a maximum of £70 for claims of under £5000, plus extras which can mount up if the case drags on. The problem is not so much the court costs but the time and trouble that it all takes. However, the good news is that few defendants will let matters go as far as this and the ultimate sanction of having bailiffs called in on them, if they can pay and unless they intend to defend the case.

You can, of course, ask for references before giving credit, though this is a matter which has to be approached with some delicacy; but if you receive a sizeable order out of the blue from some business firm with whom you have not previously dealt, it is advisable to ask for a couple of references in acknowledging the order. Ask the referees to what amount they give credit to this particular customer, how long they have been doing business with her and whether she pays promptly.

If your business consists of making or repairing goods to order – tailoring, for instance – it is not unusual to ask the customer to pay up to 50 per cent on account where an estimate of over £50 or so has been given. This helps cash flow as well as protecting you against possible default. Equally, if goods of resaleable value are left with you for repair you should display a notice reserving the right to dispose of them if the customer does not come to collect them within a reasonable time of completion of the work.

A common delaying tactic, or it may be a perfectly legitimate query, is for the customer to ask for copy invoices on receipt of your statement. Do not part with your file copy. You will have to send a photocopy if you do not keep duplicates for this purpose.

CREDIT CARDS

For larger personal transactions and for items such as the settlement of restaurant bills, credit cards are a popular method of making payment. A business which wants to offer credit card payment facilities to its customers has to make application to the company concerned, which then sets a money limit to the transaction per customer for which the business in question can accept payment on that company's cards. Above that limit, which is based roughly on the applicant's average transaction per customer, the sale has to be referred back to the credit card company. This can be done over the telephone.

Each sale, as it is made, is entered up on a voucher supplied by the credit card company. The voucher is paid into the bank by the seller and the amount is debited to the card holder's account. The advantage of credit cards from the seller's point of view is that he receives guaranteed payment. Against this, he has to pay to the bank a small percentage on every transaction, the amount of this percentage being negotiated at the time he joins the scheme.

Most credit card companies operate on lines very similar to the scheme we have just outlined. Diner's Club vouchers, for instance, though not paid into a bank, are sent to the Club organisation on certain specified dates, whereupon payment is made to the seller.

CHECKING INCOMING INVOICES AND STATEMENTS

Unless you transact your business by paying in cash or by cheque on the spot (which is likely in only a few business spheres), you will also be at the receiving end of invoices and statements from your suppliers. The moment they come in, put them on the spike. Then, daily if possible, enter the details in the suppliers' ledger, as described in Chapter 1.7. File incoming invoices in date order, for you will need them for VAT purposes.

When you receive your statement, make sure it tallies with the amounts and details which you have entered in the suppliers' ledger, mark off all the items paid and write up the amount in the cash book.

If you are paying by cheque there is no need to ask for a receipt (which only adds to the paperwork) since an honoured cheque is itself a receipt. Make sure, though, that you enter up the stubs, unless you write up the cash book at the same time as you draw the cheques.

Checklist: invoicing and credit control

Invoicing
1. Are you invoicing promptly, on or with delivery?
2. Do your invoices clearly state your terms?
3. Do you ensure that the customer's name, address and order number (if any) or date are correctly stated on your invoice?
4. Are your statements sent out promptly at the end of the month? Do they state your payment terms?
5. Are they clear and easy to follow? Would they make sense to you if you were the recipient?

Running Your Own Business

6. Are you checking payments received against ledger entries?

Credit control
1. Does every account have a credit limit?
2. Is it based on first-hand knowledge of the customer as a credit risk or personally, his track record as a payer with you or others in your line of business, on representatives' reports or reliable trade references, or on bankers' references, in that order of decreasing usefulness?
3. Do you exercise special vigilance on new accounts?
4. Do your statements show the age of outstanding balances and do you or your credit controller look at outgoing statements to check on customers whose payments situation seems to be deteriorating?
5. Do you have a system for dealing with customers who exceed their credit limit?
6. Do you have a sequence of reminder procedures for dealing with overdue accounts by telephone calls and/or letters?
7. Do you check orders received against a list of customers who have exceeded their credit limit or who are proving to be reluctant payers or non-payers?
8. Does the person in charge of credit control liaise with those responsible for supplying the account in question to make sure that there are no special reasons for non-payment before sharper warnings are delivered?
9. Do you regularly check on the debtor:sales ratio to make sure you are not heading for a liquidity problem by being too generous about extending credit?
10. Do you have a list of people you can contact in your principal customers' accounts departments if there are payment problems?

1.9 Budgeting and Cash-flow Forecasting

One principle that it is vital to grasp is the importance of liquid cash in running a business. This should not be confused with profitability. Because of the way the profit figure is arrived at on the trading account (see Chapter 1.7), it is perfectly possible for a business to be trading profitably and yet be quite unable to pay the tax bill or the rent because its resources are tied up in stock or, even worse, in equipment.

Failure to understand the distinction between profit and cash flow is not uncommon and it can be disastrous. For example, you may be offered very persuasive financial inducements to carry or manufacture additional stock. If it is a good product and one for which there is a consistent demand, you may say to yourself that you are going to need more anyway in six months' time, so why not stock up for a whole year at a bargain price? This can be a valid argument, but before you accept it consider that when the bills come in they have to be paid with money, not with stock. Profitability means very little unless cash is there when it is needed.

This is true even for businesses that do not carry stocks, like a photographic studio producing goods only to order, or a design consultancy selling more or less intangible skills. You are still going to have outgoings on travel or materials; and even if your premises are a back room in your own house there are still bills to be met, apart from the matter of needing money to live on.

PLANNING YOUR CASH REQUIREMENTS

Planning your cash requirements is crucial from the outset of your career as a self-employed person. It will determine much of your policy towards what kinds of work you take on. It is far better, if you are short of liquid capital, to take on a number of small jobs which will keep money coming in than one big, tempting, potentially profitable one where you might run out of cash three-quarters of the way through. For, unless you make provision to receive progress payments from your customer, backed up possibly by a bank overdraft, your suppliers are going to be pressing you for payment before you are in a position to send your bills to the customer.

Even at best, in most businesses which are not taking cash across the counter there is going to be a lag between the time you are being asked for payment and when your customer pays you.

In order to estimate what your needs for cash are going to be, you should set up and revise, at three- or six-monthly intervals, a cash-flow budget; and in order to refine it, you should also check it back against what actually happened. Indeed, before you begin you should have (and the bank manager will want to see) a fully worked out cash-flow projection for the first 12 to 18 months.

The words 'cash-flow budget' sound intimidatingly technical, but mean simply that you should make a realistic forecast of money coming in and going out over the period. Again, how accurate you can be depends somewhat on the circumstances and the type of business you are in. If you have bought a going concern there may be regular contracts that you hope to maintain, or in the case of a retail business or a restaurant some kind of predictable pattern of trade which can be established from the cash book or general ledger. If you have started a new business of your own, on the other hand, you may not have much to go on in the way of facts on cash coming in. You might only have enough certain information on the next two or three months, though if you have asked yourself the questions we outlined in Chapter 1.1 you will have ensured, as far as possible, that there is a continuing demand for your product so that orders will go on arriving while you are completing the work you have already lined up. But even in cases where you do not know where the penny after next is coming from, at the very least the cash-flow budget will tell you what commitments you have to meet and, therefore, what volume of sales should be your target to this end. You can include this sales target in your budget, but do not forget that, in order to achieve it, costs of materials and additional overheads will also be involved. Moreover, both in cases where income is firmly expected and where it is only a forecast of expectations, the cost of materials and wages will have to be met before you actually get paid.

Let us take a hypothetical case here to illustrate a cash-flow budget in operation over the first four months of the year, for a small offset printing business with two partners and one employee. Over these months they have a contract to print the spring catalogue from a local firm of nursery men, a monthly list from a firm selling militaria by mail order and a booklet on the town for the Chamber of Commerce. They also have some orders for what is known as 'jobbing' – small jobs such as wedding invitations, brochures, printed labels and the like – with the prospect that a regular flow of such work can be picked up. Against this, they have to meet wages, PAYE, VAT, telephone, the running of a van, the purchase of materials, rates, electricity, National Insurance contributions, etc.

As you will see from the forecast (see Table 9.1), the partners budgeted for a deficit in the first two months, but they were not worried because they knew that in March and April they could expect a couple of big payments from Rosebud Nurseries and from the Chamber of Commerce. However, in order to keep solvent they had to borrow £2000 from the bank, interest payments on which had to be paid at intervals. They also had to plan the purchase of their most costly item, paper, as close as possible to the month in which they would actually be using it for their two big jobs. There is no point in holding expensive stock which cannot be used at an early date. Even though, with inflation, it might actually have been cheaper for them to have ordered all their paper for the first four months back in January, their bank overdraft would not have been sufficient to meet the bill.

In March they had to allow for three quarterly items, electricity, telephone and their VAT return, and as the year progresses they

Table 9.1 An example of a cash-flow budget

Income (£)

January	£	February	£	March	£	April	£
From December Statement		From January Statement		From February Statement		From March Statement	
Militaria Ltd	500	Militaria Ltd	500	Rosebud Nurseries Ltd	5,300	Chamber of Commerce	2,000
Other work	400	Other work	250	Militaria Ltd	500	Militaria Ltd	500
				Other work	500	Other work	500
	900		750		6,300		3,000

Expenditure (£)

January	£	February	£	March	£	April	£
Wages, salaries, PAYE, National Insurance	750	Wages, etc	750	Wages, etc	750	Wages, etc	750
Rent	100	Rent	100	Rent	100	Rent	100
Maintenance contract	20	Maintenance	20	Maintenance	20	Maintenance	20
Petrol	40	Petrol	40	Petrol	40	Petrol	40
Postage	20	Postage	20	Postage	20	Postage	20
Travel and Entertainment	40	Travel, etc	40	Travel, etc	40	Travel, etc	40
Paper	1,500	Materials	100	Materials	150	Materials	100
Other materials	200	Bank Interest	60	Electricity	70	Paper	1,500
				Telephone	40		
				VAT	300		
				Paper	1,000		
	2,670		1,130		2,530		2,570

January	February	March	April
Cash surplus (deficit)			
(1,770)	(380)	3,770	430

will have to make plans to meet such major items as rates and taxes. Note also that expenditure which is central to the activities of the business, in this case paper, has to be forecast more carefully than incidentals such as postage where a monthly average has been extended. If postage was a more crucial factor, as might be the case with a mail-order firm, this part of the cash-flow budget would have to be worked out in more detail.

Regarding the revenue part of the forecast, the partners had enough orders for jobbing work to budget fairly accurately for the first two months. For March and April they guessed a figure, hoping spring weddings and a general upturn of business after the winter would lead to a modest growth in incoming funds after that point.

The overall March and April figures look quite rosy, but after that it was clear that they would have to turn up some more jobs like Rosebud Nurseries and the Chamber of Commerce booklet because the overheads – wages, rent, the maintenance contract on their machines, bank interest – plus the cost of paper and materials needed to fill forecast work were running slightly above the expected income. So even though they are running well ahead of the game at the end of April, they would be unwise to start reducing that bank overdraft just yet.

There are many other lessons to be learned from your cash-flow budget. They vary from business to business, but the essential points are that it is an indispensable indicator in making your buying decisions both of stock and materials, that it helps you decide your priorities between getting work (and what sort of work) and devoting all your energies to executing it, and points to the importance of getting the maximum credit and allowing the minimum!

Checklist: budgeting and cash flow

1. Is the forecast of money coming in based on firm orders or at least reasonable expectations or does it include an element of fond hope?
2. Are the customers concerned likely to pay you at the times forecast?
3. Can you persuade any large customers to offer you progress payments to help you over difficult months?
4. Have you included everything in the outgoings section of the budget, including allowing for things like VAT and the heating of premises in winter months?
5. Do you have the resources to see you through deficit months, or have you secured finance to this end?
6. Is there any way you can cut down on the expenditure element by delaying or staggering buying decisions of stock or leasing rather than buying equipment?

1.10 Costing, Pricing and Estimating

How much should you charge your customers? Or, to put it more searchingly, on what factors should your charges be based? It is surprising that many self-employed people would be hard put to it to give a clear answer to that question. There are such things as 'going rates' and 'recommended' (or generally accepted) prices, but often these are in the nature of broad guidelines and unless you know what all your costs are, not just the cost of materials, or how long the job took you, you are sooner or later going to be in the position of either under charging or making an actual loss.

There are some self-employed occupations where the scope for how much you can charge is either narrow or non-existent. This applies particularly to many areas of the retail trade, where goods tend to have recommended prices printed on them by the suppliers; but even there you may want to consider *reducing* some prices in order to undercut a competitor and the question arises whether you can afford to do so. This depends on your overall costs – rent, rates, power supplies and many other factors. Equally, some freelance jobs are subject to generally accepted 'going rates' and the more commonplace such jobs are (ie the smaller the degree of service or expertise that is involved) the more strictly you have to keep within that rate. But the corollary of this statement is also true: the more unique your product or service, the more you can afford to charge for it.

This can apply even in the ordinary retail trade where, on the face of things, the prospect of getting away with charging more than the competition is not promising. Recently a small super-market opened near my house. It is open late at night, on Sundays and on public holidays and, quite rightly, it charges for that extra time. Most things cost a penny or two above what they do in the larger shops down the High Street, but it is offering something more than they are, and meets competition not by charging less, but by providing more – a much-needed neighbourhood service for out-of-hours shopping.

The same principle can be applied to even rather routine free-lance jobs. Provide a straightforward typing service and you will have to stick pretty much to the going rate; but offer something special, like accurately typing mathematical material or unusually high turn-round speeds, and you can move into a different price bracket.

DETERMINING YOUR COSTS

You could say to yourself: 'I'm going to charge as much as I can get away with' or, 'I'm going to charge the standard rate for the job.' These are quite sensible guidelines to be going on with, but at some point you are probably going to be in the situation of wondering whether you should be charging a little more, or perhaps whether you can afford to reduce your price in order to land some work that you badly want. It is then that you have to get to grips with what your costs really are.

The most obvious one is your own time, and curiously enough it is an element that self-employed people are often confused about, because they tend to regard it as being somehow different from the time taken by employees. If a job involves your working flat out for a 100-hour week, you are underpricing the product of that work if your remuneration is less than that of an employed person doing the same kind of work at full overtime rates. There may be a reason why you *should* be undercharging: you may want a 'loss-leader' introduction to a particular customer, or to undercut a competitor, or you may simply need the money that week. But if you undercharge, you should be clear in your mind why you are doing so.

Another factor that is sometimes overlooked is that in most cases there are overhead costs incurred in running your business, irrespective of whether you have work coming in or not. We will deal with these overheads in more detail in a moment, but the point to be made here is to correct any misconception that the margin between what you charge and your basic costs in time and/or materials represents your profit. True, it is a profit of a kind – gross profit. But the real profit element in a job, the net profit, only emerges when the overhead costs have been met. So the right way to work out your price to the customer, or to determine whether a job is worth taking on, is to establish whether it will pay for materials, overheads, wages (if you employ others) and still leave you with a margin of net profit that adequately reflects the time and skill you are putting into it.

Once you have been in business for a few months you should have accumulated enough facts and figures to establish what your overhead costs are. To what extent you can control the situation beyond that depends, again, on what sort of business you are in. If you are running an ordinary retail shop, operating on margins that are more or less fixed by the supplier, there is not much you can do about pricing your goods, but at least you will know whether you can afford to spend more on extra fittings or take on more staff, or whether you should be staying open longer to attract extra trade. But if you are manufacturing something, you can work out a rule-of-thumb method in the form of a percentage to add on to your materials costs in quoting prices or, in the case of a service, an average hourly rate. It is important, though, to keep on monitoring these rule-of-thumb procedures against what actually happened, so you should keep a record detailing the specification of each job, in which actual costs can be compared against your original estimate. Over a period of time, in this way you should be able to build up a reliable set of costs which can be referred to when an assignment which sounds similar comes up.

At the beginning, though, you will have very little to go on, so let us look in more detail at the factors you will have to take into account.

Costs connected with your premises

Rent, heat, light, telephone, rates, insurance, finance (if you own or have bought a lease of the premises), cleaning and maintenance contracts and the uniform business rate.

Costs of finance

Interest charged on overdrafts or loans. You should include in this calculation interest on any money you yourself have put into the business, because it should be earning a rate of return equivalent to what you could get on the open market.

Costs of equipment

If you are renting equipment or buying it on hire purchase, this item of expenditure presents no problems. The issue is more complicated if you have bought equipment outright, because you have to figure out some way of recovering the purchase price and this is done by bringing in the concept of 'depreciation'. What this means is that you gradually write off, over a period of time based on the item's useful life, most of the amount you paid initially; not all, because it will have some resale value at the end of the depreciation period.

Supposing you bought a second-hand van for £6000 and you think it will last you for four years, at the end of which time you could expect to get £1000 for it. This leaves you with £5000 to depreciate over four years – £1250 per annum. There are also a number of other ways to calculate depreciation and your accountant will advise you on the method most advantageous to your kind of business. The important point to bear in mind, though, is that depreciation is a real factor, not just an accountancy device. Assets like motor cars and equipment do wear out and have to be replaced. Financial reserves should be built up to enable you to do this.

Administrative costs

Running your business will involve general expenditure which cannot be directly related to particular assignments: stationery, publicity, travel, postage, entertainment of clients, fees to professional advisers, and so forth.

Salaries and welfare

Salaries are best calculated at an hourly rate, based on an average working week. In the case of employees, these rates are usually determined by the market for that particular kind of employment. The problem is deciding how much you should pay to yourself. Again, this obviously varies with the kind of business you are in, but as a rough guideline you should, after meeting all your expenses, be earning at least as much as an employed person with the same degree of skill and responsibility. It is most important to cost your time properly; let us, therefore, look at a worked example of what might be involved in the case of a person in full-time self-employment.

Supposing you were aiming to earn £20,000 a year. To start with you would want to take into account four weeks' annual paid holiday (three weeks, plus statutory holidays) and you would assume an eight-hour day and a five-day working week. However, not all your time would be directly productive: some of it would be spent travelling, on administration and on getting work. So let us say your productive time is 32 hours a week. That would give you an hourly rate based on 32×48 hours a year: 1536 hours. Divided into £20,000, that means a rate of about £13.02 per hour. On top of that you have to allow for welfare items: your National Insurance stamp, possibly contributions to a retirement pension scheme and certainly insurance against sickness or death. Let us assume this comes to another £1000 a year. Divided by 1536 working hours, this adds another 98 pence to your hourly rate.

Similarly, when costing the time of any full-time staff working for you, it is not just a question of calculating basic rates of pay. You have to allow for holidays, the employer's contribution to National Insurance stamps and to the graduated pension scheme. These items can add 6 to 8 per cent to the cost of wages.

Variable costs

All the costs we have just described are fixed costs. You incur them whether you have work coming in or not. Variable costs are items like materials which can be attributed to specific jobs. There are circumstances in which what we have described as fixed costs can vary slightly. If you are running a lot of overtime, this will mean an increase in your fuel bills and extra payments to your staff or to yourself. But the benefit of achieving properly costed increases in productivity, for example in the case of a shop staying open late to attract more trade, is that, provided you are able to keep fixed overheads stable, this element will form a smaller proportion relative to your turnover, and that means a more profitable business.

ESTABLISHING YOUR PRICES

You now have a set of basic data on costs which can be applied to your prices when you are asked to quote for a job or in making up your invoice. If you are supplying a service, the best way to do this is to take all your fixed costs, establish an hourly rate based on your usual working week and then estimate how long the job will take you. The effect of this is that if jobs do not materialise in the way the 'usual working week' concept implies, you yourself are going to be carrying the can for the fixed overheads which are being incurred during all the hours in that week when you are not working. And if you only get 20 hours' work during a week in which you had budgeted for 40, loading your charges to the customer to make up for the shortfall could mean that you will come up with an unacceptable quotation or a price that will discourage your customer in the future.

The other lesson to be learned is that fixed overheads should be kept as low as possible. For instance, if you are planning a freelance design service to earn extra money in the evenings, you should be chary of acquiring expensive equipment. In the limited hours of work which a part-time freelance operation implies, you may never be able to charge enough money to do more than pay the overheads. As far as possible, keep your costs in the variable category by hiring or renting equipment only when and for as long as you need it.

This is also true of businesses that produce manufactured articles (and activities which operate on lines similar to manufacturing such as a restaurant, where the product is created in the form of a meal), though in these cases some machinery and equipment are usually essential. The price here will be based on a unit per item rather than on an hourly rate, but the principle is the same. Instead of fixing an hourly rate based on an expected working week, calculations should be made on a projected volume of costs spread over the number of units sold. Thus, if you aimed to sell in a week 20 chairs which cost you £5 each in materials your variable costs would be £100. If your fixed overheads, including your own remuneration, came to £300 a week, you would have to charge £20 per chair. And do not forget that even if your object is only to make a living wage out of your business, you should still be putting aside reserves to replace equipment as it wears out, and that the cost of doing so will, in periods of inflation, be a great deal higher than its original cost.

PREPARING QUOTATIONS

With many jobs, whether they are a service or a commission to manufacture something, you will be asked to supply a quotation before a firm order is placed. Once that quotation has been accepted it is legally binding on both parties, so it is important not only to get your sums right but to make it clear in the wording attached to them what exactly you are providing for the money. In the case of a decorating job, for example, you should specify who is providing the materials and, if you are, to what standards they are going to be. Consider also whether any out-of-pocket expenses will be involved (travel, subsistence) and whether these are to be met by your customer or whether they have been allowed for in your quotation.

Apart from variable factors such as these, every quotation should set out the conditions of sale under which it is being offered. Different businesses will involve different kinds of conditions, but here are some basic points to bear in mind:

1. Particularly in times of inflation, you should make it clear that the prices quoted are current ones and may have to go up if costs rise during the course of the job.
2. Terms of payment should be set out, for example 30 days net.
3. You will have to cover the not uncommon situation of the customer changing her mind about the way she wants the

job done subsequent to her accepting your quotation. You should leave yourself free to charge extra in such circumstances.

4. If you have agreed to complete a job within a certain length of time, set out the factors beyond your control which would prevent you from meeting the agreed date.

5. You should make it clear what circumstances of error, loss or damage will be your responsibility and what would fall outside it.

6. You should stipulate that once the quotation is accepted, the order cannot be cancelled except by mutual consent and that the customer will be liable for all charges up to that point.

7. You should mention that the total is subject to VAT at the rate ruling at the date of invoice. This is particularly important when the customer is a private person who is unable to claim back VAT inputs. (See Chapter 1.14 for details of VAT.)

Having gone to all the trouble to set out the quotation and conditions of sale, you should not neglect to check, before you start work, that the customer has actually accepted it in writing! It is all too easy to forget this or to imagine that an amicable verbal OK is sufficient. If a dispute arises, however, you will be very thankful to have carried out all the formal steps of documentation.

Every few months sit back for half an hour and consider your pricing policy. If you have set up as a consulting engineer and have no wish to get involved with renting offices and employing others, your workload capacity is limited to the number of hours you put in. To start with, you will probably be glad of work at any price, but as your business builds up to the point where you are working all hours, the only way you will be able to increase your real income is to increase your prices. So if you have a reliable supply of work coming in which is giving you a reasonable income, do not be afraid to put in some highish quotes for new work. It is not always the case that the lowest tender wins the job, particularly in the field of consultancy.

Checklist: costing, pricing and estimating

1. How unique is your product or service? If it is not particularly uncommon, how can you make it more so?
2. How essential is it to the customer?
3. What is the competition charging for the same or similar product or service?
4. How badly do you need the job or order?
5. Is your customer likely to come back for more if the price is right, or is it a one-off?
6. Will doing business with this customer enable you to break into a wider market, and thus enable you to reduce your unit costs?
7. What is the element of risk involved (ie is the customer, to your knowledge, a quick and certain payer)?
8. Do you have any idea how long the job will take you?
9. Can you relate the time element to your fixed costs?
10. Have you made a full assessment of all your fixed costs?
11. Do you have any idea what your materials are going to cost you?
12. Have you costed your own time properly?
13. Will the job leave you a margin of net profit? Or should you forgo this in the interest of meeting fixed costs?
14. Have you prepared a quote, specifying exactly what you are going to provide or do, including terms of payment?
15. Has the customer accepted your quotation?
16. Are you keeping records of what the job cost you so that you can adjust your prices or quote more accurately next time?

1.11 Marketing Your Work

Good ideas, it is sometimes dismissively said, are ten a penny, the implication being that the really difficult part is putting them into effect. Apart from the obvious virtues of persistence, hard work and technical know-how, this also requires a modicum of marketing skill. In other words, you will have to know whether there is a big enough demand for your product or service at the price you need to charge to make a living and how to identify and reach your potential customers.

MANUFACTURERS

You may be the world's most skilful maker of hand-carved model sailing ships, but unless enough people want them you are going to have a hard time trying to make a living out of producing them commercially. It is worth doing some research before you start in business and the following methods should help you direct your products more effectively:

- ☐ Look around. Go to gift shops, luxury stores or wherever it is that the kind of item you are aiming to produce is being sold and find out about prices, quality standards and the extent of the demand. Shop managers might help advise you on any modifications required to your idea.
- ☐ Consider whether there is a long-term future for your product. Are you able to keep ahead by being in a position to meet the next craze before the big manufacturers become aware of it?
- ☐ Keep an eye on competitors of your own size to ensure your own commercial viability and to see if there is a gap in the market for your product.

But no matter how good or unique your product may be, the ultimate key to success lies in effective sales and distribution. At the smallest level you might be selling direct to the public through your own shop, as is the case with many craft goods, but you have to bear in mind that you need to achieve a considerable turnover for a shop in a good location to be viable. This is difficult if the range of specialisation is very narrow, and many small-scale manufacturers, therefore, combine having their own shop with direct mail and mail order (which we shall come to in a moment) and with marketing to other retail outlets. Shop and workshop premises can be combined in the same floor area, so that you can switch readily from the sales counter to the workbench when the shop is empty. This requires permission from the local planning authority if a 'change of use' of what were originally shop premises is involved.

Starting-up costs will eat deeply into your capital, so unless you have enough experience of the marketing (as opposed to the manufacturing) end of your speciality to be absolutely convinced that you can sell it, it is a good idea to begin by making a few prototypes of the product and its packaging and by trying to get orders from retailers. Though your friends and family may think your idea is wonderful, the acid test is whether it will survive in the marketplace. In the course of investigating this, the natural conservatism of most branches of the retail trade may at times depress or irritate you, but it is worth listening to what people who are involved in it have to say. If the same criticisms keep on cropping up, you should think seriously of modifying your prototype to take them into account.

Distribution can be another big headache and your premises should be big enough to enable you to hold roughly as many days' or weeks' supply of stocks as it takes to replace it at its rate of demand. If a business is selling ten chairs a week and it takes two weeks to get that number of replacements, there should, ideally, be space for something like 20 chairs. A customer might be prepared to wait a week before delivery, but she is unlikely to wait a month.

Accessibility of non-selling areas is important too. Adequate entry for goods and materials at the rear or side of the premises is often essential and will always save time and energy.

DEALING WITH LARGE COMPANIES

Winning an order from a large company can put a small business on its feet at a stroke, not only directly but in terms of gaining credibility with other customers. But pursuing orders of that kind is not without its perils. For one thing, large firms are not necessarily rapid payers; nor, as some bankruptcies have shown, is a household name inevitably a sign of financial soundness. Careful checks with your bank are essential.

The implications of a big order also need to be thought out very fully in cash-flow terms, and if progress payments are not offered other forms of finance will have to be found. A further point to consider is that it is highly likely that a major customer will seek to impose conditions not only of price, but of quality and delivery. Fair enough; but in combination these three can make what seems like a high-value order look much less tempting on the bottom line of profitability.

The whole thing becomes even more complicated if you find you have to subcontract part of the job, as is often the case when a small business lands in the big time. Unless you can control the subcontractor's work very tightly by writing and being in a position to enforce a very clear set of specifications, you can land yourself in the position one small book publisher got into once. It won an order from a major chain of multiples for many tens of thousands of copies of a number of titles. For cost reasons these had to be manufactured in the Far East and when they were delivered they did not match up to the very strict merchandising standards that had been stipulated. What had looked like a wonderful stroke of good fortune turned into a horrifying, litigation-laden loss.

Of course, large companies are anxious to avoid this sort of thing, so they seldom deal with small companies whose approach is less than 100 per cent professional. A lot of them, by all accounts, fall down at this first hurdle. However good your idea or product, it will never even come up for discussion unless your letter is clearly and neatly presented, reasonably well written and, above all, sent to the right person. Firms are full of stories of letters being sent to executives who had long left the company and whose names had been gleaned from some out-of-date directory. One phone call would have done the trick.

The lesson that small things make big impressions is also worth remembering when the big customer you have been courting finally sends his inspection team or his purchasing officer round. Nothing looks worse than a scruffy reception area or sounds worse than badly briefed staff. Indeed, you yourself should make sure that you can answer convincingly all the questions you are likely to be asked on such things as capacity, delivery, the quality of your workforce and whatever is connected with the business you are trying to win.

SHOPS AND SERVICE INDUSTRIES

The first large shopping centre built in Britain was a flop because, among other disadvantages, it had no parking facilities and was situated in a working-class area a few minutes' walk away from a large, long-established and very popular street market. The developers, for all their vast financial resources, had ignored hotel magnate Conrad Hilton's three factors in siting a business serving the public: location, location and location. If you are thinking of setting up a shop, restaurant or some other service outlet, find out as much as possible about the area and ask:

- ☐ Who lives there?
- ☐ Is the area declining economically or is it on the up and up?
- ☐ What is the range of competitors and how well are they doing?
- ☐ If you are thinking of opening a high-class restaurant and there are nothing but fish and chip establishments in the neighbourhood, does this mean that there is no demand for a good restaurant or a crying need for one?

Take the case of a bookshop. You would want to conduct some rule-of-thumb market research about the area before going any further. For example, you would want to know whether there were enough people in the area to support such a venture, whether they were the sort of people who regularly bought books, and how good the local library was. You would also want to know what impact the result of your market investigations might have on your trading policies. Thus, if there were a lot of families with young children around, you should be considering getting to know, and stocking, children's books; or, if there were a lot of students in the neighbourhood, it would be worth your while finding out what textbooks were being used in local educational institutions. Alternatively, if your bookshop is highly specialised – medicine, academic history, chess, or some other specific activity – an expensive High Street location is likely to be wholly inappropriate. You will want to be near the centre of that activity, or, more likely, will want to sell to your well-defined audience through direct mail.

The same broad principles apply to almost every kind of retail or service outlet and you will have to conduct this kind of research, which is really just plain common sense, whatever your venture. Do not be tempted to overlook it just because you are buying what is supposed to be a 'going concern'. One reason why it is up for sale may be that, despite the owner's or agent's protestations to the contrary, it was doing badly. If that was because the previous owner was a poor manager or stocked the wrong kind of goods for the neighbourhood you might be able to turn the business around, but if there was simply too much competition in the area from similar shops and there is no chance of trading viably in something else from the same address, you would be well advised to forget about those premises, however good a buy they may seem from a purely cost point of view. You will also be able to check on the vendor's assertions by looking, preferably with your accountant, at his profit and loss accounts, not just for the past year but the previous three to five years, to get a picture of the general trend of things. On the whole, buying a going concern has to be approached with great caution, particularly by the inexperienced, because of the difficulties of valuing stock and goodwill with any accuracy. See Chapters 1.3 and 2.1 for more detailed treatment of these points.

FREELANCE SERVICES

Most freelancers agree that the way you get work is by knowing people who are in a position to give it to you. That sounds rather like a chicken-and-egg situation and, to begin with, so it is. You would be ill-advised to launch into freelance work, certainly on a full-time basis, until you have built up a range of contacts who can provide you with enough work to produce some sort of living for at least the first few months. Often these are people whom you have got to know in the course of a full-time job, or while doing temporary work. Many advertising agencies, for instance, have been started by a breakaway group taking a batch of clients with them when they start up.* And it may even be that your employer, having been compelled to make you redundant, will still be willing to put work out to you on a freelance basis.

Once you have got going and established a reputation for doing good, reliable work, things get much easier. For one thing, word-of-mouth recommendations have a strong effect in the freelance world. Moreover, you will be able to produce examples of work sold, or be able to refer prospects to other clients who have engaged you successfully. Evidence, for instance, that your fashion photographs have actually been used by national magazines is generally more impressive than a folder of prints, no matter how good they are. In freelance work, as in other spheres, nothing succeeds like success.

One problem with freelance work, though, is that clients often want something done in a hurry – over a weekend or even overnight. This can be highly inconvenient at times, but it is generally a bad idea to turn work down simply for this reason. If you have to be selective, turn away the smaller, less remunerative jobs or commissions from people who are slow to pay their bills. One thing you should never do is to let a client down. If you cannot, or do not want to, take on an assignment, say so immediately.

---

*To combat this trend many firms now include clauses in their employment contract expressly stating that it is not permissible to work for a client of the employer for two years after leaving that employer.

PRESS ADVERTISING

Advertising is a marketing tool and like any other tool you have to use it in the right place, at the right time and for the right job if it is going to be of any use to you. If you are a local building contractor, there is no point in advertising in national news-papers, because most of the circulation, which is what you are paying for in the rates charged, will be outside the geographical area you are working in. On the other hand, if you are making a product to sell by mail order, the bigger the circulation the better. There are, however, still provisos; there is, for example, no point in advertising a product aimed at 'top people' in a mass-circulation tabloid.

When considering advertising think about:

☐ The right medium for the product or service you have to sell.

☐ The quality of the circulation rather than the figures. A small specialist or local paper might provide as good a return as a mass circulation publication.

☐ A regular 'classified' insertion will remind readers of your services and will be relatively inexpensive.

☐ Display advertising can be placed in eye-catching positions. These are more expensive than classified adverts and will need to be designed by a graphic designer (look in *Yellow Pages* or *Thomson* local directory) but you can control where they are placed.

☐ Experiment with different days for your advert to appear as some days can produce a better response than others.

☐ Experiment with wording, but do not use too many words. Be specific about how goods and services can be obtained. Your address and availability times should be prominent.

☐ Include an order coupon stating price *and* postage. This will also provide information on where your sales come from and will help future marketing efforts.

PUBLIC RELATIONS

It may be possible, particularly if you have a specialist line of business, to obtain free coverage in trade journals and local newspapers by sending them press releases to mark events such as the opening of an extension or the provision of some unique service. You simply type the information on a slip marked PRESS RELEASE; 'embargo' it – ie prohibit its use – until a date that suits you, and send it to newspapers and magazines you choose as the likeliest to use it. Newspapers and other news media – don't forget about local radio and even local TV – are, however, only interested in *news* and the mere fact that you have opened a business may not interest them much. Try to find a news angle; for instance, that you have obtained a large export order, or are reviving a local craft or are giving employment to school-leavers. If you have any friends who are journalists, ask their advice on the sort of information that is likely to get the attention of editors. Better still, ask them if they will draft your press release for you.

There are many other PR activities – sponsorship, stunts, celebrity appearances at your premises, public speaking, and so on. All are designed to publicise who you are and what you do, and suggest to the public that you provide a worthwhile and reliable service. PR for the small business is covered thoroughly in Michael Bland's *Be Your Own PR Man* (published by Kogan Page).

DIRECT MAIL AND DIRECT RESPONSE PROMOTION

Direct mail selling is a considerable subject in its own right. It differs from mail order in that the latter consists of mailing goods direct to the customer from orders engendered by general press advertising, whereas in the case of direct mail selling the advertising is a brochure or sales letter specifically directed at the customer. Direct response promotion consists of an ad plus coupon placed in a newspaper or journal, to be posted to the manufacturer as an order. If you use these methods, remember to allow for postage in your pricing, and since the response to direct mail averages around 2 per cent, the postage cost per sale is quite a considerable factor. It can, however, be a very effective way of selling specialised, high-priced items (£15 is around the viable minimum these days) or of identifying people who are likely to buy from you regularly if you are selling variations on the same product. Unless you are very skilful at writing brochures or sales letters you should get this done for you by an expert. Such people are employed by mailing list brokers (you will find those in the Yellow Pages), who will often provide a complete package: they will sell to you, or compile for you, specialised lists, address and stuff envelopes and produce sales literature.

Their services are not cheap and before you plunge into a direct mail campaign there are relatively inexpensive ways of testing the market for yourself. Pick 100 specialist addresses of the type you want to reach on a bigger scale – again, you may find them in the Yellow Pages. A small want ad in one of the advertising industry's trade papers will soon raise the services of freelance copywriters and designers if you need such help. From the percentage reply to the sample mailing, you will be able to gauge whether a bigger campaign is worth mounting and you will also get some idea of how to price the product to take into account the likely mailing costs per sale. It is generally essential, by the way, with direct mail advertising, to include a reply paid card or envelope with your sales literature. Details of how to apply for reply paid and Freepost facilities are available from the Post Office.

Mail Order Protection Schemes

Before you can start selling by direct response advertising in a newspaper or periodical, you will have to get permission to do so from its mail order protection scheme (MOPS). These schemes have been set up under the auspices of the Office of Fair Trading to protect consumers from fraudulent advertisers. Essentially, the various media act as insurers and undertake to refund readers' money if the advertiser absconds or fails to deliver for some reason or other. Before accepting the insurance risk, papers and periodicals will therefore try to satisfy themselves that the advertiser is above board. In the case of national media their requirements will be quite searching; they may want to see accounts, take up credit and other references and even look over your premises. Applications for MOPS clearing at this end of the advertising market have to be accompanied by a fee which can go well into four figures and which has to be renewed every year. Requirements in local and trade media are less exacting, but you still need clearance before they will take your advertisement.

MARKETING ON THE INTERNET

The number of people on the Internet is exploding. If you have a product or a service which is of more than local interest, then getting on the Internet is becoming an essential part of your marketing strategy. You do this by having your own Web site which describes your product or activity, how much it costs and how to get it. You can also take orders over the Internet and even get customers to pay by credit card. The mechanics of this are complicated by issues of security – customers are naturally anxious about disclosing credit card details on a system which gives open access to millions of people – but they are not insurmountable. Other business uses offered by the Internet include:

- ☐ carrying out research before you launch a new marketing campaign;
- ☐ checking patents, demographics or statistics on a new sales area;
- ☐ researching new manufacturers and distributors;
- ☐ creating a new way of marketing your products to a niche group of users;
- ☐ publicising your company and its products;
- ☐ keeping in touch with your customers and employees;
- ☐ cutting long-distance phone bills.

Research can be carried out on the Internet before you market your product. You can visit government Web sites for statistics, look for information on search engines and carry out research through news services, newspapers, magazines and user groups.

health, wealth and happiness

That's what we enjoy at Neways – is it what you're looking for?

- Unique products from a world-wide company.
- Build your own business – don't be tied to someone else!
- Very low start-up cost – only £10.00
- Work the hours that suit you – not the hours that suit your boss!
- Products that really make a difference to people's lives.

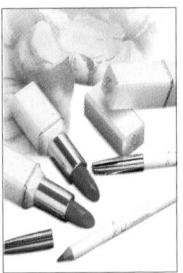

NETWORK MARKETING – A SELF-EMPLOYED BUSINESS WITH "BIG FIRM"HEART

In your search for the best business opportunity available, you may have come across the term network marketing or multi level marketing (MLM), and wondered exactly what was involved. What are the advantages over other forms of self-employment? What kind of commitment, financial or otherwise, is required? Who are the people this kind of business opportunity suits best?

Network marketing involves self-employed "distributors" buying a company's products, often exclusively, for personal use and retail sale. Part of their income is derived from the profit made on their own retail sales and then, by building a network of other distributors below them (their "downline"), they qualify to receive bonus payments based on their own "personal volume" plus the "group volume" sales of their downlines. This is the second arm of a distributor's income, and it is these bonus payments that change network marketing from a limited, sales-based income to an exciting career with unrestricted financial potential.

One of the big advantages of network marketing is that, unlike many others in self-employed businesses, you would be working for yourself, but with the support, not only of the company whose products you are selling, but also from the distributors above you, your "upline". These experienced networkers have a vested interest in your business as, although you are independent of them financially, your sales contribute directly to their income through the bonus schemes that network marketing companies have. Therefore, they are keen to see you do well, providing you with help and information, particularly when you are just starting out.

Let's look at one company, Neways International (UK) Ltd, in more detail. Neways is an ethical multi-level marketing company that has been in the United Kingdom since 1993. It has ten superb ranges of products: personal care; hair care; dental care; body contouring; skin care; nutritional supplementation; cosmetic care; household and automotive systems and essential oils. With one of the best marketing plans in the business, and an exciting car bonus scheme that gives senior distributors the chance to obtain new cars, paid for partly or wholly by the company, Neways is one of the fastest growing network marketing companies in the country.

Rod Catherall, partner in Optimum Health Products Limited and with Neways for over two years, tells us more about the kind of support that new distributors receive, even when they aren't members of an established team. "Early in 1998, I was invited by Neways to advise on the feasibility of contracting out their warehousing, storage and distribution in their rapidly expanding business. In the process, I learned about Neways' background and something of their very impressive products. I bought some products thinking that my partner, Maggie, would be as taken with them as I was. She is a complementary health practitioner and I believed they would extend the services provided from her clinic. When I explained that Neways is a network marketing operation, it was the kiss of death - she simply did not want to know. Maggie had been modestly involved with networking previously and it had not been a happy experience."

"Some months later, I became decidedly under the weather, having one cold after another. Maggie decided the time had come for some drastic action. This prompted her to look closely at the Neways products, which I had bought and which had lain unopened ever since. After taking one of the products I personally found the results truly astonishing. Within a week the cold had gone and what's more, I have not had one since."

"At about this time, an invitation came from Neways asking if we would like to attend their annual convention in London. What a day it was! We met Tom and Dee Mower, the founders, Dr Samuel Epstein the renowned cancer prevention campaigner, top distributors and many others relatively new to the business. We decided there and then that Neways was for us and signed."

"As the weeks went by, it became apparent that we were disadvantaged, as we had unwittingly signed up to a group whose leaders where in Australia and not the UK. We felt like orphans! It meant that we did not have the benefit of experienced networkers to show us how best to operate and build our business. We quickly came to terms with the situation and set about attending every Neways meeting we could find. In the process, we have made many friends, all of whom have been very supportive. As it has turned out, being orphans has almost been an advantage! Neways is truly an extended family of like-minded, friendly and helpful people ready and willing to support others without any question of personal gain. This has played a major part in enabling Maggie and I to build our business. We have also had the opportunity of repaying some of the kindness by doing all we can to help others new to the business. One of the ways we can achieve this is by running monthly meetings where we regularly get 200 attendees."

"We are delighted to say that our business is now growing at a pace and we fully expect within the next few months to achieve the top rank of Diamond Ambassador. Neways really is a first rate company and we are proud to be part of that "extended family""

Another big advantage that encourages many people to get involved with network marketing is that the amount of time and money required can be flexible. In the early stages of their networking career, many people will start by just selling products to friends and family and the time taken will be minimal. As they start to develop their own downlines, more and more time will be taken up with training and encouragement, but the income generated will rise proportionally.

Dick Jeeps CBE is an ex-England Rugby captain and former Chairman of the British Sports Council. His wife first joined Neways soon after the company came to this country in 1994, but Dick was not initially impressed. He himself takes up the story: "My wife, Jennifer, joined Neways about a month after they came to England in 1994 - she was attracted to them as her background is in Beauty Therapy and Cosmetics Consultancy. She joined because of the quality of the products that Neways produce and also because they are totally ethical products that have never been tested on animals."

"She had not enjoyed good health for some years and was having hormone replacement therapy (HRT) twice a year. After starting with Neways' cosmetics, she soon decided to try some of Neways' nutritional products to see if a natural approach would help her condition. Within a short time, she was feeling much better and what really impressed us both most of all was how well she felt in terms of mood i.e. very balanced."

"During this time, and after I had retired as Chairman of the British Sports Council, we were running a restaurant. In 1995, I had a colon cancer removed and was still quite ill 6 weeks after the operation. Jennifer contacted Tom Mower, the founder of Neways International, and he sent over from the US supplies of a powerful anti-oxidant, which has subsequently become available in this country. I started taking Revenol and, within a few weeks, I began to feel much better; within four months, I was back working in the restaurant. I continued to take a maintenance dose and this seems to have rid me of all my aches and pains from old rugby injuries, left over from my days as England Captain. In addition, I haven't suffered from colds or sore throats since."

"In 1996, and having sold our restaurant, I joined Neways full-time, a decision I will never regret. Initially, I had severe reservations about network marketing but soon discovered that my wife had joined a company that is run by the Owner/Founder and his family, is totally debt-free and is innovative and constantly evolving to meet the needs of its distributors. Since 1996, Neways has grown so much that a new, purpose built, 27,000 sq ft warehouse/office complex is presently with the planners and is expected to be ready for occupation in the early part of next year. With an exciting new product catalogue just issued and several other projects, like a new starter kit and a new party-plan package in the pipeline, Neways is always keen to provide the tools its distributors need to sell the best products currently available in this field."

"With their tremendous marketing plan, we, like many other distributors, are reaping the financial rewards whilst promoting a wonderful, safe range of products. The future will see further expansion into many other countries but if I were to be asked the question "Have we reached saturation point in Great Britain?" my reply would be "We have not even scratched the surface!"

With some people, it may be the ability to work from home, at times that suit them, that attracts them to network marketing in the first place. Everyone's personal circumstances are different but full-time employment is not always flexible enough to deal with that. This particular aspect of network marketing was part of the appeal for Dr Surjit Virk, a Ph D in Biochemistry, and father of two young girls. "As a student at the University of Birmingham, I revelled in the time spent researching in my chosen field of Biochemistry. The freedom to work the hours that I wanted, whether that was at night or weekends, was something that I really enjoyed and, whilst I needed to report to a project supervisor, I was left pretty much to my own devices. What a shock, therefore, when I left university and went into full-time employment, virtually tied down to a desk. I very quickly decided that I felt cramped and, although I tried different jobs to see if I could find something that suited me more, I was not happy working for others and wanted to regain the freedom I had felt before."

"In 1992, my wife, who has her own full-time career as a careers adviser, gave birth to our first daughter and I was faced with a choice; either carry on working full-time and find a child minder or find some form of self-employment that would give me the flexibility to look after my daughter as well as providing an income. It was at this time that I first became involved in network marketing. Finally, I had found something that gave me the flexibility to look after my daughter during the daytime but the opportunity of working in the evenings, and at weekends, to build my networking business. When our second daughter was born a couple of years later, I knew I had made the right decision."

"I worked for a number of different network marketing businesses and learnt a lot along the way. I enjoyed the opportunity of seeing other successful people, of always having goals to aim for and making life-long friendsy. At the back of my mind, however, was the concern that so many of the senior people in the companies I tried seemed to be totally money-oriented."

"In 1999, I found Neways and realised my search had ended. Here, finally, was the right company with the right product and the right organisation; a company whose owners were totally debt-free and whose concern was with introducing as many people as possible to their superb range of products. Of course, the money is very nice but far more fulfilling is the opportunity to introduce people to products that can really make a difference to their quality of life. In fact, at a recent training meeting I ran for twenty of my downline, we spent the whole day talking about the products and the marketing plan wasn't mentioned once! We all knew that, if we can get the products to people, that side would almost take care of itself."

The sign of a truly successful network marketing company is when a superb compensation plan takes second place to the products!

User groups are a particularly useful source of information on the Internet and there are over 250,000 of them. They cover a wide range of subject areas and you can access them through a Web Browser and post messages to them. Mailing lists can also be bought and you can send information by e-mail on your new product through this method.

Creating a Web site

If you want to sell over the Internet, your best plan would be to hire a consultant to help you design a Web site and register it with various search engines so that your name comes up when customers are looking for information on products in your field. Ask the consultant to show you how to update it, how to record users, how to follow-up enquiries and which item is attracting the most interest from visitors to your site.

You should also have a look at other Web sites to see what works and what doesn't before discussing your own needs with your consultant. Your own visits to other people's Web sites should also warn you about trying to use graphics that take too long to download, as Internet users have a notoriously short attention span and are unlikely to wait for your three-dimensional revolving logo to appear on their screens. The following points should also be considered when discussing the design with your consultant:

- ☐ content should be of good quality and be up-to-date;
- ☐ try to encourage feedback by making the Web site interactive;
- ☐ remember that your audience is international and make sure that you include relevant information such as the contact details of your worldwide distributors;
- ☐ register your Web site with search engines;
- ☐ create links with other Web sites; two-way traffic is mutually beneficial;
- ☐ swap banner advertising.

You can also stimulate interest in your product or service on the Internet in other ways. The design of your site can build in a link to other sites so that if, for instance, you are selling antique tools, there is a link to sites about books on antique tools. A customer for the one may well also be interested in the other. User groups are not only useful as sources of information about topics in the interest field in which your business is located (for example, antiques) but can be used for discrete marketing. For example, it is considered bad form to advertise directly in a user group, but you could drop in some comment about antique repairs and refer interested parties to a Web site, which might just happen to be yours.

The Information Society Initiative (ISI), is a public-private partnership run by the Department of Trade and Industry and provides hands-on information and communications technology experience for businesses. For more information and advice, telephone 0345 15 2000 or visit its Web site www.isi.gov.uk. For a full account of Internet marketing, see *Doing Business on the Internet*, by Simon Collin (Kogan Page).

Checklist: marketing your work

Manufacturers
1. Have you tested your idea by discussing your proposed product with potential customers? Or, better still, by showing it to them?
2. Is the market for it big enough? How accessible is it?
3. Can the customers you have in mind afford a price that will produce a profit for you?
4. Have you studied the competition from the point of view of price, design quality, reliability, delivery dates, etc?
5. Should you modify your product so as to get the edge on the competition? What will this do to your costs?
6. Is there a long-term future for your product? If not, do you have any ideas for a follow-up?
7. Can you handle distribution? Do you have access to a van if the market is local? Do you have adequate parking facilities if it requires dispatching?

8. Have you taken dispatching costs into account in working out how much the product will cost the customer?
9. Do you have adequate space to hold stock, taking into account production time?
10. Do you have someone who can deal with customer queries and complaints? Or have you allowed for the fact that you will have to take time out yourself to deal with them?

Shops and service industries
1. How much do you know about the area?
2. Is the location good from the point of view of attracting the kind of trade you are looking for?
3. What competitors do you have?
4. How are they doing?
5. Based on your study of the area, and the people who live in it, how does this affect the type of goods or the nature of the service you are going to offer?
6. If you are buying a going concern, have you checked it out thoroughly with your professional advisers?

Freelance services
1. Do you have any contacts who can give you work?
2. Have you made a realistic appraisal of how much you can expect to earn over the first six months?
3. Have you allowed for the fact that you will need spare time to go around looking for more business?
4. What evidence can you produce of your competence to do freelance work in your proposed field?
5. Have you shown that evidence to the sort of person who might be a customer to get her reaction on whether it is likely to impress?
6. Who are your competitors, what do they charge and what can you offer that is superior to their services?

Advertising and promotion
1. Have you chosen the right medium to promote your product or service?

2. Do you have any idea of the circulation and how this is broken down, geographically or by type of reader?
3. Have you worked out any way of monitoring results, for instance by including a coupon?
4. Have you included the cost of advertising and promotion in your cash-flow budget and in costing your product?
5. How many orders do you need to get from your advertising/promotion campaign to show a profit?
6. In the case of a display advertisement, have you specified a position in which it is to appear?
7. Again, in the case of a display ad or a brochure, have you had it properly designed?
8. Does your advertising/promotion material state where your product or service can be obtained and the price?
9. Is the wording compelling? Does it clearly describe the product or service and does it motivate the customer? Would you buy it, if you were a customer?
10. In the case of a classified advertisement, have you specified under which classification it is to appear?
11. Are all the statements and claims you are making about your product or service true to the best of your knowledge and belief, bearing in mind that untruths can leave you open to prosecution under the Trade Descriptions Acts?
12. Have you looked at other companies' Web sites to see what works for users?
13. Is your Web site attractive to customers and easy to use? Do you update it regularly?
14. Have you registered with search engines?

1.12 The Fun of Exporting

'Exporting is fun,' said Harold Macmillan when he was Prime Minister, though it may perhaps be doubted whether he knew much about filling in bills of lading in sextuplicate or waiting for an onward flight in a corrugated iron shed in Burkina Faso. At any rate, it has taken a long time for the export message to sink in with British firms and even now many small companies put export fairly low on their list of priorities. But while it is true that it is usually essential to get one's place established in the domestic market, there are many attractions about exporting.

- ☐ It increases sales and therefore lowers unit costs.
- ☐ It decreases dependence on the UK market.
- ☐ It can produce increased profits in countries where you can charge higher prices or where sterling has a poor exchange rate.
- ☐ It broadens one's awareness of other markets and sometimes gives warning of competing products being developed or on sale elsewhere.
- ☐ It gives you a chance to see the world 'on the company'.

Even if you find none of these reasons compelling enough to make you want to leave your home patch, there are circumstances under which you can become an exporter without really wishing to. If you have a good product, it is very possible that someone abroad will get to hear of it and want to buy it. Indeed, that is how many small companies first become involved, having made the wise decision that business should never be turned away.

If, however, you decide to play a more active role as an exporter than just meeting the demand as it occurs, what special factors should a small business look at? Actually, in many respects they are not very different from those that apply domestically: that the product has to be competitive in price and quality or that it has a unique feature which places it in a class of its own, but for which there is also a viable demand at a price you are reasonably sure the market will pay. Where export does raise special problems is that you also have to make sure that the product meets local specification in terms of technical requirements and consumer laws; that it can thrive under what may be quite different environmental and climatic conditions; that manuals and user instructions are intelligible, either in English or in translations; and that it does not breach any cultural taboos. The last named is often more important and wide ranging than people realise. One Australian meat company nearly lost a huge Middle East order because their house symbol was stamped on their cheques. It was a pig, an unclean animal in Moslem countries.

Indeed, all markets have their peculiarities and the advice generally given to exporters is first to visit one country or region and get to know it rather than trying to sell to the world. Even Sir Terence Conran, one of Britain's outstanding marketing men, lost heavily at first with his New York venture because he had not appreciated the Americans' appetite for continuing 'sales', however bogus. Apart from that, exporters to the US market often fail to realise that America is such a huge country that the characteristics of the Midwest are different from those of California and that both are different from the South or New York City. Freight is a factor there too – freight costs can eat deeply into margins and you have to consider that the price of your goods to the customer has to include the cost of physically getting them to her.

Similar lessons can be drawn from Africa with its widely different climatic conditions and its heavy ingredient of political risk, from Asia and Australia where sheer distance from the UK means that it can take months to get the goods there and further months to get payment, and even from the EU.

WHERE TO GET HELP

Fortunately, there are quite a few sources of help and advice for those who want to become exporters. Addresses and Web sites can be found at the back of this book.

- ☐ Local Chambers of Commerce are often well informed about major markets.
- ☐ Many of Britain's major trading partners maintain trade associations in London (eg the German Chamber of Trade and Industry, the Arab-British Chamber of Commerce) and though some of them are more concerned with exporting to this country than importing into their own, they do also know what the requirements are in the latter case.
- ☐ The customer service division of the overseas departments of the big four banks.
- ☐ The Department of Trade and Industry (DTI). They produce inexpensive booklets of basic information on all the major countries which do business with British firms and you can also get special reports on particular countries, which cost somewhat more. They can also tell you about buying missions from overseas buying organisations established in this country by major foreign department stores, for instance.

  Equally usefully, they organise trade missions through local Chambers of Commerce or trade associations. These enable you to visit major markets as part of a group with a substantial government subsidy. Since contacts can be arranged in advance, this is a considerable saving in time as well as money. Usually, if you go on your own to another country, it takes days simply to find your bearings and set up meetings.
- ☐ The Overseas Trade Services Department of the DTI produces a _Guide to Export Services_ which is well spoken of. The DTI also organises local seminars for small exporters – call 020 7215 5000 for details. When contacting the DTI, ask to be put through to the country desk dealing with the country you are planning to export to.

SETTING UP SALES ARRANGEMENTS

Few firms will want to move so far, so fast, though. Usually it is a question of setting up some kind of sales operation by appointing a local agent; you may already have been approached by one keen to handle your business. Flattering though such interest is, and though it certainly helps to start out with someone who feels optimistic about your prospects, agents do have to be checked out. Bad ones may not only hinder your progress, but may cost you a lot of money by alienating dealers or by taking commission on business which you would have got anyway and which they have made little effort to expand.

For a small fee the DTI provides status reports on agents, but the best plan is undoubtedly to go out to the territory and meet the prospective agent personally. Apart from any impressions you form of him and his office – you should certainly see the latter – you should find out who else he is working for and preferably get a statement of that in writing. You will be known in that territory by the company you keep. Quite apart from the fact that the agent's other clients should be appropriate to your business – there is no point in having someone handling medical supplies when all their other agencies are office equipment – they should also be reputable. Preferably, the principals in some cases should be known to you so that you can make further inquiries back in the UK.

Once you have satisfied yourself of his *bona fides*, there should be a written agreement defining:

- ☐ The territory.
- ☐ The period of time the agreement is to run for.
- ☐ Payment terms.
- ☐ Whether the agency is exclusive or not; and, if customers are still free to buy direct from you, whether the agent gets commission on such business.
- ☐ Whether or not he is to be a stockist and, if he is, on what terms he has the right to return unsold goods.
- ☐ What you undertake to provide, free or otherwise, in the way of promotional back-up.

Once you have appointed an agent it is equally important to keep taking an interest in his activities. If he never hears from you, he will assume that you have forgotten his existence. A word of praise, or even complaint, never comes amiss. Remember the American saying, 'The wheel that squeaks loudest gets the most oil.'

DOCUMENTATION

What chiefly deters small businesses – and some larger ones – from actively pursuing export sales is the documentation it involves. This is particularly true in countries with a strong bureaucracy or where the purchasing is done by the State. Invoices have to be correct in every detail and to conform exactly to quotes or other documents to which they relate; otherwise the goods may not be collected or, worse, not paid for. There are also problems in some countries with certificates of origin of the goods, usually because of political considerations. Quite a number of countries, for instance, do not buy – or at any rate profess not to buy – goods from countries of which they disapprove politically, and demand certified invoices attested by a Chamber of Commerce in multiple copies. In some cases, it must be said, the documentation is literally not worth the trouble it costs – it has to be a matter of judgement related to the value of the goods being supplied or the importance of the customer other-wise.

As an exporter you will also have to familiarise yourself with the arcane vocabulary of export documentation – phrases like CIF, CIP, FOB, FRC and so forth. An excellent account of this and other matters is given in _Getting Started in Export_ by Roger Bennett, published by Kogan Page.

Fortunately, freight forwarders – a list of them can be obtained from the British International Freight Association – will handle the documentation for you, for a fee, which is quite modest considering the hassles involved: about 5 per cent of the total freight costs. Some freight forwarders are less than competent, though. Ask your colleagues in other firms for their recom-mendations and the name of the person they deal with. Good service quite often depends on one particular individual who is well worth rewarding with some good Scotch at Christmas time.

Sales to VAT registered customers in other EU countries are zero rated. You must show their VAT number (with their country code prefix) on the invoice and the goods must be sent to a destination outside the UK. You cannot, for instance, zero rate goods which are being sent to a customer's hotel in the UK and which he intends to take with him on his journey home. The prefix GB has to be shown on your own VAT number, so if you do a lot of exporting it may be worthwhile using it for all your invoices. In that case, however, you will also have to make a further quarterly return to Customs & Excise, the so-called EU Sales List (ESL). This is a record of all the sales you have made to customers within the EU.

You can also claim refunds of VAT incurred while doing business in other EU countries, but the documentation involved is very cumbersome. The matter may not be worth pursuing unless very substantial sums are involved.

GETTING PAID

One thing freight forwarders cannot do for you is to collect payments, and the mechanics of this are a great deal more complicated than in the UK. The reason for this is largely that invoices, which trigger the payment process, also have to serve as a Customs clearance document and must therefore have all kinds of data on them which are not required in the UK: weight, value, origin of the goods and so forth. The requirements vary from country to country and are set out in a book called *Croner's Reference Book for Exporters*. Your bank should be able to help you with them. They should also be able to advise you on the best method of getting paid once the invoice has been presented. Generally, it involves some method of transferring money from the customer's bank to yours, so you need feel no hesitation in calling on your bank for assistance.

If you just receive the occasional order from abroad and don't want to get involved in extended payment procedures, the best plan is to send a *pro forma* invoice. This still has to have details which are shown on the commercial invoice, but it means the customer has to pay in advance if he wants the goods. However, you should wait to clear his cheque before despatching them unless payment is made by some form of mail transfer; again through the bank.

The devaluation of sterling on 'black Wednesday' in 1992 brought handsome profits for those who had quoted prices in one of the currencies that appreciated against the pound. However, sterling rose by a good 10 per cent against some of these currencies during 1993, so those who went on quoting in them lost some of the money they had gained earlier. Again, businesses which had quoted in local currencies lost out badly when sterling soared in 1997/8. Most exporters agree that the safest bet is to quote in your own currency. You won't make any windfall profits that way, but at least you know you will be able to pay your UK suppliers in the currency at which you have bought from them, namely pounds sterling.

THE SINGLE EUROPEAN CURRENCY

The single European currency was introduced by 11 European states on 1 January 1999. Although Britain is unlikely to adopt the single currency before 2002–2005 at the earliest (if at all), businesses are advised to prepare for its introduction now. The 'euro' will not be introduced as hard currency until 2002 and until then will be purely a trading currency. Several larger international firms have already switched all accounting across Europe – including the UK – to euros. This means any British businesses trading with large European companies or exporting to Europe will come under pressure to adopt the euro for electronic payments and invoicing. The advantage of the euro – once the UK joins – will be an end to currency fluctuations. However, until we join, sterling could be in for a bumpy ride, so make sure you prepare for this when trading with the Continent.

Checklist: exporting

1. Have you considered local conditions and regulations to ensure your product is suitable for the market?
2. Seek out help from the DTI, your local Chamber of Commerce or your bank.
3. Have you researched the territory you are planning to export to and checked up on the local agent through the DTI status report for the area?
4. Make sure a written agreement specifies issues such as territory and the period of time the agreement will run for.
5. Contact the British International Freight Association for a list of freight forwarders and ask colleagues for recommendations.
6. Consider setting up a euro account if you are trading with EU members and ask your bank about the best way to receive foreign payments.

1.13 Employing People

A fairly common observation about employing people has been to say that this is when your troubles begin. Apart from the difficulty of finding Mr or Ms Right – a task which even experienced personnel people admit, in their more candid moments, is something of a lottery – employers also have to comply with various articles of employment legislation. Whole books could be and have been written about the legal technicalities involved, but all we can do in this section is to draw your attention to some of the major pitfalls you should look out for when you start employing people.

THE TERMS OF EMPLOYMENT

The terms of employment statement which has to be issued in writing to every employee who is going to work for you for eight hours or more per week within eight weeks of joining is in fact not a pitfall, but a rather sensible document which clarifies right from the outset what the terms of employment are. From the employer's point of view, the necessity of drafting a terms of employment statement should concentrate the mind wonderfully on issues about which it is all too easy to be sloppy at the expense of subsequent aggravation, such as hours of work, holidays and, above all, exactly what it is the employee is supposed to be doing. The following points have to be covered in the contract, and you must say if you have not covered one or other of them:

- [ ] The normal hours of work and the terms and conditions relating to them.
- [ ] Holidays and holiday pay.
- [ ] Provision for sick pay.
- [ ] Pension and pension schemes.
- [ ] Notice required by both parties.
- [ ] The job title.
- [ ] Any disciplinary rules relating to the job.
- [ ] Grievance procedures.

A further requirement is that employers must issue on or before each payday and for each employee an itemised statement showing:

- [ ] Gross wages/salary.
- [ ] Net wages/salary.
- [ ] Deductions and the reasons for them (unless these are a standard amount, in which case the reasons need only be repeated every 12 months).
- [ ] Details of part-payments, eg special overtime rates.
- [ ] The rate of pay and how it is calculated.
- [ ] Whether it is paid weekly or monthly.
- [ ] The period of employment, if it is temporary.

UNFAIR DISMISSAL

Probably the area of legislation which it is easiest and most common to fall foul of is that relating to unfair dismissal. Every employee, including part-timers, must be given a written statement of your reason if you want to dismiss him or her.

You must also give them one week's notice (or payment in lieu) if they have been with you continuously for four weeks or more and, after two years, one week's notice for every year of continuous employment. Fair enough, you might say, particularly as, on the face of things, what the law regards as fair grounds for dismissal are perfectly reasonable: incompetence, misconduct or genuine redundancy. The problem is that the employee is at liberty to disagree with you on the fairness issue and to take the case to an industrial tribunal, which stipulates that the employer's grounds for dismissal must be _reasonable_.

There are four areas of employment law of particular relevance to small businesses employing staff:

1. The qualifying period for alleged unfair dismissal is one year.
2. Industrial tribunals are directed to take account of the size and resources of the employer. For example, where an employee proves unsatisfactory in one job, a large employer might be able to offer him another position, but a small employer would find this more difficult in most cases.
3. Post-maternity reinstatement is waived for firms of five employees or less, if reinstatement is not practicable.
4. Frivolous claims are to be deterred by a liability to costs.

If the employee has been guilty of gross misconduct, such as persistent lateness, you will probably win your case, provided you warned him in writing to mend his ways well before you dismissed him. The point here is that not only must you have good reasons for dismissing him, but also you must have acted reasonably in the dismissal situation. This means that you have got to follow a proper sequence of written warnings – not less than three is the number generally recommended – stating his inadequacies, telling him what he has to do to put them right and spelling out the consequences if he fails to do so.

When it comes to matters of competence, though, things are rather less clear-cut, particularly if the task involved is not one where performance can be readily quantified or where there are many imponderables. It would be relatively easy to argue a case against a machine operator who was consistently turning out less work than her colleagues on similar machines, but far more diffi-cult in the case of a sales rep who could plead that a poor call-rate was the result of difficulties in finding car parking or inefficient back-up from the office.

The fact is that in all matters affecting competence you really have to do your homework very carefully before dismissing someone. The inexperienced employer may unwittingly contribute to a judgement by the tribunal going against her by such steps as including the person concerned in a general salary rise not long before informing him he is not up to the job.

There may be cases where you, as the employer, are satisfied that dismissal is fair, but where the law does not agree with you. One where you have to be very careful is dismissal on medical grounds. No reasonable employer would dismiss anyone in such circumstances if she could help it, but if you get stuck with someone who is persistently off sick and is able to provide satisfactory medical evidence, you would have to show proof that the absences were of such a nature as to cause disruption to your business before you could discharge him. Even more tricky is the case of employees who are engaged in public duties, such as being on the local council. You have to give them reasonable time off to attend to those duties, though not necessarily with pay.

The Sex Discrimination Act and the Equal Pay Act mean that women have in all respects to be treated on an equal footing with men, though since 1982 firms with fewer than five employees have been exempt from the former provisions. There are also occupations where discrimination is legal because of the nature of the work.

There are some additional conditions when employing women of child-bearing age. It used to be the case that women had to have had two years' continuous service with the same employer to qualify for maternity leave. These rules have now changed. Every expectant mother can take up to 18 weeks maternity leave and is entitled to Statutory Maternity Pay (SMP). Those employed for one year or more can take a further 11 weeks without SMP. This is 90 per cent of average weekly earnings for the first six weeks of maternity leave and £59.55 a week for the remaining 12 weeks. Businesses can recover 92 per cent of the SMP paid to employees, with smaller firms allowed to claim 100 per cent. Employees must give 21 days notice of their intention to take maternity leave and are entitled to get their old job back when they return – although these rules are slightly relaxed for the smallest firms who do not need to keep the job open if they can show it is not practicable to do so.

There is also now the right to take parental leave for a child born after 15 December 1999. Before the child reaches the age of five, parents are allowed 13 weeks leave in periods of not less than one week and up to a maximum of four weeks per year.

Nor does it end there. You will have to maintain all benefits other than remuneration... and if you bring in a replacement for her, or any other employee who is off for any longer period of time, be very careful. Her replacement could sue you for unlawful dismissal unless you notify him or her in writing that the appointment is a temporary one and give notice when it is coming to an end.

The penalties for losing an unfair dismissal case can be ruinous for a small firm. Under the new White Paper, _Fairness at Work_, there is no longer any limit to the amount that can be claimed. One effect may be a rise in substantial five-figure claims by aggrieved claimants with an aggressive lawyer. Thus if you are in any doubt at all about a dismissal, you should consult a solicitor who is versed in this aspect of the law.

REDUNDANCY

Redundancy is a ripe area for misunderstanding. Redundancy occurs when a job disappears, for example because a firm ceases trading or has to cut down on staff. It does not have the same restrictions as dismissal, but nevertheless does involve some financial penalties for employers if the employee has been continuously employed by the firm concerned for one year or more. In that case he will be entitled to redundancy pay on a formula based on length of service and rate of pay. About half of this can be recovered from the Department for Education and Employment, which you should notify if you intend to make anyone redundant. As usual, there is a good deal of form-filling involved. The law also requires you to give advance warning to the relevant unions if any of their members are to be made redundant.

What happens if you buy a business, lock, stock and barrel, together with the staff? You may find that you do not like some of the people the previous owner took on, or that you want to change or drop some of the things she was doing, with the result that staff will be made redundant. Irrespective of the fact that you did not hire the people concerned, you are still stuck with the responsibility towards them as their current employer, so that being the proverbial new broom can be a very costly exercise. Before buying a business, therefore, it is very important to look at the staff and at the extent of any redundancy payments or dismissals situations you could get involved in.

STATUTORY SICK PAY

Under the Social Security Contributions and Benefits Act (1992), employers are responsible for paying Statutory Sick Pay (SSP) to virtually all employees earning more than £66 a week, for up to 28 weeks' sickness in the year, and note that there is no longer a minimum number of weeks for which an employee has to have worked, before being able to claim sick pay. The obligation begins after the employee has been off work sick for more than three consecutive days. These need not be working days, though. They could include the weekend, or days when he would not normally be working. SSP is treated as earnings, so you should deduct PAYE and pay the employer's National Insurance contribution on it.

After these three days, and once the employee starts qualifying for SSP, it is only payable for the days when she would have been working. This means that when you employ part-timers – a growing part of the workforce – you would be well advised to specify their working days in the terms of employment, rather than having a loose 'as and when needed' arrangement.

Good paperwork in SSP situations is all the more important because you can claim back the payments you have made provided they exceed 13 per cent of your gross National Insurance contribution for the month (that is, NIC for employer *and* employee). The excess is deducted from the employer's National Insurance contribution.

The employee can offer self-certification for up to seven days. After that the employer should ask for a doctor's certificate. Careful records have to be kept of SSP payments and retained for three years. When you start employing people, you should get guidance from the DSS on how they require this to be done.

Guidance leaflets on employment

A great many leaflets giving guidance on employment matters are available free from the Department for Education and Employment. For an up-to-date list, write to the General Office, Information 4, Department of Employment, Caxton House, Tothill Street, London SW1H 9NF.

In the same context, another Act of Parliament you should keep an eye open for when buying a business is the Health and Safety at Work Act, which lays down standards to which working premises have to conform. Before putting down your money you should check with the inspectors of the Health and Safety Executive that any premises you are buying or leasing as part of the deal meet those standards.

In this connection it is important to be aware of the concept of 'constructive dismissal'. If an employer changes the terms of employment by action such as substantively lengthening hours, reducing pay or benefits or even adversely changing the status of an employee, that can be tantamount to unfair dismissal. Working Time Regulations are discussed later in this Chapter.

RECRUITMENT

The cost of discharging staff, whether because of redundancy or by dismissal, makes it imperative that you should make the right decisions in picking people to work for you in the first place. We have said that the sphere of personnel selection is something of a lottery. It could equally be described as a gamble and there are ways in which you could cut down on the odds against you.

The most obvious question to ask yourself is whether you really do need to take someone on permanently at all. The principle we have put forward for the purchase of equipment – never buy anything outright unless you are sure you have a continuing use for it and that it will pay for itself over a reasonable interval of time – also applies to personnel. The legal constraints that cover part-time or full-time employees do not extend to freelancers, personnel from agencies or outside work done on contract, and this could well be the best way of tackling a particular problem such as an upward bump in demand until you are sure that it is going to last.* It is worth remembering, too, that when you take on staff you take on a good many payroll and administrative overheads in addition to their salary. These can add quite significantly to your costs. The introduction of the minimum wage in April, 1999, should also make you consider the costs of recruitment. The standard rate is £3.60 an hour for those aged 22 and above. For those aged 18–21 the rate is £3.00 an hour. Exemptions include 16 and 17 year olds and apprentices between the ages of 18 and 26 who are in the first year of their apprenticeship.

Sooner or later, though, if you want your business to grow (and growth of some kind seems to be an inevitable concomitant of success) you are going to need people. But even then you should ask yourself what exactly you need them for and how much you can afford to pay. Clarifying these two issues is not only important in itself, but will also give you the basis of a job description which you can use in your press advertising or approach to a recruitment agency, at the interview and, finally, in the contract of employment. Around it you should also build a series of questions to ask the interviewee that should give you some indication of her competence to do the job. Such questions should call for a detailed response rather than a 'yes' or 'no' type of answer. For example:

☐ How many previous employers has he had? Has his progress been up, down or steady? Is this move part of the overall employment pattern?

☐ If he is willing to take a large drop in salary find out why – there could be a perfectly good reason, but it is worth being cautious.

---

* However, in some cases freelancers have successfully argued retrospectively that since they were subject to the same conditions as the ordinary employees of a firm, they were covered by employment law. It is not enough to say that 'A' is a freelance and 'B' is not; there must be recognisable differences in the way they work. The freelance must not be under your direct supervision and control, or he will be likely to be classified (for the purposes of redundancy pay, etc) as an employee.

- [ ] If you are interviewing a sales representative, as well as asking her how long she has been in the business, try to find out which buyers she knows and how well she knows them.
- [ ] Always ask for and check references. Telephone references are reckoned to be more reliable than written ones as referees are more forthcoming without the potential threat of libel.
- [ ] Be careful that the job specification stays within the growing range of employment protection legislation. Many employment agencies will advise you on the dos and don'ts of these contentious areas before you start interviewing candidates.

WORKING TIME

Since 1 October 1998, The Working Time Regulations have given a wide range of rights to employees and other workers, including, for the first time, a statutory right to paid leave. This right arises after 13 weeks of continuous working or employment. The minimum annual paid leave is three weeks, although this will rise to four weeks by the end of 1999. Working time must be recorded – including overtime – and must not exceed an average of 48 hours (averaged over a period which is usually 17 weeks) unless there is a written agreement between the employer and employees opting out of this restriction. Night workers also have restrictions on hours worked and have the right to free health assessments. The Regulations also give workers rights to rest-breaks and daily and weekly rest periods.

CONDITIONS OF WORK

Numerous regulations affect working conditions and you should be conversant with those relevant to your area, particularly if it is a potentially dangerous trade. Length of hours, minimum wages, employment of young persons, etc will tend to apply to all businesses and, though you may escape prosecution for a while, to fall foul of the law is likely to be embarrassing and expensive.

Checklist: employing people

1. Do you really need to take on staff? Will there be enough to keep them busy a year from now?
2. Have you worked out a job description which sets out the purpose of the job, the duties involved and who the person appointed will report to?
3. Have you decided how much you can afford to pay?
4. Does your advertisement or approach to a recruiting agency spell out the job description, the salary and an indication of the age of the person you are looking for?
5. Does it in any way contravene the Sex Discrimination Act or the Race Relations Act?
6. Have you prepared a series of questions that will throw some light on the interviewee's competence, personality and previous record of employment?
7. Have you taken up and checked references?
8. Are you satisfied, before making the appointment, that you have seen enough applicants to give you an idea of the quality of staff available for this particular job?
9. Do you have a procedure for reviewing the employee's progress before the expiry of the 52-week period after which he can claim unfair dismissal if you decide he is not suitable?
10. Do you make a practice of putting important matters in writing to the employees concerned?

1.14 Taxation

How you are affected by taxation depends on the nature of the commercial activity in which you are engaged. Virtually everyone pays tax on income from some source, whether this be from full-time employment, from dividends or interest or from self-employment, or from a combination of several of these elements. The various kinds of income are assessed under several headings or schedules and the ones we will be particularly concerned with are:

1. Schedule D. Case I and Case II: Income from trades, professions or vocations. (In the interests of simplicity we will refer to this as Schedule D, though there are four other 'Cases' of Schedule D income.)
2. Schedule E: Wages and salaries from employment.

There are also other ways in which you may be involved in tax matters. You may be paying capital gains tax on the disposal of capital assets. If you are employing people full-time, you will be responsible for administering their PAYE payments; also, in certain circumstances, your own PAYE. If you are a shareholder in a limited company, it will be paying corporation tax on its profits. Lastly, you may – and if your turnover exceeds £52,000 a year, you must – for the supply of certain goods and services collect VAT from your customers and pay it over to Customs and Excise, less any VAT on goods and services supplied to you in the course of business.

One cannot, in a book of this nature, deal exhaustively with a subject as complex as taxation. But, with this proviso, let us look in broad outline at some of its principal implications. There are certain income tax advantages in working for yourself, or even in earning a supplementary income from part-time self-employment. To some extent these advantages are eroded by the National Insurance contributions for the self-employed (Class 4) which impose, what is, in effect, an additional tax on the self-employed. The amount of contribution is subject to a certain amount of annual tinkering. It is payable by men under 65 and women under 60 and it currently stands as a levy of 7 per cent of business profits between £4,385 and £27,820 in 2000/2001 – a maximum of £1,640.45 per year. Businesses can no longer deduct 50 per cent of Class 4 contributions from income for tax purposes. Class 4 contributions are collected by the Inland Revenue. Contributions are payable if your profits exceed the threshold of £4,385 even if you work full-time or part-time in addition to being self-employed. However, there is a maximum amount of contributions that you have to pay in a year, so those who are employees and self-employed may be exempt from paying some or all of their Class 4 contributions. See below for details.

In addition, the self-employed must also pay a flat-rate weekly Class 2 National Insurance contribution if their profits are more than £3,825 a year. Those earning less than this can apply to be exempt. Ask for leaflet CA02 'National Insurance contributions for self-employed people with small earnings' from your local Contributions Agency (see your telephone directory) and fill in the exemption form CF10. The standard flat rate Class 2 contribution for 2000/2001 is £2.00 per week payable to the Department of Social Security. Most people pay this contribution by direct debit from their bank but alternatively you can be sent a quarterly bill.

As with Class 4 contributions, there is an overall maximum of Class 2 contributions payable in any tax year if you are self-employed and an employee. If you have earnings as an employee taxed under PAYE you will pay Class 1 National Insurance contributions if you earn more than £67 a week in the 2000/2001 tax year.

If you earn £535 or more a week from employment you will not normally have to pay any Class 2 or Class 4 contributions so you should ask for a deferral by asking for form CF259 from your local Contributions Agency office and send it to the Deferral Group of the Social Security office at DSS, Newcastle upon Tyne, NE98 1YX. If your earnings are less than this amount you can either ask for a deferral or apply for a refund at the end of the tax year.

158

As with income from employment, the profits of the self-employed are subject to an ascending rate of tax with income falling into different tax bands. If you have income from employment and self-employment, this is added together when calculating how much income falls into each tax band.

All income up to the basic Personal Allowance of £4,385 for the 2000/2001 tax year is tax free. If you are both an employee and self-employed, remember that you can have only one allowance which is offset against your total income. Income above this tax threshold then falls into tax bands starting with the first £1,520 of income (above your personal tax allowances) which is taxed at 10 per cent. The next £1,521 to £28,400 of income is taxed at 22 per cent and any income above £28,400 is taxed at 40 per cent. The total amount of income that will be taxed will also depend on any tax reliefs due – for example, personal pension contribution tax relief.

The main difference between taxation of employees and taxation of the self-employed, is that the self-employed can deduct a vast array of costs and expenses when calculating their taxable profits. The self-employed can deduct any expenditure 'wholly and exclusively incurred' in carrying on a trade or profession. It is essential that you are aware of what you can – or cannot deduct – as it will enable you to reduce the amount of your taxable profits and therefore the amount of tax you will have to pay.

THE MAIN ALLOWABLE BUSINESS EXPENSES

You can deduct 100 per cent of the cost of buying the following items unless they are purchased for part business and part private use, in which case only the business proportion may be deducted.

1. *The cost of goods bought for resale and materials bought in manufacturing.* This does not include capital expenditure on items such as cars, machinery or computers, although you can deduct some of the cost of buying these as a capital

allowance (see page 153). However, small items of expenditure such as filing trays, software or small tools can be deducted.

2. *The running costs of the business or practice.* Under this concession come heating, lighting, rent, rates, telephone, postage, advertising, cleaning, repairs (but not improvements of a capital nature), insurance and the use of special clothing. If you are using your home as office, you can claim up to two-thirds of the running costs of the premises as a business expense – provided you can convince the tax office that you are indeed using as high a proportion of your house as this exclusively for business purposes. Some people have been advised not to make this type of claim at all, because of the probability that, on selling, they might have to pay capital gains tax on the 'business' part of the sale, thus outweighing any income tax advantage. One way round this is to use a room mainly for business rather than exclusively. You will generally need to agree with your tax office what proportion of costs you can deduct.

3. *Carriage, packing and delivery costs.*

4. *Wages and salaries.* Any sums paid to full-time or part-time employees. You cannot, however, count any salary you and your partners are taking from the business, but you can pay your spouse a salary (provided they are actually doing a reasonably convincing amount of work for you). This is an advantage if their income from other sources is less than £4,385 a year, because that first slice of earnings is free of tax.

5. *Travel.* Hotel and travelling expenses on business trips and in connection with soliciting business. You are not, however, allowed the cost of travel between home and office, if you have a regular place of work. In addition to these expenses you can claim for the running costs of your car (including petrol) in proportion to the extent to which you use it for business purposes. WARNING: you cannot deduct the cost of entertaining as this is a disallowable expense.

6. *Interest.* Interest on loans and overdraft incurred wholly in connection with your business. This does not include interest on any money you or your partners have lent to the business.

7. *Hire and hire purchase.* Hiring and leasing charges and hire element in hire-purchase agreement (not the actual cost, because this is a capital expense).

8. *Insurance.* Every kind of business insurance, including that taken out on behalf of employees, but excluding your own National Insurance contributions and premiums paid on your personal life insurance. You cannot deduct personal pension contributions when calculating your business profits, but when calculating your tax these contributions – which qualify for tax-relief at your highest rate of tax – can be used to reduce the amount of tax you will have to pay.

9. *The VAT element in allowable business expenses (unless you are a taxable trader for VAT purposes).* This would include, for instance, VAT on petrol for your car. The VAT on the purchase of a motor car is allowable in all cases, since this cannot be reclaimed in your VAT return.

10. *Certain legal and other professional fees.* You are allowed to claim for things like audit fees or court actions in connection with business, but not for penalties for breaking the law (eg parking fines!)

11. *Subscriptions to professional or trade bodies.*

12. *Bad debts.* These are bad debts actually incurred, though provision is generally allowed against tax in the case of specific customers whom you can show are unlikely to meet their obligations; for instance, if their account is overdue and they are failing to respond to reminders. A general provision for a percentage of unspecified bad debts is not allowable against tax, however sensible it may be to make such provision in your accounts.

    Trade debts owing to you count as income even if they have not been paid at the end of the accounting period. Likewise, debts owed by you count as costs, even if you are not going to pay them until the next accounting period.

13. *Gifts.* Business gifts costing up to £10 per recipient per year, provided they are marked with the firm's name (but excluding food, drink and tobacco). All gifts to employees are allowable, but generous employers should remember that the employee may have to declare them on her tax return if their value is substantial.

Capital allowances

Generally you are allowed to write off against taxable profits 25 per cent of the cost of capital equipment on a reducing balance basis after the first year. For instance, in the year of purchase, if you buy a piece of equipment for £1000, you will be granted £250 writing-down allowance. For the following year, it will be 25 per cent of £750 (£1,000–£250=£750) giving an allowance of £187.50 and so forth. However, a 2000 budget change means that small and medium-sized businesses may claim a first year allowance of 40 per cent on plant and machinery. In addition, small businesses that invest in various computers, software and Internet-enabled mobile phones during the 3 years from 1 April 2000 will be abole to claim 100 per cent first-year allowances.

The writing-down allowance also extends to private cars used for business, up to a maximum of £3000.

Equipment bought on hire purchase is eligible for the writing-down allowance in respect of the capital element.

The hire charges themselves can be claimed as business expenses, spread over the period of the agreement.

In calculating your writing-down allowances you will have to take into account whether or not you are a taxable trader for VAT purposes, which depends on whether your annual turnover exceeds £51,000. If you are, you will already have claimed the VAT on your purchase in your quarterly or monthly VAT return. Thus capital allowances will be calculated on the net amount excluding VAT (except in the case of motor cars).

STOCK VALUATION

If you are in a business which involves holding stock (which may be either finished goods for resale, work in progress or materials for manufacture), it must be valued at each accounting date. The difference in value between opening stock and closing stock, when added to the value of purchases during the year, represents the cost of sales. Obviously, therefore, if you value your closing stock on a different basis from the opening stock, this will affect the profit you show. If you value the same kind of items more highly it will depress the cost of sales and increase the apparent profit. If you value them on a lower basis, the cost of sales will be increased and the profit decreased.

Table 14.1 *An example of stock valuation (assuming no purchases)*

Example A		Example B	
Sales	£150	Sales	£150
Opening Stock 100 Rose bushes @ £1.00: £100		*Opening Stock* 100 Rose bushes @ £1.00: £100	
Closing Stock 50 Rose bushes @ £1.50: £75		*Closing Stock* 50 Rose bushes @ 60p: £30	
Cost of Sales	£25	Cost of Sales	£70
Profit	£125	Profit	£80

Plainly, then, it does not make sense for you to up-value your closing stock in order to show a paper profit. Equally, you are not allowed to depress it artificially in order to achieve the reverse effect. However, if you can make a genuine case that some stock will have to be sold at a lower margin than the one you normally work to in order to be able to sell it within a reasonable time, a valuation in the light of this fact will generally be accepted by the tax office.

COMPUTING TAXABLE PROFIT

Normally your accountant will prepare a set of accounts for you for each year you are in business. Your accounting date need not coincide with the tax year (ending 5 April). The profits shown in these accounts will be the basis of your assessment.

As we stated earlier, certain costs which are genuine enough from the point of view of your profit and loss account are nevertheless not allowable for tax purposes: for example, entertaining customers. You are also not allowed to charge depreciation against your profit (though remember that when claiming capital allowances you will receive a writing-down allowance which, in the end, has a similar effect). These and other non-allowable expenses must be added back to the profits.

Equally, certain profits which you have made are to be deducted for the purposes of Schedule D assessment because they are taxed on a different basis and are subject to a return under another heading. Examples are gains from the disposal of capital assets, income from sub-letting part of your premises or interest paid by the bank on money being held in a deposit account.

In recent years some new kinds of business spending have come in for tax relief, notably incidental costs of raising loan finance and start-up costs incurred before you begin trading.

LOSSES

If your business or professional occupation has made a loss in its accounting year (and remember that from the tax point of view non-allowable expenses are added back to profits and you will have to do the same in your return), you can have the loss set off against your other income for the tax year in which the loss was incurred and for the subsequent year. It is also possible for a trading loss to be offset against capital gains if you have no other income to offset it against.

If your income for the year in which you made the loss and that of the subsequent year still does not exceed that loss, you can set off the balance against future profits; or you can carry the loss back and set it against earlier profits.

In the case of traders and partnerships, losses incurred in the first four years of business can be carried back against income from other sources, including salary, in the three years before commencing business as a self-employed person or partner. However, it should be noted that this does not apply to losses incurred by a limited company of which you are a shareholder – such losses can only be set off against profits chargeable in the the form of corporation tax. Even if you invest your money in your own company and it fails, you can only set off your loss against capital gains from other sources – not against income tax.

SELF-ASSESSMENT

In 1997 the taxation of the self-employed was radically changed. The main effect on the self-employed was that instead of being taxed on profits in their accounting year ending in the preceding tax year, they are now taxed on what is known as a 'current year basis'. This means that if, for example, your accounting year ends on 31 March 2000, you will be assessed for tax on those profits at the rates applying to the April 1999 to April 2000 tax year. Under the old regime you would not have been assessed until the following tax year. So, in effect the self-employed must pay tax on profits more quickly than they did under the old regime.

The self-employed pay tax on three different dates – two advance or 'interim' payments made by 31 January within the year of assessment and by 31 July following the end of the tax year of assessment. The third payment, the final balancing payment, is made by the following 31 January. To go back to the example above, a business with an accounting year to 31 March 2000, the first payment – usually half the tax on trading profits paid in the previous year – will be payable on 31 January 2000, the second payment on 31 July 2000 and a final balancing payment (if any further tax is due) on 31 January 2001. If your profits are likely to be much lower than in the previous year you can apply to have your interim payments – also known as 'payments on account' – reduced.

The other change introduced by self-assessment is that you can calculate your own tax should you want to. However, this is not mandatory. If you want the Inland Revenue to calculate your tax liability you must complete and submit your Tax Return by 30 September following the end of the tax year on 5 April.

If you – or your accountant – wish to calculate the tax owed, the Tax Return does not have to be submitted until 31 January (see Table 14.2). If you miss this deadline, you will be fined (see Table 14.3).

Self-assessment also requires taxpayers to keep and retain records to support information on their Tax Return. The self-employed must keep records for five years after the date of sending back their Tax Return.

The amount of information you need to give on your Tax

Table 14.2 *Key dates to remember*

31 July 2000	Second interim payment on account for the 1999/2000 tax year now due
30 September 2000	Final deadline for Tax Returns to be submitted by those wanting the Inland Revenue to calculate their tax bill
5 October 2000	Deadline for those who need to inform the Inland Revenue of new sources of income
31 January 2001	Final deadline to send back completed Tax Return sent out following the end of the tax year on 5 April
	First payment on account for the 2001/2002 tax year now due
	Final balancing payment for the 2000/2001 tax year now due

Return will depend on your turnover. Those with a turnover of less than £15,000 a year need only submit three line accounts – turnover, expenses and profit/loss. Other sole traders and partners have to produce more information including a detailed breakdown of expenses claimed. As accountancy fees are tax deductible by the self-employed, you are strongly advised to use an accountant to help you – to ensure that you claim all that you can to reduce your taxable profits and to ensure you are not fined by the Inland Revenue.

Table 14.3 *Inland Revenue fines and penalties*

Failure to submit Tax Return by 31 January	£100
Failure to pay tax due on 31 January	9.5% interest
Failure to pay tax by 28 February	5% surcharge plus interest
Failure to submit Tax Return by 31 July	a further £100
Failure to pay tax by 31 July	10% surcharge plus interest
Returns still not submitted after this date	up to £60 a day
Failure to keep accurate records	up to £3,000

SPARE-TIME WORK

Even though you have a full-time job which is being taxed under Schedule E and thus being taken care of under your employer's PAYE scheme, you may also have earnings from part-time employment in the evenings and weekends which you have to declare. Your employer need not know about this second income because you can establish with your tax inspector that the tax code which fixes the amount of PAYE you pay (see below) only relates to the income you receive from your employer.

Your spare-time income is also eligible for the allowances on expenses 'wholly and exclusively incurred' for business purposes. This means that it is most important that you should keep a proper record of incomings and outgoings. If your spare-time activities are on a small scale, you will not need to keep the kind of detailed books of account described in Chapter 1.7; but you should certainly maintain a simple cash book, from which at the end of the year you or your accountant can prepare a statement to append to your Income Tax Return.

Tax on spare-time work is payable in two half-yearly assessments: on 1 January within the year of assessment and on 1 July following the end of it.

Probably the largest item you will be able to set off against spare-time income is any sums you can pay your spouse for assistance up to the level of their tax-free allowance of £4385, provided they are not earning as much as this from another source.

PARTNERSHIPS

Partners pay tax on their share of the partnership profits in the same ratio as that in which they have agreed to split profits. Until the introduction of self-assessment, the partnership was taxed as a single entity with tax collected from the partnership as a whole, not the individual partners. However, the new rules stipulate that each partner is liable for his or her own tax. Most of the other tax rules relating to partners are the same as for the self-employed, so that means that salaries cannot be deducted when calculating profits and any interest on money put into the business by partners is considered as part of the partnership profits. Partners are deemed to start in business when they join the partnership and cease in business when they leave.

CORPORATION TAX

Corporation tax is payable by limited companies. Its provisions are somewhat complicated and it must be assumed, for the purposes of this brief chapter on taxation, that readers who are intending to set up businesses in this form will seek professional advice on tax aspects. However, the salient points are as follows:

1. For small companies corporation tax is currently charged at a rate of 10 per cent on taxable profits up to £10,000. Thereafter various rates apply up to 30 per cent for taxable profits over £1.5 million.
2. Unlike Schedule D income tax, corporation tax is normally payable nine months from the end of each accounting period.
3. If you are a director of a limited company, your income from this source will not be liable to Class 2 or Class 4 National Insurance. Instead your National Insurance contributions will be at the employed Class 1 rate and you will be paying PAYE on your salary (not tax on your business profits as you do if you are self-employed).

INHERITANCE TAX

This tax is in some ways similar to the older concept of death duties in that a charge is made on transfers of assets at death, up to a maximum of 40 per cent on amounts over £234,000 for the 2000/2001 tax year. If you make an outright gift more than seven years before death, no inheritance tax will be paid on this. A reduced amount of tax is paid on gifts made within seven years of death. These gifts are known as 'potentially exempt transfers'.

Business assets of those who have an interest in a small business or a farm qualify for substantial concessions which can reduce or eliminate the tax. You are advised to seek professional advice. However, generally, business relief means there is no inheritance tax to pay on business assets such as goodwill, land, buildings, plant, stock or patents (reduced by debts incurred in the business). What are regarded as private and business assets at death are, however, bound to be a subject of potential dispute with the Inland Revenue, so it is vital to seek professional advice on the implications of this tax when making a will.

CAPITAL GAINS TAX

If you sell or give away assets – usually cash, shares, property or other valuables – you are liable to capital gains tax on the gain made. This gain is generally calculated as the price you sell the asset for (or its market value) _less_ the cost of purchasing the asset (or its value on 31 March 1982 if it was bought before then and you want to use this value) and any costs incurred in buying, selling or improving the asset. However, you do not pay tax on the first £7,200 of gains you make in any tax year. If you are liable for capital gains tax it will be at your top rate of tax. So higher-rate taxpayers will pay it at 40 per cent.

The March 1998 Budget made significant changes to capital gains tax – with many of these new rules having a major impact on those running small businesses. Until the Budget, those selling assets could deduct the effects of inflation when calculating their gains. However, in future, inflation will only be deductible if the asset was bought before 1 April 1998 and then the effects of inflation can only be deducted until April 1998. For small businesses a major concession, retirement relief given to those selling their business after age 50 or retiring earlier due to ill-health, is being phased-out over five years until the tax year 2002/3. In the past this relief meant that the self-employed paid no capital gains tax if they owned the business for ten years before the sale and sold it for less than £250,000. Tax on gains between £250,000 and £1 million was halved. This relief is being replaced by a new tapering system of relief which will reduce the amount of tax paid the longer the asset is held. After ten years only 60 per cent of the gain will be taxed.

Other tax concessions include relief if a business is sold and another one is bought within three years. As reliefs vary and provide valuable tax breaks, you are advised to consult an accountant.

One area where those running a business can be caught out is if they run a business from home. Profits made on the sale of your main residence are generally exempt from tax. However, if you use your home for business and have been claiming part of the costs of running the business including a share of heating, lighting, rates and your mortgage or rent, you could have to pay capital gains tax. The easiest way to get round this is to not use a room 'exclusively' for business but only 'mainly'. So if you have three rooms in your home (other than bathrooms and kitchens) and use one for business, instead of claiming a third of the running costs of your home, claim slightly less than this. Always agree the business proportion of these costs with your Tax Office.

APPEALS

All taxpayers, be they an individual or a corporation, have the right to appeal against their tax assessment, if they have grounds for believing they are being asked to pay too much. Such appeals have to be made in writing to the Inspector of Taxes within 30 days of receiving an assessment. They are usually settled by more or less amicable correspondence, but ultimately can be taken to a hearing by the General or, in more complex cases, Special Commissioners.

PAYE

If you employ staff you will be responsible for deducting PAYE from their wages. The same applies to your own salary from a partnership or a limited company. The sums have to be paid monthly to the Inland Revenue by the employer.

You will receive from the tax office a tax deduction card for each employee, with spaces for each week or month (depending on how they are paid) for the year ending 5 April. On these cards, weekly or monthly as the case may be, you will have to enter under a number of headings, details of tax, pay for each period and for the year to date. You will know how much tax to deduct by reading off the employee's tax code number, which has been allotted to him by the tax office, against a set of tables with which you will also be issued. Without going into technicalities, the way the tables work is to provide a mechanism, self-correcting for possible fluctuations of earnings, of assessing the amount of tax due on any particular wage or salary at any given point of the year.

At the end of the tax year you will have to make out two forms:

1. Form P14 for each employee for whom a deductions working sheet has been used in the year just ended. Two copies are sent to the tax office. The third copy is called Form P60, and is issued to each employee. This gives details of pay and tax deducted during the year, as well as any SMP or SSP.
2. Form P35 for the Inland Revenue. This is a summary of tax and graduated National Insurance contributions for all employees during the year. It is a covering certificate sent with the Forms P14.

Before 6 May you have to send the tax office Forms P11D or P9D, which give details of your employees' expenses and benefits for the tax year just ended.

When an employee leaves, you should complete another form, P45, for her. Part of this form, showing her code number, pay and tax deducted for the year to date, is sent to the tax office. The other parts are to be handed by the employee to her new employer so that she can pick up the PAYE system where you left off.

Employers are also responsible for deducting Class 1 National Insurance contributions from their employees and will have to pay these along with their own employer's contributions (which are also based on a percentage of each employee's pay) at the same time as making PAYE tax payments. The introduction of the Small Business Service should ease this process with advice and an automated payroll service available to small businesses.

VAT

If the taxable outputs of your business, which for practical purposes means what you charge your customers for any goods or services that are not specifically 'exempt', exceed, or are likely to exceed, £52,000 in a year, you will have to register with the Customs and Excise (not the tax office, in this case) as a taxable trader for VAT purposes. This means that you will have to remit to Customs and Excise, either monthly or quarterly, 17.5 per cent of the price you charge on your 'outputs', this being the current standard rate of VAT. However, you will be able to deduct from these remittances any VAT which you yourself have been charged by your suppliers – your 'inputs'. This item covers not only VAT on materials used in producing the goods or services you supply to your customers, but everything which you have to buy to run your business, including such things as telephone charges. VAT also extends to goods purchased from outside the EU.

Not all goods and services carry 17.5 per cent VAT. Some are 'zero rated' – basic foodstuffs, newspapers and exported goods being notable examples. Full details are contained in VAT Notices 700 and 701, issued by Customs and Excise, New King's Beam House, 22 Upper Ground, London SE1 9PJ, and you should obtain from them these Notices together with any others about VAT which are relevant to your trade or profession. You will find your local office listed in the phone book. The significance of zero rating is that even though you do not charge VAT on goods of this nature that you supply, you can still claim back VAT on all your inputs, excluding the purchase of cars and business entertainment of domestic customers.

Zero rating is not, however, the same as 'exemption'. Zero rating carries a theoretical rate of VAT, which is 0 per cent. Exemption means that no rate of VAT applies at all and examples of exempt suppliers are bookmakers, persons selling or renting land and buildings, and various types of medical services. The exempt status is not particularly desirable, because if you are exempt you still have to pay VAT on all your inputs but have no outputs to set the tax off against.*

In this sense exempt traders are like private individuals, and the question, therefore, arises as to whether you should, as you are entitled to do, ask to be registered as a taxable trader even though your outputs are less than the mandatory £52,000 a year level. Customs and Excise may, of course, refuse to register you on the grounds that your outputs are too low, though no hard-and-fast minimum figure for this has been fixed. Your accountant should be able to advise you on this point, but the main consideration would be the level of your taxable inputs. Thus if you are a part-time cabinet-maker you would be buying a lot of materials which carry VAT. But, if you were doing something like picture research, the VAT inputs might be quite low and the administrative work involved in being a taxable trader might not be justified by the amount of VAT you could claim back against your outputs.

The point to be realised is that if you register as a taxable trader, voluntarily or otherwise, you are going to be involved in a fair bit of extra administration. At the end of each VAT accounting period (quarterly or monthly, the latter being more usual with traders in zero-rated goods), you will have to make a return of all your outputs, showing their total value and the amount of VAT charged. Against this you set the total of your inputs and the amount of VAT you have paid. The difference between the VAT on your outputs and that on your inputs is the sum payable to Customs and Excise. This obviously causes problems for retailers making a great many small sales and particularly for those supplying a mixture of zero-rated and standard-rated goods (eg a shop supplying sweets, which are taxable, and other items of foods, which are mostly zero rated). It also underlines the vital importance of keeping proper records and retaining copy invoices of all sales and purchases, because although your VAT return needs only show totals, Customs and Excise inspectors are empowered to check the documents on which your return is based and require you to keep these records for six years. There is obviously, therefore, a link between the records you have to maintain for ordinary accounting purposes and those that are needed to back up your VAT return.

* The distinction between zero-rated goods and exempt goods is important in determining whether you should be registered for VAT. Exempt goods do not count towards total 'turnover' for this purpose, but zero-rated goods do. Thus, if your turnover is over £52,000 including exempt goods but under that figure without them, you are not liable to pay VAT.

There is also a close connection between VAT and the problem of cash flow. When you receive an invoice bearing VAT, the input element can be set off against the VAT output on your next return, irrespective of whether you yourself have paid the supplier. Therefore, if you are buying an expensive piece of capital equipment it will make sense for you to arrange to be invoiced just before your next return to Customs and Excise is due.

The boot is on the other foot, though, when you yourself are extending credit to a customer. The sale is reckoned to have taken place when the invoice has been rendered, not when you have received payment. Therefore you will be paying VAT on your output before you have actually received the cash covering it from your customer. However, VAT can be reclaimed on bad debts, which in this case means amounts overdue by 6 months.

However, as a concession to small businesses with a taxable turnover (exclusive of VAT) of under £350,000, Customs will allow you to operate what is known as cash accounting. This enables small firms to account for tax when cash is paid and received rather than on presentation of an invoice.

It is also worth noting that if you are liable for VAT, inputs can be claimed on goods purchased for the business before it opens which are in place at the time of opening. VAT can also be claimed back on services such as professional advisers' fees supplied within six months of starting to trade.

Once you have registered for VAT, you will receive, at the end of each quarter, a form on which to make your return to Customs and Excise. It is very important to do this within the time stated, because there are financial penalties for making late returns, which can go as high as 30 per cent for repeated defaults.

There are also penalties for 'serious misdeclarations'. If you find, however, that you have accidentally underdeclared any of your taxable outputs, you can apply to the Customs and Excise to make a 'voluntary disclosure for accidental underpayment'. This would not make you liable to a penalty.

Before making a quarterly return, it is a good idea to check your own figures. Dividing the VAT total by the net total should show that the VAT is 17.5 per cent of the net, or at least very close to it. Customs and Excise will accept a tolerance like 0.25 per cent. But anything more than that suggests a mistake in your arithmetic somewhere. Better to pick it up yourself than to invite a visit from the VAT inspector.

THE BLACK ECONOMY

One cannot these days write about taxation without some reference to the 'black economy'. There is a good deal of evidence to suggest that the response to the way rising wages and salaries are pulling an increasing number of people into higher tax brackets has been tax evasion on a large scale by a variety of means, such as straightforward non-declaration of earnings, making or receiving payments in cash, arranging remuneration in kind or, simply, barter deals. Some of these methods are easier for the tax inspectors to spot than others, but this is not the place to give advice on a highly contentious topic, except to say that all forms of tax evasion are illegal. In fact, there are enough loopholes and 'perks' available to self-employed people with a good tax consultant at their elbow to render law-breaking an unacceptable and unnecessary risk.

THE CHALLENGE TO SELF-EMPLOYED STATUS

In recent years there has been an increasing tendency for the Inland Revenue to challenge taxpayers' claims to be assessed under Schedule D and to try to bring them within the PAYE scheme. The challenge hinges round the nature of the relationship between the provider of work and the performer of it. If the provider of work is in a position to tell the performer the exact place, time and manner in which the job is to be done, then the relationship between them is, to use an old-fashioned phrase, a master-and-servant one and clearly does not qualify for Schedule D taxation. On the other hand, if the performer of the work is merely given a job to do and is absolutely free as to how she does it, except in so far as it has to be completed within certain specifications of time, quality and price, then the performer can be regarded as self-employed. There are, however, some

175

potential grey areas here; for instance, a freelance working mostly for one client may be straying into a master-and-servant situation. The Inland Revenue is also now treating any income derived under a contract of service as liable to PAYE – even if it is only for one or two days a month. This means that formal contractual arrangements should be avoided when worthwhile payments are involved. A guidance note has been issued (IR56) under the title *Tax – Employed or Self-Employed*, but the inspector of taxes is still entitled to take his own view of your situation.

The Inland Revenue has a degree of autonomy which is not generally realised by the general public. It is not, for instance, answerable to Parliament except in the widest political sense, so it is no use writing to your MP, no matter how unjustified you may feel a tax decision is. Your only recourse is to take the matter to an Independent Appeals Tribunal, but unless a large sum of money is involved it is probably not worth the trouble – though self-employed people who are members of a professional association may find it willing to take up on their behalf something that looks like a test case.

Complaints

If you have a complaint about the way your affairs have been dealt with by Customs & Excise, there is a leaflet about complaints procedures relating to VAT: *Complaints Against Customs & Excise*, available from any local VAT office.

Beyond that, there is a complaints supremo, who deals with Inland Revenue and Benefit Office as well as VAT matters: The Adjudicator's Office (see Appendix 1).

Checklist: taxation

1. Inform the Department of Social Security if you have recently become full-time or self-employed.
2. Collect receipts for allowable business expenses. Check with your accountant if you are not sure what is permissible.
3. Become acquainted with the important dates related to self-assessment and make sure that you do not miss the deadlines.
4. Contact your tax inspector if you have a second, self-employed, job and establish that your tax code fixes the amount of PAYE you pay only for the income you receive from your employer.
5. Be aware that you might be liable to pay Capital Gains Tax on the sale of your home if you claim tax relief on using part of it as a business premise.
6. If you are likely to exceed £51,000 a year taxable outputs, register with the Customs and Excise for VAT and consult your accountant.

1.15 | **Choosing Premises**

The choice of premises tends to be determined by individual requirements. Over 400,000 businesses are currently home-based, accounting for over one in ten small businesses in this country. This chapter will mainly concentrate on the requirements of this group. However, for many, such as those in retailing, this simply is not an option and help is available at the end of this chapter for those who need to choose separate premises.

WORKING FROM HOME

Research by Barclays Small Business Banking has identified the growing trend amongst the self-employed to work from home. Key findings include:

☐ Businesses operating from home are generally smaller than those with separate premises and have a quarter of the average turnover of these businesses.

☐ The average start-up cost for small businesses operating from home is £5,000 compared with £13,000 for those operating from separate premises.

☐ Only a fifth of those business owners working from home see it as a stepping stone to operating from separate premises.

☐ Business owners working from home work on average 11 hours less each week than those working from separate premises.

When it comes to Studies
we've done
our Homework

We've been making quality fitted furniture, built to last, for over a quarter
of a century and our latest range of superior home-offices
are unquestionably the finest of their kind.
You can choose from numerous wood finishes and styles and
whatever shape or size your room, our consultant will work with
you to design a study that will be perfect for all your needs.

BROOKLANDS

FOR YOUR FREE COMPLIMENTARY PORTFOLIO

PHONE
TODAY **0800 923 4000**

BROOKLANDS LIMITED FREEPOST CL2 126 BASILDON SS14 3GY

Lines open 7 days a week or you can fax us on **01268 472010**

Commenting on this research, Mike Davis, Managing Director of Barclays Small Business Banking, identifies the reasons for the increasing number of home workers:

> The way we work is changing. Technological advances, especially in the communications field – coupled with growing frustration with time wasted travelling to and from work – has meant that more and more people are choosing to work from home.

Working from home needs to be given careful consideration. While start-up costs are smaller than for businesses operating from premises, you should be aware of the effects on family life and the prospect of working in isolation. Furthermore, should you need to have business visitors, a home-based office might create a bad impression of your operation unless you think carefully about presentation. You should also check whether by claiming part of the costs of running your business from home you will incur capital gains tax.

Barclays identify two types of home worker. The first spends most of the working day at home and the second uses the home as a base but works at clients' premises. The second group is older, with over half aged over 45. Typical occupations in this group are building and gardening.

On the other hand, the group using their home as an office tend to be women, of which a sixth were formerly housewives. The researchers observe:

> These characteristics suggest many of the owners of these businesses are trying to juggle domestic responsibilities with those of work, or have more than one job and set up in business to supplement the family income. It is more likely that they plan to maintain the size of their home-based business rather than expand it to become the main breadwinner.

Indeed, the above comment points to one of the biggest problems experienced by working from home: the difficulty in separating work from home life. Domestic distractions are one thing (the attractions of finishing off the dusting can far outweigh having to do your accounts), but if you only have one telephone for both home and business, a child acting as receptionist to potential

3rd TIME LUCKY?

No chance. We believe the only way to win 'Your Mortgage' magazine's 'Best Direct Lender' award for three years running is good, old-fashioned hard work. The award is judged on customer satisfaction and tested by a panel of mystery shoppers. So our efforts to provide a fast, simple and friendly service have paid off. We can give you a quote in five minutes and an Agreement In Principle just ten minutes later. So why not give us a call? And discover why we believe that where finding the right mortgage is concerned, there's no such thing as luck.

 **NatWest Mortgages**

0800 400 999
Monday – Friday 8am to 8pm,
weekends 10am to 4pm
(quote reference CHAMP)
www.natwest.com

HOME TRUTHS
NatWest Mortgage Services

This is not the usual broadbrush banker's article about how to prepare a business plan, where to find sources of finance, who to ask for advice and so on.

Instead it has a sharper focus - your home - which is perhaps not a surprising choice for a writer who is a mortgage specialist. What may be surprising, however, is that much of the article is as relevant to those who choose not to work from home as those who do.

The truth is that, if you are considering making a break and working for yourself (or indeed already doing so), your home is important in the sense of how you finance it.

Your mortgage (assuming you have one) may well be one of your biggest outgoings so it is important to make sure it is the most appropriate type for you. Becoming self-employed gives you the opportunity to reassess the position. Let me explain why.

When you work for somebody else you know what your monthly salary will be and you can rely on receiving it on a particular day. This is reassuring and makes budgeting easier.

Clearly, when you are self-employed, you may not know with any certainty what your future profits will be, nor when your invoices will be paid.

Your monthly income will also fluctuate; some months could be spectacularly good and others more disappointing. Taken over a long period, you will hope to do better than

if you worked for somebody else but how do you manage these monthly fluctuations in your income so far as your mortgage repayments are concerned ?

The answer could well be one of the new generation of so-called 'flexible mortgages' which offer advantages to people whose income varies from month to month.

There are various types on the market and each has slightly different features. Some enable you to use surplus funds, from a succession of good months for example, to be credited into your mortgage account, after making your usual monthly repayment, so reducing the outstanding debt and, if the lender calculates interest daily, immediately reducing the interest you are being charged.

This can be a particularly valuable feature because, if you were to invest the funds elsewhere, you would have to be effectively earning at least your lender's mortgage rate - and even more if you pay tax - to be making your finances work just as hard for you.

Furthermore, some mortgages give you the flexibility to take back some of the surplus funds you have paid in which can be very useful if you are unlucky enough to hit a bad patch. Technically this is known as a 'redraw facility' but certain lenders are confident about offering it as long as you stay within a comfort zone of an agreed credit limit.

Taking the longer view, if over the years you can pay in more surplus funds than you need to withdraw, then you will be able to pay off your mortgage early, possibly without any early repayment charges.

Remember, these are mortgages for grown-ups. Check with the lender, but the chances are that you will be given the freedom to choose your own repayment method - whether it's the traditional capital and interest way or interest-only with a separate repayment vehicle, for example ISAs or personal pension, running alongside.

Another mortgage -related issue concerns how you would meet the repayments if you could not work for a time. If you work for someone else, there are policies which cover your repayments if you become ill, have an accident or lose your job.

As a self-employed person, it's different because you can't lose your job in the conventional sense. The good news though, is that you can be covered, usually for up to a year, if you can't work through sickness, or accident or if you cease trading permanently and don't have enough money to make ends meet.

It is also wise to ensure that you have enough life cover to repay your mortgage if you die.

Finally, you don't need to tell your mortgage lender if you're working from your spare room, but you should check with them and with your local council planning department if you want to change part of the building's usage - for example, to use an extension as a nursery school.

The old days of rigid rules which insisted that working part time from a single desk in the corner of a tiny attic would automatically mean your mortgage being switched from a domestic to (more expensive) commercial one are well behind us. These days, it's a question of the degree to which your home will be used for commercial purposes and lenders all have their own criteria on this.

Check the house deeds too to ensure they do not prohibit your home being used for business purposes and tell the local authority what you are intending to do. In some cases you may need planning permission, particularly if you need to make extensive alterations, but then again you might not - again it's a question of the degree to which the fundamental nature of the property would be changed.

It is also sensible to ask your neighbours if they would have any objections to you working from home and also to find out if there are any local bylaws which impose covenants or restrictions.

Also, don't forget to tell the company insuring your home or you may risk invalidating your policy. You should also ask for a quote based on the additional business equipment in your home.

In summary, whether you intend to work from home or not, it is sound practice to consider how the inevitable fluctuations in your income will affect your ability to repay your mortgage.

Look at the mortgage options, particularly the new flexible products and ensure you take out a policy which covers your repayments if the worst happens.

For those thinking of working from home remember the biggest home truth of all - share your ideas with your lender, your insurers and your local authority. Don't be afraid to ask now. You may be pleasantly surprised with the flexibility of the response and it's much better than getting a nasty shock later.

clients will not present a professional image and might critically damage your prospects.

Setting aside a dedicated room to act as a separate office can help, if your home allows it. This will help to separate domestic and work life both physically and psychologically. Going to work in a separate space – even if it is the room next door – can help create the division. However, while there are problems in juggling domestic responsibilities and work in the same environment, one should not ignore the benefits. For example, the Barclays research found that nearly half of the women working from home stated that it was an important benefit because it allowed them to look after children and/or other dependants. Flexible working hours and practices, a reduction in travelling time and improved quality of life were also cited as benefits of home working. The following table identifies the perceived benefits of working from home:

Table 15.1 *Perceived benefits of working from home*

Perceived benefit	All	Men	Women
Lower overheads	26	37	16
Allows me to look after children/dependants	24	4	48
Allows me flexible working hours/practices	22	20	23
Allows me to be my own boss	17	21	13
No need for separate premises	16	20	12
Less travelling time	12	13	11
Lower start-up costs	8	10	6
Better quality of life	6	8	5
Greater potential profits	5	8	3

Choosing a room

What, then, should be taken into consideration when setting up an office from home? The following checklist should help:

- ☐ Noise – choose as quiet a room as possible, away from the distractions of family and other external noises.
- ☐ Position – try to think about heating and ventilation. A south-facing office might be appealing but will become a heat trap in the summer, as can uninsulated attics. Save on heating bills by purchasing a heater for your office rather than heating the whole house in winter.
- ☐ Lighting – be aware of the glare on computers and of the need for good lighting for close work such as design.
- ☐ Storage – you will never have enough space to store paperwork. However, consideration for the best use of storage facilities should be given.
- ☐ Security – being burgled is an unpleasant experience that could be disastrous if your means of making a living are also taken. Invest in a burglar alarm, good window and door locks and mark any equipment with an identifiable label.

Visitors

One of the main reasons cited by people who do not choose to work from home is that a separate premises provides a professional image. Indeed, a visitor who has to negotiate children's toys and overeager pets might not leave with the image of the professional business that you would want. Should you expect your home business to have visitors, bear in mind the impression you are likely to give and clear passageways and the route through to your working area where possible. Your office can be a comfortable environment in which to meet clients and as they know that you work from home will not expect otherwise. However, you can also arrange to meet elsewhere such as in a hotel or club such as the Institute of Directors, should you be a member. Furthermore, if you do not want to use your home address for business purposes, using a Post Office Box number can help to guard privacy and, should you move, maintain continuity for your customers.

Networking

One of the biggest problems for people working from home is the sense of isolation. Whereas going to work in separate premises automatically introduces contact with other individuals, it is quite possible not to see another adult in your working day if you work from home. This can impact on your work, as informal feedback from colleagues about ideas and projects is an underrated but invaluable source of advice and motivation. Daily discussion that occurs naturally in shared offices and workspaces can be helpful on a range of issues and is often sorely missed. The lack of this informal feedback is often neglected when considering how to work from home and it is important to build into your work practice a way of networking with other people in the same occupation or in similar circumstances. Being a member of a trade association or union can help, as regular local meetings can be attended; local chambers of commerce can also help you keep in contact with other businesses in your region. The Internet is also another way to contact people through user-groups and e-mail. However, non-professional communication is also important and building in a break to the day where contact is made with other people can also help. Peter Chatterton describes how he has overcome this problem in *Your Home Office* (Kogan Page), by forming a lunch society with other home-based workers:

> We get together on an ad-hoc basis for lunch or early evening drinks. This may sound trivial, but it is important to one's sanity in home working. But there are other benefits – our growing band of home workers have suddenly found that we can work together and give each other business. It's the start of a new wave of home business networking.

Chatterton also recommends putting adverts in local papers to make contact with other home workers and taking advantage of the flexible hours by going to a local sports club during the day when there isn't the weekend rush, adding: 'Think originally and openly – after all, you don't have the constraints of a normal job.'

CHOOSING A SEPARATE PREMISES

Working from home simply isn't an option when space needs to be found for employees, machinery, vehicles and other equipment. Indeed a sixth of small business owners cite this as the reason for working from separate premises. Research has also found that a further 15 per cent believe that it is easier to keep business and private lives separate, while 8 per cent thought it would mean fewer distractions. However, choosing a premise can be a complicated matter. It is important to consider your own specific requirements and ask some key questions before committing yourself to a lease or purchase. For example:

☐ Is passing trade a requirement for your business?
☐ Is a prestigious/prominent building important to your needs?
☐ What can you afford and are you going to lease or purchase?
☐ Do you have specific space requirements such as the need for warehousing?
☐ Is there sufficient utility capacity for your needs (ie gas, electricity, water, drainage, waste disposal)?
☐ Does the property present security risks?
☐ Do you need unrestricted parking for deliveries and customers?
☐ Will you need planning permission for your usage?
☐ Will it accommodate your growing business?

LEASES

Whether you plan to trade from your home or a separate premise, if the property is rented you will need to look carefully at the terms of your lease. There are likely to be restrictive covenants in the lease which will prevent you from carrying on a trade in premises let to you for domestic use. This may not be an insuperable obstacle, but you would certainly have to get the owner's permission if you wanted to use your home for any purpose other than just living there.

Even when you rent commercial premises there are likely to be restrictions on the trade you carry on in them. An empty flower shop, for instance, could probably be used as a dress shop without complications, but its use as a furniture repair business might be disallowed because of the noise involved in running wood-working machinery. You and your solicitor should examine the lease closely for possible snags of this sort.

Equally important is the existence of any restrictions which would prohibit you from transferring the lease to a third party. This would mean that the purchaser would have to negotiate the lease element in the event of the sale of the business with the property owner, not with you, and this could drastically affect the value of what you have to sell. For instance, if you took a gamble on renting premises in an improving area which fulfilled your expectations by coming up in the world, you would not be able to reap the benefit of your foresight and courage if you could not transfer the unexpired portion of the lease.

Commercial leases, unlike most domestic ones, run for relatively short periods: usually between three and seven years, with rent reviews at the end of each term or sometimes even sooner. This adds an unknown factor to the long-term future of any business in rented premises and is one you need to take into account in buying a business – again, particularly in an improving area. In Covent Garden, for instance, a number of small shops which moved in when it was a very run-down part of central London with correspondingly low rents were hit by huge increases when these rents were reviewed in the light of the improved status of the area subsequent to the redevelopment of the market building and its surroundings.

The other point to watch for in leases is whether you are responsible for dilapidation during the period of your lease. If you are, you could be in for a hefty bill at its end and for this reason it is advisable to have a survey done and its findings agreed with the owner, before you take on the lease.

MEET YOUR OWN REQUIREMENTS

Whether working from home, or from a separate premise, your environment is an important element in being able to motivate yourself and work efficiently. If you are able to discipline yourself to set hours within your home office, then this might be the answer for you. However, if being in contact with people on a daily basis is important it might be worth looking at a shared space with other like-minded self-employed individuals. Your local paper should have details of workspaces, or try your trade association or trade union for contacts. Deciding to work from separate premises will need careful consideration. Requirements for specific trades, such as retailing or catering, are discussed in Part Two. However, the Royal Institution of Chartered Surveyors also publishes a book, *The Business Property Handbook*, which covers all of the main areas such as the complicated issue of signing a lease, planning permission and tax allowances. The choice of premises in relation to marketing is also discussed in this book in Chapter 1.11.

Checklist: choosing premises and equipment

1. Are you able to separate domestic and work duties within your own home?
2. Are you able to work in isolation?
3. Have you identified forums for networking and are there other self-employed home workers with whom you can maintain contact?
4. Talk to your local crime prevention officer for advice on securing your office and equipment and inform your insurance company that you will be using part of your home for work.
5. Have you a room which allows adequate storage, good light, comfortable heat and ventilation and that is reasonably quiet? Check the route to your office to assess the impression a visitor might get.
6. Consider a separate telephone line for your business use.

7. Talk to other home workers in similar businesses about their equipment before you commit yourself to buying anything. If you have low usage of a piece of equipment, such as a photocopier, assess local availability before purchasing.
8. Assess your needs when considering separate premises. If passing trade is a requirement, think about parking restrictions. Is there enough room for equipment and any future growth in staff and business?
9. Seek out legal and professional advice whether you are considering purchasing or leasing a property.
10. Check if planning permission is required before altering the premises.

1.16 Information and Communication Technologies

E-COMMERCE

Technological advances have made self-employment accessible to many more businesses and individuals. The range of new technologies and equipment can be quite daunting and it seems that no sooner than something appears on the market than it is replaced by an updated and more efficient version. Whereas five years ago a personal computer, fax and answerphone were probably all the equipment that start-up businesses needed, the phenomenal growth of e-commerce has made it important for individuals and small businesses to re-examine their needs and to investigate the use of information and communication technologies (ICTs). The easy accessibility and affordability of ICTs have had a two-fold effect on small businesses. First, it has made working from home far easier and second it has provided even the smallest enterprise access to a global market.

This accessibility and the growing interest of SMEs in e-commerce is demonstrated by the fact that Web site ownership and the use of Web sites to sell online by SMEs have more than doubled since 1997, according to government figures. Indeed, the Christmas of 1999 has become known as the first 'e-xmas' with many small traders reporting phenomenal sales through their Web sites.

mondus.co.uk - The one-stop shop for business services

mondus.co.uk is the first global, business-to-business marketplace which can bring buyers and suppliers together on the Internet.

Buyers can use the net to choose the most attractive deals from its network of high-quality business suppliers saving their company time, money and hassle. Meanwhile, for suppliers, mondus offers a great way to reach new prospects and customers.

If you purchase products and services for your organisation, mondus could make a real difference to the way you contact and select your suppliers. mondus gives you direct access to top quality suppliers in a wide range of markets from IT to printing, office equipment to human resources. With such a host of products and services on offer, mondus can help you find what you want quickly and easily.

By making just one visit to www.mondus.co.uk, you can receive tenders from many more suppliers than you would have time to contact directly. This is "shopping around" the twenty-first century way.

Using mondus ensures you get the best value for money by opting for the most competitive quote. It's an excellent way of making sure you buy products as cost effectively as possible, and get exactly the service you want. And mondus is totally free to anyone looking for business suppliers.

If mondus is invaluable for buyers, it's just as essential for suppliers. This new marketplace provides a great way for companies to reach new prospects and customers.

The fact is, for many small or medium-sized businesses, building a web site may be problematic from a technical point of view. With mondus, however, you can still reach the millions of web users all over the world, easily and cost effectively. Registering with mondus means that prospects who need your products or services can be put in touch with you through a simple e-mail. It's an effortless way of generating new customer leads.

You get all the benefits of your own web site without the trouble of building or maintaining it. And even if you do have a web site, mondus can significantly increase the chances of a prospect contacting you.

How buyers use mondus

Registering with mondus.co.uk as a buyer costs nothing. Simply access the Internet and log on to the mondus homepage at www.mondus.co.uk. Fill in the registration form by answering a few basic questions and you're ready to seek quotes from suppliers.

The list of product categories is growing all the time. So just choose your category and fill in the simple order form. mondus will then e-mail your form to all our qualified suppliers, keeping you anonymous. The suppliers can then submit on-line quotes for the goods or service. The quotes are held securely and only you can view them.

Simply choose the quote which best suits your priorities, and mondus puts you in touch with the supplier to complete the deal.

If you have any difficulty in filling in the order form, you can always call the mondus helpline on 0800 100 123, or e-mail mondus@ukcentral.com for more information.

How suppliers use mondus

Visit www.mondus.co.uk to register with mondus as a supplier. Once your registration is activated, you will be alerted by e-mail when purchasers are looking for the type of products or services you supply. Only after a buyer is introduced to you and makes a purchase will you pay a small commission. Clearly, this is a very cost-effective way to locate qualified buyers.

Helping small businesses get on to the Internet

Audrey Roser, mondus's Global Customer Relations Manager, answers some of the most frequently asked questions.

Audrey Roser joined mondus last year, and is very excited to be working in such an innovative and fast-growing enterprise. She believes mondus is building an internet application which companies really do find useful, for both buying and selling products and services.

Here are Audrey's answers to the questions she is asked most often:

What's the catch – how much will it cost me?

There's no catch – it's free for both buyers and suppliers to register, and suppliers only pay commission when they actually close a deal. This commission fee is typically less than 5% although some categories attract a higher rate, and we'll invoice you for it when you win the deal.

Buyers don't pay us anything, ever.

How do I register?

Just go to www.mondus.co.uk, answer a few basic questions and then you're ready to use your account.

Your categories don't cover what my company needs/sells – can you add more?

We are expanding our list of categories all the time, and welcome suggestions from our customers.

Are your buyers and suppliers reliable and trustworthy?

We are currently implementing a comprehensive checking policy. However, mondus also has a facility to run a Dun & Bradstreet credit check on buyers and suppliers.

mondus – save yourself time, money and hassle

Every day, more and more buyers and suppliers are signing up to mondus. So don't miss out on this huge potential market – register with mondus right away, by clicking on to www.mondus.co.uk.

You don't need any special skills to use mondus – just a computer with access to the Internet. To find out more about mondus.co.uk, simply click on to their web site at www.mondus.co.uk, or call their free helpline on 0800 100 123. They're open 7 days a week.

In the time it took to get this many quotes...

...mondus brings you this many.

mondus.co.uk can put you in touch with hundreds of top quality suppliers in minutes. Register free now at **www.mondus.co.uk** and save yourself time, money and hassle.

However, as much as there is plenty to be optimistic about there are still concerns over the ability of the Internet to be secure and to maintain confidentiality. Furthermore, many businesses have been the victim of their own success and found that although having Web sites has boosted sales, they have not been able to back this up properly with adequate distribution and warehousing facilities. An interesting example of this is that the online sales of books in the run-up to the Christmas of 1999 far outstripped conventional purchasing in shops. However, this dropped off rapidly in the ten days before Christmas as customers lacked confidence in the ability of online retailers to get them their goods on time. Indeed, high-street traders found that they made up the sales lost to their electronic counterparts. Experience will undoubtedly iron out some of these problems and many are convinced that unless small businesses adopt e-commerce into their work practices they cannot possibly remain competitive. Commenting on the 1998 report *Net Benefit: The Electronic Commerce Agenda for the UK*, the former DTI minister, Barbara Roche, identified why it is so important for companies and individuals to embrace these changes:

> The phenomenal speed of change poses huge challenges to business – the need to change working practices, open up new markets, create new products and new forms of distribution. In markets where the traditional model can be turned on its head overnight, where a business can move from start-up to global player in a matter of months, it is vital that all companies, whatever their sector of business, whether large or small, understand how electronic commerce can bring them competitive advantage and use that knowledge.

Definition of e-commerce

There is still debate about the true definition of e-commerce. The Information Society Initiative, a government scheme to encourage SMEs to adopt e-commerce practices into their businesses, identifies two definitions:

1. Narrow definition: focus on buying and selling of goods or services over electronic networks such as the Internet between businesses, business and consumers or between the public and private sector.

2. Broad definition: includes the above but also activities between businesses for intermediate goods and the electronic processing of information, ie how businesses are using information gathered electronically to improve their business processes and relationships with suppliers and consumers.

A simpler definition is offered by the Association for Standards and Practices in Electronic Trade on its extremely useful Web site 'eCentreuk' HYPERLINK http://www.eca.org.uk www.eca.org.uk:

> Electronic commerce covers any form of business or administrative transaction or information exchange that is executed using any information and communications technology.

Building an ICT infrastructure

Building an ICT infrastructure could be as easy as buying a suitable PC with a modem. This might set you up with an e-mail capability, access to the Internet, ordering facilities, etc. Alternatively, you might need additional technology to build your infrastructure, such as a mobile phone with a modem if you are on the road a lot.

The most recent ISI review of usage trends internationally found that ICT uptake was growing in all areas of UK industry:

ICT Ownership and Use

	1997 %	1999 %
PCs	94	93
PCs with modems	73	79
Internet access	35	62
Web site	27	51
External e-mail	52	72
Electronic Data Interchange (EDI)	31	32
Selling online	3	9

Source: Moving into the Information Age 1999, ISI

It's interesting to note that while many businesses have begun to use communications technologies such as e-mail and the number of businesses with Web sites have doubled in two years, the number of companies using the Internet to sell their goods is less than one in ten. This figure will have undoubtedly risen when the next figures are released for 2000 but it does demonstrate how some of the concerns about payment and distribution have affected uptake of e-commerce in this area.

Before considering what equipment your business may need, it is worth carrying out a needs assessment. Peter Chatterton in *Your Home Office* advises that the process of purchasing technological tools should be carried out in a sensible and planned way. He advises that you should:

- find out what's available;
- work out your own needs;
- put a realistic plan together;
- buy with confidence;
- learn gradually;
- get yourself organized.

Advice on your ICT needs can be sought from both the ISI and eCentreuk. However, the following is a base-line guide to equipment necessary to join the information superhighway.

A computer with modem

Either a PC or Mac with at least enough memory to make full use of graphical interfaces, like Windows. However, if you want to use your computer for the Internet or other functions such as e-mail you should think big. Generally, the bigger the processor and more megabytes of RAM (Mbs) you have, the faster and more advanced your computer will be. Likewise, the speed of your modem is also important as it can affect the speed of connections and downloading of documents. Current modems are running at 56K and are unlikely to change in the near future. However, check the current system entry levels for your PC or Mac as these change almost monthly.

There are a vast number of personal computers on the market, all offering much the same features. Your choice boils down to the following criteria:

Don't be dazzled by the good looks

Sure. The TravelMate 342 has a stunning and robust **magnesium alloy** design.

Yes. It weighs only **1.8 kg** and is less than **1″ thick**.

But, don't imagine we've compromised on **power** or **personal productivity**.

No way. Not with the new **Intel® Pentium® III Processor**.

Or. An **integrated 56K modem** and **LAN** for complete communications.

TravelMate 342T
Intel® Pentium® III processor 500 MHz, 64MB RAM (expandable to 256MB), up to 9GB hard disk 12.1″ TFT display, full size keyboard, integrated 56k modem and inbuilt LAN, CD-ROM and floppy disk Combo Drive, USB video camera, and Microsoft® Windows® 98 or Windows® 2000.

1 year International Traveller's Warranty

we hear you

Choose a notebook with power and style – the TravelMate 340 series. Call today on 0870 900 2237 (quoting ref: DTq2) or visit www.acer.co.uk/q2

☐ what you actually want to do;
☐ cost;
☐ desktop, laptop or palmtop;
☐ PC or Mac;
☐ processor type and speed;
☐ peripherals (such as scanner);
☐ speed of modem;
☐ software applications.

Desktops are considerably cheaper than laptops or portables but if you are on the move a lot it may make more sense to buy a laptop. The current generation of laptops has impressive specifications and match desktops in terms of MHz and RAM. Nearly all recent models of PCs – both desktop and laptop – include a modem and a fax facility.

What you actually want the computer to do is probably the most important factor in choosing one, but the issue here is one of choosing software, rather than hardware. There are software packages for virtually every conceivable standard business application, but if you think yours is in any way different, make sure that you do buy the right software package. 'Bending' software to a particular application can be done, but it is extremely expensive and it may be cheaper to change your procedures, rather than to get a special program written. Before you buy a piece of software, prepare a very detailed specification of what you do and what you need – and what you might need or be doing in the foreseeable future.

Cost largely depends on the range of features that are available, like the modem and fax capability mentioned earlier, it will also depend on how much software is 'bundled in' with the purchase price, such as word processing, financial and desktop-publishing packages. It is not advisable to buy second-hand computers, unless you really know what you are doing and what to look for.

Telephone lines

Although a simple choice in the past, the option now exists to have an Integrated Services Digital Network – an ISDN line. This will speed up your connection to the Internet and is a high-speed

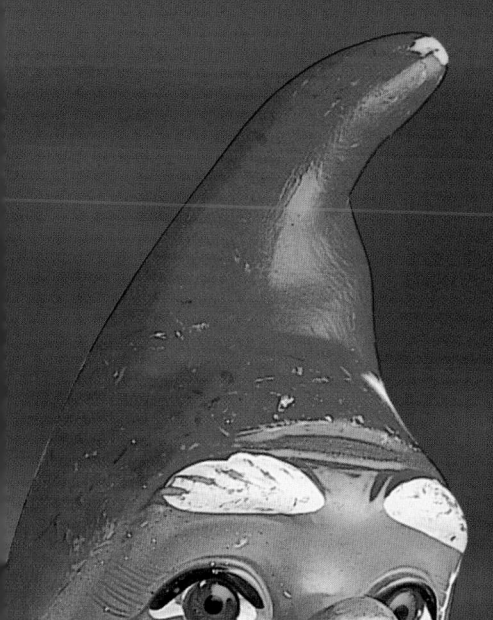

E.T. The Extra-Terrestrial TM & © Universal Studios

See more of the garden.

can help you get much more out of your working day, so you can
more of the things you want to do. Visit www.bt.com/timesmart
find out how.

BT *Stay in touch*

CALL COSTS APPLY.

See more of the TV.

BT can help you get much more out of your working day, so you
do more of the things you want to do. Visit www.bt.com/timesm
to find out how.

BT *Stay in touch*

INTRODUCTION

Today's workplace is very different from five years ago — remote or home working is now common-place. The reliance on IT systems by the small business owner has never been greater and is growing constantly. Therefore, it is essential to choose the right equipment to allow you to optimise how and where you work.

The modern office needs reliable technology capable of utilising the latest advancements to optimise the effectiveness of the users — notebooks provide the solution.

Notebooks have been trans-formed over the last few years and their specifications now rival traditional desktop PCs. Demand from SoHo users is at an all-time high and continues to grow; 30% year on year.

UMAX has worked very hard to bring ActionBook prices down to enable everyone to benefit from mobile computing — it has never been more affordable! At the same time UMAX have also given the user advanced specifications, only normally seen in desktop PC's.

SO, WHAT ARE THE ADVANTAGES OF MOBILE COMPUTING?

Firstly, the main and obvious advantage with being portable is the ability to work anywhere. With today's laptops weighing less than 3Kg, they can be easily carried and used anywhere – on the train, at home, or at the office.

Today's laptops are true desktop replacements; they have the ability to do everything that a desktop PC can do. In the past, laptop users had been limited by processor power when compared to a desktop PC — this is no longer the case.

In addition, the expansion capabilities of a laptop used to be limited and certain upgrades weren't available. As technology has improved over the last couple of years, mainly through miniaturisation, these limitations have been overcome. Virtually every major IT component manufacturer has introduced the equivalent products available for both desktop PC's and laptops. This has resulted in the laptop achieving the same levels of performance as a PC. In all laptops today the processor, HDD and memory are equivalent to a desktop PC, the only difference being the size.

In previous years, one disadvantage with a laptop used to be poor screen quality. This meant that for prolonged viewing the laptop had to be plugged into an external monitor, which took away the whole portability of the laptop. Today's laptops have the most advanced screens available, available in sizes up to 14.1" and resolutions of up to 1024×768 (XGA). This very high quality TFT design results in the image being just as sharp as a conventional desktop monitor, or in many cases, even better!

THE GROWTH OF THE NOTEBOOK

Latest research from Intel, the biggest processor manufacturer in the world, shows by the year 2003 four out of five computers sold will be laptops — that makes them one of the fastest growing product groups in the IT market today. So, it appears the days are numbered for the desktop PC as we know it.

One of the main reasons for this huge growth is convenience, users don't want bulky boxes taking up room on their desk and they also need flexibility in where they can work. A laptop combined with a mobile phone, to access email and the Internet, results in the ability to work anywhere.

THE UMAX RANGE

With the Internet becoming a part of everyone's life, it is very important for today's laptops to have a built-in modem. The whole UMAX laptop range has built-in 56k modems, which is essential in today's office environment for rapid access to the Internet and email.

Laptops today also have excellent expansion capabilities. The UMAX range has PCMCIA expansion slots, which are the equivalent of the desktop PC's PCI slots. The size of credit cards, these allow easy connection of network cards, enhanced sound cards and a whole host of peripheral items, such as scanners.

Some UMAX models also have one touch access buttons, or 'hot keys', to the Internet and email, which can be programmed to your favourite communications software.

With the performance of UMAX laptops comparable to most desktop systems, small businesses often use them as true desktop replacements. Unplugging the printer, scanner and ethernet connection every morning and night used to be an arduous job, however, using a port replicator makes it very simple and quick – with only one connection, the user can plug all external devices into the back of the laptop.

All UMAX laptops are supplied with a full-sized Windows 98 keyboard as standard, with the additional convenience of being able to connect an external keyboard or mouse via the PS2 port.

PROJECTORS

An ideal extension to the portability of a notebook is a projector — these lightweight, modern systems enable high quality presentations to customers, suppliers and can be used for a whole host of other uses such as training and marketing. Connecting to your notebook is as easy as connecting an external monitor — via one cable that plugs into the back.

The projector market is also experiencing a huge growth in demand with substantial price reductions. The latest Polaroid range is now available from under £2400.

In summary, the laptop PC is the perfect solution for today's small office. It has all the functionality a desktop PC, yet the mobile convenience and flexibility that is needed in today's office environment. The difference in price between a desktop PC and laptop is narrowing all the time and this is fuelling the huge growth in the laptop PC market. The desktop system as we know it today is fast dying — make way for the new PC.

For full details of the UMAX and Polaroid ranges contact IMC Plc tel: 01344 871329

Would you like free Internet call 24 hours a day, 7 days a week?

Yes   No

Do you spend £5 or more on phone calls every month?

Yes   No

If you answered 'yes', you're in luck.

With LineOne there are no Internet call charges 24 hours a day, 7 days a week and no monthl subscription fees. In fact, you can even save up to 60% on national and international phone cal

All you have to do to access the Internet completely free of charge is spend £5 or more a month on national or international phone calls with Quip! - the new low cost phone company There is no need to change your current phone line or number, simply pay a one off charge o £20 for a telephone adapter that plugs into your existing phone socket.

Call **0800 111 210** now or register at **www.lineone.net/freeinternet**

www.lineone.n

TOTALLY FREE INTERNET!

Free Internet calls
24 hours a day, 7 days a week!*

WHATEVER your experience of the Internet already, if you haven't yet tried LineOne, you haven't discovered just how much more LineOne can offer compared to other ISP offerings in the market.

LineOne really knocks the spots off the competition. It's fast, reliable and provides a great Internet service in terms of broad and superb exclusive content. Originally a paid-for Internet service, LineOne has maintained it's high level of quality service and product offerings since going free last year, providing many time-saving tools and unique features that put other services well and truly in the shade. Plus — as well as free Internet access – members can now get free Internet calls, 24 hours a day, 7 days a week.

As well as the usual forms of Internet communication like email, instant messaging and chat, LineOne offers RocketTalk. With RocketTalk you can send and receive voice messages via your PC. It's quick, easy and reliable but, best of all, there's no special software or downloads needed to hear the messages and your recipients don't have to be a RocketTalk member.

Talking about things audio — and visual for that matter — where other services offer a diet of the usual news, sport, weather, etc, with LineOne you can not only read the latest news headlines but you also have the choice to **listen** to the latest ITN headlines or **watch** video clips of all the top stories. You can even have the latest news emailed to your inbox every morning with eNews. And you can listen to all the top UK radio stations currently available live on the Net.

The sense of community is very strong on LineOne too. You can make new friends with other members who share your interests in the many chat rooms, or you can debate and swap advice in the many forums (otherwise known as message boards) ranging from education, computing and business to sport, food, lifestyle and even pets! You're sure to find several to suit your tastes.

As well as many features like those mentioned above, LineOne has over a *million* pages of highly impressive UK content.

Take LineOne's Business section for example. Thinking of starting your own business but don't know quite where to start? You'll find all the

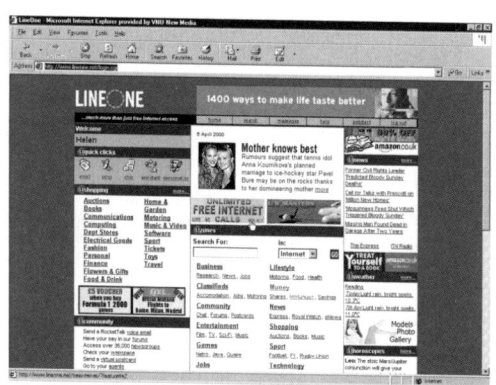

information you need to get you started and turn your business ideas into a reality. There's help with marketing and business plans from KeyNotes and LineOne, plus the latest business news and business banking rates, company and market reports, up-to-the-minute share prices and stock indices and hints and tips to make your life a little easier! LineOne also provides links to other organisations which you may want to access information from, such as Business Link, The Princes Trust and DTI sites.

In the one-stop Travel section, for example, you can access an excellent range of travel information and special offers 24 hours a day. There are discounts on over a million flights and thousands of hotels, car hire and holiday packages — all bookable online or by phone. Undoubtedly one of the best travel sites on the net.

In LineOne Shopping, you can get some fantastic offers and member discounts. And to make your online shopping experience quick and safe, LineOne has set up its own Shopping Charter to offer an additional level of excellence in online customer service.

Need to keep the kids happily occupied on a wet day? LineOne is crammed with exciting and safe things for the young 'uns to do. Need help with homework or academic study? LineOne has a wide array of educational resources in Learning. Then there's help with personal money management, hugely popular online games, support for people running a business, adult-only areas, lots of

places to chat and meet friends, and much much more.

It's no wonder LineOne has rapidly become the second largest free Internet Service Provider in the UK, with over 950,000 members and growing fast. Get more from the Net with LineOne.

**Call 0800 111 210
for your free start-up pack or
join online now
www.lineone.net**

---

* Simply register and spend £5 or more per month with Quip! on national and international voice calls for unlimited free Internet calls to LineOne. There is a one-off charge of £20 for a telephone adapter. Subject to availability and the terms and conditions stated at www.lineone.net/freeinternet This offer is not available to business users. Non-offer calls charged at local rates.

EVER DREAMED OF OWNING YOUR OWN BUSINESS? DISCOVER A FAST GROWING, SUCCESSFUL AND LUCRATIVE OPPORTUNITY :

TransNet Communications is a fast developing worldwide network marketing company with its sights firmly set on rapid growth in the multi-billion pound communications industry

The reality of employment today and in the future is increased redundancies, outsourcing, global recession and pension erosion. With 18 million unemployed in Europe and part-time workers outnumbering full-timers, how can we be sure of job security? Owning one's own business usually means , amongst other things, serious capital investment, premises, employees, stock and bad debts.

The ideal business would therefore be one in which none of these are required, where there is no risk and which is part of the fastest growing industry in the world. More importantly, a business where one can see the potential for an immediate income. Network marketing is a 50-year-old industry, involving 21 million people in 125 countries, responsible for £45 billion annually and it is an industry, which produces many millionaires each year. It is a dynamic method of product distribution utilising "word of mouth" advertising and personal recommendation.

Henk Keilman, one of Europe's pioneering and most successful telecommunications entrepreneurs, has the ideal business. Highly accomplished and well respected in the industry, Henk has successfully spearheaded five companies one of which he sold in 1998 for a staggering $250 million. Possessing a remarkable ability to accurately identify emerging trends and create opportunities for those associated with him, Henk immediately set about starting a new company - TransNet Communications. His vision - to establish the first pan-European telecommunication and technology Network Marketing company.

Says Henk "It is no secret that telecomms and communication prod-

Henk Keilman

Paula Pritchard

sharing information with other consumers about the products and services they use themselves, they can build a business of their own.

TNC has already established itself in the UK, Netherlands, Belgium, Germany, Austria Sweden and its latest market Denmark was opened in March 2000. Further European expansion is planned over the next eighteen months. TNC has attracted in excess of 75,000 customers and employs over 80 people who are based in its headquarters situated in the business district of Amsterdam.

ucts such as the Internet are the massive growth markets of the modern era. Without doubt this is the market arena to be involved in as we move into the 21st century. Market research shows that this trend is here to stay and like any growth market, the enormous demand for communication products and services outstrips supply." Indeed in 1997 there were 160 million Internet users worldwide, this is now increased more than fourfold.

TNC specialises in the provision of low cost telephony services, the Internet, GSM mobile communications and innovative communication technology products that are sold through an ever-growing network of Independent Distributors. These Distributors have an opportunity to benefit from what is considered the most lucrative Marketing Plan in the industry whilst at the same time they are able to take advantage of the deregulation of public utilities worldwide and the explosion of the information superhighway. By

In May, Henk Keilman announced that the company had attracted substantial funding from a group of private investors and three venture capital firms. Henk Keilman commented at the time "The European telecommunications market offers great opportunities for companies that understand that market and have adequate financial backing. With the addition of our new investors we are in an excellent position to support our plans for pan-European growth".

There are no barriers to anyone becoming an Independent Distributor in terms of the number of hours they put into the business, or by the standard of their education, their cultural background or whether or not they have had previous experience in the telecommunication and technology industry. The opportunity is open to anyone and everyone to achieve their own goals and aspirations and gain

Elaine Fishberg

financial independence, whilst having fun and enjoyment on the way.

On joining, a new Distributor receives a Welcome Pack which contains all the information needed to start their business, though they are encouraged to purchase the Telephony Business Programme which has a number of additional benefits to "fast start" their business. This includes a training programme, a manual, a diskette featuring the company presentation as well as a three pages TNC business website, transnetonline.com, Pop3email addresses. Telephony Marketing Materials and smart portfolio case containing a stock of high quality brochures, a corporate video, an audio tape about the business opportunity and a mobile phone and accessories voucher or free landline use voucher and last but not least free TNC Genie for six (6)months! There is a parallel Internet Business Programme for those interested in developing an Internet based business.

TNC Marketing Plan works as well for people wanting a part-time additional income as for people seeking a new career with significant remuneration.

In either case, the residual income potential of getting paid again and

again in fact indefinitely for the same business is highly appealing.

Discover how easy TNC products are to use and how much money they will save you!

Get the inside story on how TNC's proven results could work for you!

Paula Pritchard, who has reached the top position of International Marketing Director, and has an impressive background in Network marketing with over 20 years experience, helps present the programme and the business opportunity by giving presentations throughout the TransNet markets. Paula Pritchard comments "I want to share with other people this ideal business that I am in. With the training I show people how to activate their position, how to start right and develop their TNC business. They in turn will duplicate by teaching their people how to do the same, and so on. It is a constant duplication which of course is what networking is all about."

A final word from Henk Keilman, "We are equipped with the leadership, the drive, the experience and the resources to make a difference to the lives of our distributors and our customers through technology and communication. The future belongs to TransNet and to those who share our vision."

TransNet Communications B.V.
www.transnet.nl
For further details, please contact :
Maido Garay
TransNet Communications
2 Queen Caroline Street
London
W 6 9 DX
Direct Phone : +44 (0) 20 8323 8153
Direct Fax : + 44(0) 20 8323 8326
Email : Mgaray@transnet.nl

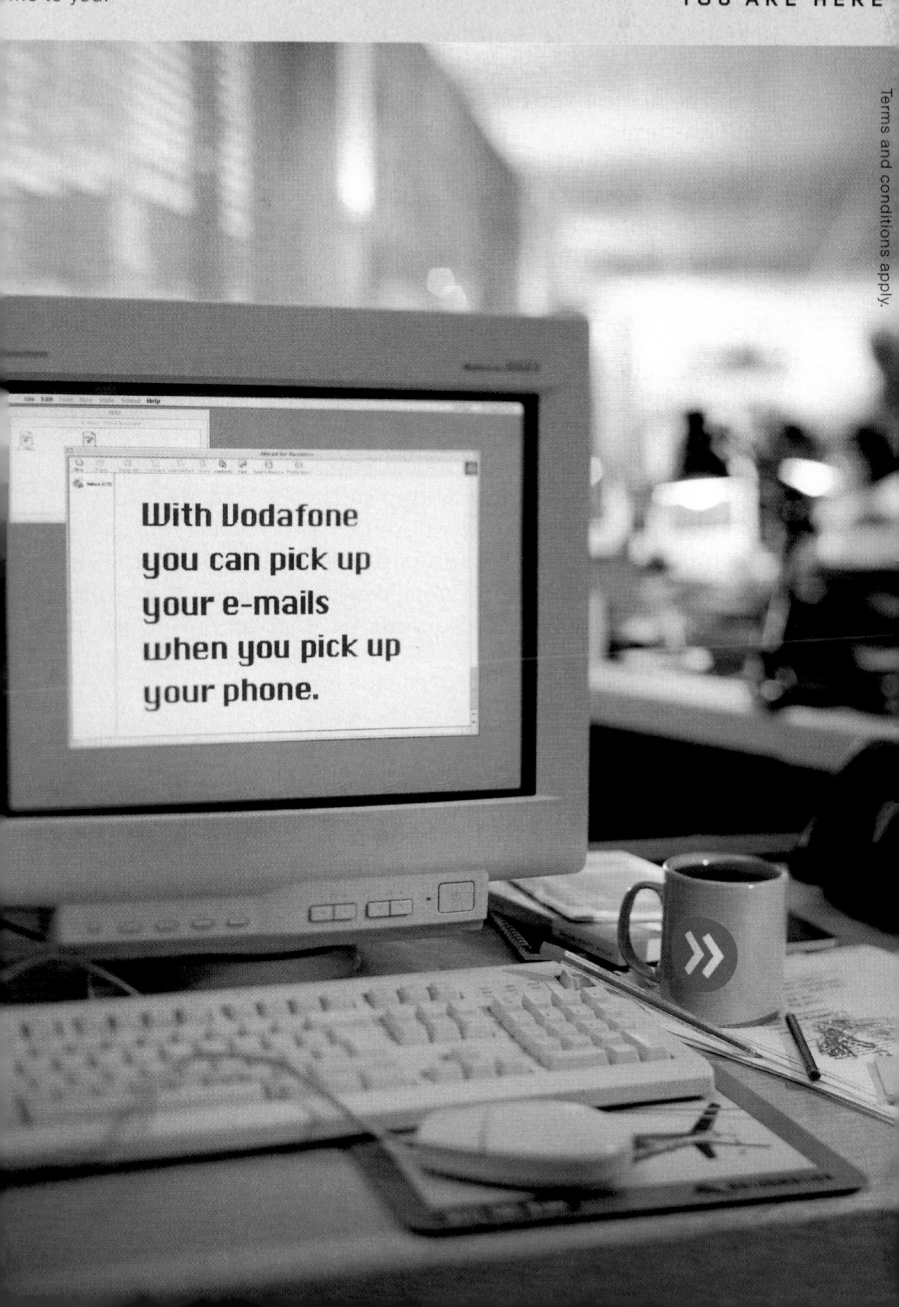

digital equivalent to a normal telephone line. It is also advisable if you want to link several users to the Internet. It is estimated to be as much as four times as fast as most modems and can connect you to your Internet Service Provider (ISP) almost immediately, although you will have to check with your ISP to see if it supports ISDN links.

Mobile phones have also become essential to businesses on the move. The newest versions can offer Internet access and fax and e-mail functions. We will not attempt to list the different networks and handset providers here as they are far too numerous to mention. However, if a mobile phone is necessary to your business you should include it in your overall strategy to integrate it fully into your ICT infrastructure.

Internet Service Provider

To take advantage of the Internet and to install e-mail you will need to sign up with an ISP. There has been the recent emergence of free services. However, take heed, many of the free services charge over the odds for technical support and whatever you might save on a subscription (typically £12-15 a month) you might lose in this additional cost. An ISP will provide your access to the Internet and e-mail. Setting up a Web site is discussed fully in Chapter 1.11 'Marketing Your Work'. However, it is worth mentioning here that it is also your ISP that rents you the file space for your Web site.

E-mail

The provision of e-mail by your ISP is also an important consideration and one of the great innovations of recent years. It allows messages, files or documents to be sent electronically to other Internet users for the price of a local telephone call. It is incredibly easy to use and the instantaneous sending of material makes it extremely attractive. Your PC should have the appropriate software. The advantages of using e-mail over fax are that you can send high resolution colour and long documents. Any computer file can be attached to an e-mail including spreadsheets, pictures and audio files.

THE COMPLETE BUSINESS COMMUNICATIONS SOLUTION

DN is the perfect communication platform for small to medium sized isinesses and is ideally suited to Internet access, email, sending large files or nnecting to other locations. Eicon Technology enables any organisation to ke advantage of the speed, flexibility and advanced features of ISDN.

th Eicon's DIVA range of ISDN products, a complete communications solution n be provided for anything from a single PC, to a solution for an office corporating Internet access, email, fax and analogue equipment.

WHY CHOOSE ISDN?

ISDN is cost effective, combining data, fax and normal voice on two phone lines.

Speed and Security – ISDN is fast, very fast and combined with digital security it is ideal for business.

ISDN is available worldwide and is ideal for fast Internet access and inter-office communications.

For dial-up access, ISDN offers the most reliable connection that can expand to meet your needs.

WHY CHOOSE EICON?

- Eicon is the European market leader for ISDN solutions.

- Ease of use and installation features are second to none to make life simple for users.

- DIVA ISDN products are renowned for reliability and carry a 5 year warranty.

- The DIVA ISDN family has won more than 50 independent 'Best in Test' awards.

Connecting People to Information.®

THE IMPORTANCE OF COMMUNICATION

The importance of effective communications to a businesses' future are widely recognised, whether that be communicating internally with other members of the organisation or externally with customers and suppliers. In recent years, the forms in which this communication can take place have expanded from the traditional telephone and fax to include digital based communication such as the web and internet email.

Advantages of Digital Communications for Small Businesses

These new developments in digital communications are especially important to small businesses as they give them the ability to level the playing field somewhat and compete with larger organisations. Internet email enables a small business to provide better customer service through faster response times and the ability to circulate information regularly, quickly and cheaply.

Web sites can be used to create a 'virtual company' and give small businesses a marketing presence 24 hours a day, 7 days a week. Even a basic site can provide an invaluable and low cost way to interface with customers, disseminate information and take orders or enquiries. It gives a small business the marketing exposure and reach that would be difficult to achieve by conventional means such as advertising or direct mail which would become prohibitively expensive.

This all sounds great, but how does a home user or small business take advantage of the opportunities offered by this new technology? The main obstacle most will perceive would be resource, both financial and technological. As a rule, small enterprises do not have significant sums of money to invest in IT infrastructure and lack the in-house technological expertise to install complex systems and maintain them.

The ISDN Answer

The good news however, is that it is probably not as difficult or expensive as many think. A simple, flexible and inexpensive communications infrastructure covering both traditional analogue and the new digital communications can be built around ISDN services from a local telecommunications provider such as BT and ISDN modems and terminal adapters like Eicon's DIVA family.

What are the Advantages of ISDN?

Traditional analogue telephone lines are intended to carry voice traffic and are not very well suited to transmitting digital data. This results in slow connection and low transmission speeds which translates to more time on-line and increased call charges as well as the frustration this bandwidth bottleneck causes.

ISDN (Integrated Services Digital Network) is a digital communication service which supersedes ordinary analogue telephone lines giving far greater transmission and connection speeds combined with digital security.

An ISDN line will connect within 1-2 seconds compared to 30-45 with analogue. Once connected, ISDN guarantees a transmission speed of up to 128 kbps compared with 56 kbps with the fastest analogue modem. Even this is misleading as a 56 kbps modem will rarely reach speeds of more than 36 kbps for uploading and 40 - 44 kbps for downloading making ISDN three to four times faster.

Apart from greater speed, another major advantage of ISDN over analogue is that it allows multiple simultaneous communications over a single physical line. This is because within an ISDN line there are several 'virtual' channels called bearer or 'B' channels. There are several different levels of ISDN service available from telecommunications providers with Basic Rate (BRI) having two 'B' channels and Primary Rate (PRI) having up to 30. This means that in a small office one physical ISDN line connected to an ISDN modem or card can be shared by many users giving everyone high speed digital access to the internet for surfing and email. The alternative is to have one analogue line per user with the resulting expense of having to pay line rental and installation costs on each line.

Consolidated Communications

Lastly, with ISDN, a whole office's communications can be sent over the ISDN line. This means that data files from a PC, analogue voice calls, fax calls and even GSM mobile calls can all be sent or received over an ISDN line eliminating the need for separate analogue telephone lines.

Application Scenarios

Home User

For the worker who has set up on their own and is possibly working from home, an ideal communications solution is a Basic Rate ISDN line and the DIVA T/A ISDN Modem from Eicon.

Once the ISDN line has been ordered from the telecommunications provider, simply plug the ISDN line and the PC (via the serial port) into the back of the DIVA T/A Modem. There are also two analogue ports for plugging in a telephone and fax machine. Configuration of the DIVA T/A is simple via plug and play and built in set up wizards so no great technical skill is required.

Once set up, all data, voice and fax communications can be managed through the DIVA T/A and ISDN line. The two 'B' channels allow the user to surf the internet whilst simultaneously talking on the telephone or sending a fax. Advanced features allow different numbers to be allocated to the telephone and fax which the DIVA T/A will use to route calls to the appropriate device. Other features such as call forwarding and call waiting are also supported.

Small Office

In a small office where a group of PC users need email and internet access, the DIVA LAN ISDN Modem and a Basic Rate (BRI) ISDN line will provide for all the office's communications needs.

The DIVA LAN Modem is a similar device to the DIVA T/A but also includes an Ethernet hub. With the PCs connected to it via the Ethernet ports a network is created where all the PCs can share peripherals such as printers. By adding an ISDN line into the DIVA LAN, these same PCs can share the line for high speed internet access and email. As with the DIVA T/A, analogue devices such as fax machines can be added for incoming and outgoing faxes.

A Solution to Fit Every Need

In this brief overview, we have tried to give a flavour of what is possible. ISDN is an established, standards based technology available world-wide. It is inexpensive, fast, easy to use and manage, flexible and scalable from the single user, to a large office with hundreds of users.

Together with ISDN products from companies such as Eicon, a small business can implement a communication solution to take full advantage of the opportunities offered by new digital age.

The Daily Telegraph

Guide to Funerals and Bereavement

Sam Weller

Funerals are probably one of the largest yet most unexpected costs that we have to face, yet arranging a funeral usually takes place when the bereaved are at their most vulnerable. Unfortunately, the funeral directing trade is not licensed or regulated and there is concern about the level of pricing and standards. Relatives do not wish to appear mean where their loved ones are concerned so often end up paying more than they can afford.

In this practical book Sam Weller examines the entire 'death care industry'. He provides clear information on arranging a funeral, cremation, burial and memorialization, and the costs involved. He takes a holistic view of death and its aftermath. The book spans:

- **planning for a funeral and what to do when someone dies**
- **memorialization**
- **ownership and inheritance of grave plots**
- **rights and responsibilities in cemeteries and churchyards.**

£8.99 • Paperback • ISBN 0 7494 3057 5 • 208 pages • 1999

KOGAN PAGE
120 Pentonville Road, London N1 9JN
Tel: 020 7278 0433 • Fax: 020 7837 6348 • w w w . k o g a n - p a g e . c o . u k

NET◯bjects™ – putting the 'e' into e-business

With small and medium-sized enterprises (SMEs) making up 80% of UK businesses, Martin Powell, northern Europe sales manager at NetObjects, looks at two simple and viable solutions that enable SMEs to get online.

Creating a Web site with NetObjects Fusion 5.0

If you've ever wanted to create your own Website, but your experience is minimal or non-existent, then NetObjects Fusion 5.0 could be the simple answer. Fusion is the award-winning software that enables you to build and develop professional Web sites quickly and easily. It is great for individuals and small businesses that want to establish an online presence or build onto an existing Web site.

Fusion 5.0 is one of the most popular web design products available today. It is a WYSIWYG (What You See Is What You Get) html editor which allows you to design your site visually by dragging and dropping elements like images and text directly onto your page.

Focus on businesses

NetObjects Fusion 5.0 is designed to help business owners create full-featured sites that promote, inform, and sell. Many small businesses want more flexibility, individuality, and advanced features than other site-building templates deliver. At the other end of the spectrum there are the complex and time-consuming applications that cater to full-time Web designers. NetObjects Fusion 5.0 offers the combination of productivity, flexibility, and ease-of-use that SME businesses need.

e-business

Today's businesses need more than just an online presence, they need an 'e-business site', or a place where customers, employees, suppliers and distributors can reach, interact and transact with the business. E-business sites represent a convergence of publishing electronic commerce and application functionality and enable businesses to leverage the potential of the Internet.

With Fusion, a Web site can become an e-commerce site in minutes, offering several unique features, such as the ability to sell multiple items, full on-line

Martin Powell

ordering capabilities, shopping cart functionality with several payment options, automatic tax and shipping charge calculations, and extensive reporting.

Virtual encyclopedia for online success

NetObjects Fusion 5.0 includes an Online View, a link to everything a business needs to build a successful site. With an ever-evolving collection of valuable information and special offers, the Online View helps customers every step of the way – from finding an ISP and getting a domain name, to posting and promoting their sites. It's an integrated resource that users can turn to as their business grows to discover how to gather information from site visitors, set up an online store, and much more.

Multimedia

Fusion gives you the tools to make your Web site look simple or very sophisticated, it is up to you. It offers a full set of powerful components, allowing insertion of text, graphic images, multimedia files (such as Shockwave or Quicktime), connections with ODBC-compliant databases, Java applets, and online forms. Using DHTML, actions can be associated with any image. This allows site builders to increase Web site interactivity as well as create sophisticated animations to stimulate visitor interest.

NetObjects Fusion software includes tools that will help you to structure your site efficiently and update it automatically. The product has sold over six million copies since its initial release in 1996, and more than four million e-business Web sites and pages have already been built using NetObjects Fusion.

Gobizgo

In addition to the Fusion offering for SMEs, NetObjects recently launched GoBizGo.com, an online service that enables small companies to build successful e-businesses. Using GoBizGo.com, these small businesses can do everything from build a Web site and online store, to integrate offline and online marketing efforts, all with the advantage of online personalised assistance from experts and other business owners. The site gives small businesses an all in one solution and marketing tools, and it also encourages members to participate in communities that bring together like-minded small business owners to share resources, ideas and knowledge.

Simply put, GoBizGo.com makes creating a professional and effective Web site of up to 25 pages and 100 products as easy as a few mouse clicks. In addition to fast and effortless Web site development, membership provides a variety of other benefits, including: instant updating and maintenance, automatic search engine submission, domain name registration, e-mail services, contact management, eBay auction upload, and remote site management via any browser connected to the internet.

Finally, GoBizGo.com is a completely scalable solution. If a company finds that it has outgrown the ASP platform, they can simply transfer their current site into NetObjects Fusion to leverage its additional functionality.

It doesn't matter whether your company employs one person or one hundred, NetObjects Fusion 5.0 and GoBizGo.com can turn your business into an e-business in the click of a mouse, quickly and easily. For more information on what NetObjects can do for you, visit www.netobjects.com, or call NetObjects on 0800 0289851.

www.netobjects.com
www.gobizgo.com

Making the Internet part of your business

Set your business free on the Internet with Oneview.net

The message is simple. To survive and prosper in today's global market place, your business can no longer afford to be without a web site on the Internet.

And with Oneview.net there's no cheaper, faster or more cost effective way to get your business there.

Our Web range packages.

We'll register your domain name, provide all programming, design and hosting of 3-15 page web sites, e-mail and e-marketing. All for a monthly subscription that starts at just £20+ VAT.

Giving your customers access to your business 24 hours a day, 365 days a year - not only locally but also globally. *Compare that to the cost of a small classified advertisement in your local newspaper!*

As your business and Internet requirements grow, we can grow your web site too. We've a complete range of Internet packages for you to choose from including the very latest e-commerce solutions.

Open your business to a whole new world of customers.

The world is turning to the Internet. Turn to Oneview.net and get your business on the Internet, hassle free, jargon free, for a minimal fee. *Before your competitors do.*

- Web site design

- Domain name registration

- E-mail

- Completely upgradeable to include e-commerce

- Expand your web site as your business grows

- No hassle, jargon or hidden costs

- No set up fee, just a monthly subscription

Don't get left behind. Call Oneview.net
01384 251111

Email: sales@oneview.net Internet: www.oneview.net

The simplest, quickest and most cost effective way to get your business on the Internet.

MAKE THE INTERNET WORK FOR YOU

The Internet has become a whole new sales channel, but what is important is how it is used to create and open up new revenue streams. It is becoming clear that e-commerce is transforming key business processes and potentially re-engineering businesses and sales chains - even creating new ones. Some companies are traditionally good at grasping change in this way, others have been forced to in order to survive.

Small business should not be daunted by this prospect, for someone who is working for themselves they should not see it as a threat, rather as a great advantage to compete with the big players in the first ever environment that means size doesn't matter. The thought of making a business an e-business, however, must still be daunting to someone running their own one man show - won't they need to hire in help or use an expensive agency? This may have been the case, but now creating a presence on the web is being opened up to all and through a simple enough process for someone working for themselves to take advantage of.

Companies, such as Telewest Business Communications, have seen the value in opening up the Internet to new and existing customers and helping them grow by offering a free service to take their business on-line.

You don't have to be a multi-million pound concern to warrant implementing an e-commerce strategy. We see examples of small retailers, building and plumbing firms, independent travel agents, professional services companies, manufacturers, specialist consultants and so on, using the Internet to reach a wider customer audience, to open up new markets and revenue opportunities and to help them keep in step with their larger competitors. And the opportunities are not reserved exclusively for business to consumer sales either; business to business is another sector that has benefited tremendously from growth through the Internet.

As consumers become 'wired', so they become more comfortable with web-based technologies and will feel happy buying goods and services via their PC, interactive digital television at home, a multimedia kiosk in the high street, or even using their Internet-enabled mobile phone. This whole area is growing exponentially and presents a real challenge to the small business market. There is a marked shift in power back to the consumer as they seek choice and flexibility. E-commerce represents a massive opportunity that any business can ill afford to sweep under the carpet. They risk losing business to their competitors without it.

There is a need for an all-in-one Internet and e-commerce service for new and old businesses alike and that includes those people working for themselves, whether they are working from a back bedroom, a warehouse or swish new offices in central London.

Biz-Explore, the service provided by Telewest Business Communications, has been designed to help companies get on-line quickly, simply and without any fuss. The idea is to provide the business with the tools to use the Internet for their own needs and above all help cut out the costs and any risk of setting up on-line. It is a total e-commerce solution that takes customers through a simple step by step approach to trading on-line.

However, not all companies understand the value or importance of the Internet to their work, particularly those that believe they are too small to warrant taking their business on-line.

According to recent research commissioned by Telewest Business Communications, over half of the UK's small to medium sized companies have yet to grasp the importance of e-commerce - indeed they find it all a mystery. And yet the research also finds that 73 per cent of small companies across the country use a computer for business, so clearly there is an education gap rather than a technological one.

From the person working for themselves to the medium sized business, Biz-Explore from Telewest Business Communications has been set up to help them, and to answer any concerns or questions they may have. The core elements come absolutely free. These include an Internet subscription, an unlimited number of e-mail accounts and access to a special Website where customers can gain access to a wealth of content, information and services dedicated to aiding small and growing businesses.

Provided within the first tier are free response generating tools including an electronic business card giving the opportunity to almost instantaneously put company details on the Internet. This business card will be registered with over 20 major Internet search engines and listed within the Biz-Explore Directory. For users of the directory they simply need to input details of the type of business they are looking for and the location. In response the directory will show the names of the businesses that have a Biz-Explore Business Card within that category and area for the user to choose from.

Each basic electronic business card is a page on-screen containing a company's contact details - making it easy for prospective customers to get in touch, a description of the products and services on offer, a 'home' button to enable fast navigation around the Telewest Biz-Explore site and a search facility for ease of use of the business directory.

An additional paid for service that can be attached to the business card is a Biz-Call button that allows visitors to the site to contact the company direct from the web at the click of a button. Biz-Call uses technology known as a hyperphone link that allows the potential customer to specify exactly when they want a call back - this could be immediately, in half an hour or later in the day. For anyone working for themselves it can be a highly effective way of keeping customers happy without having the support of someone to man the phones. They are never left in a queue, they can be contacted at their convenience and it costs the customer nothing to make contact. If the business requires the calls to go to a specific person who is continually on the move the service is versatile enough to follow someone from one number to another.

Telewest have designed this service to offer a whole range of additions and enhanced services to grow with a business as its needs grow.

As companies get used to Biz-Explore they can enhance their service with these new services and features. One way of doing this is by building an on-line store promoting a range of up to fifty goods and services. As confidence grows or for any business with a greater number of items to promote this can then be grown to a Superstore where a business can have as many as 25 departments containing up to 100 products. For the individual working for themselves and without the help that would appear to be needed - such as the requirement of technical skills or professional advice, this may seem impossible to do, but this is not the case. With the Telewest service buying, setting up and designing the store is all done over the Internet using a simple to use point-and-click process.

With all the hype about the Internet, this is a system that offers companies a simple, sensible way to get on-line and grow at their own pace, adding on services as and when they feel comfortable. The Internet is different for every company, as business is different for every company, but Biz-explore offers firms something in common - the ability to cut costs whilst growing in size and revenue.

Networks

Local networks are used by companies to link their employees. This can be within a company building, or to teleworkers based in various locations. Local Area Network (LAN) allows files and resources to be shared. It can also provide access to the Internet by being connected to an ISP via an ISDN or leased line.

Videoconferencing

Using the Internet as a telephone or video conference service, two or more people can be linked visually. Your PC will need to have a microphone, sound card, speakers, camera and video card. A fast link to the Internet is also advisable as it reduces the time it takes to update the video pictures.

Electronic Data Interchange (EDI)

EDI facilitates the exchange of business documents between computers of trading partners. It allows purchasers and suppliers to handle transactions down the phone lines by sending set forms and invoices in an electronic form. However, for the small business or start-up, where there are not a large number of transactions, EDI might not be cost-effective and using e-mail might be more appropriate.

Areas of activity

The rapid increase in Web sites also signifies that many businesses acknowledge the marketing benefits of being on the Internet. However, there are other areas of business to which ICTs can bring a competitive advantage.

1. E-mail
   - Efficient communication with customers and staff.
   - Images – photographs, technical details, etc – can be sent to anywhere in the world enabling faster design approval times.
   - Standardized forms can be e-mailed cutting times given for estimates and quotes. Cuts paperwork and postage.

- Electronic products can be exported quickly and easily overseas.
- After-sales service can be made by processing queries and keeping customers informed by e-mail. Newsletters can also be sent.

2. Networks
   - Provides access to information which can be updated as often as necessary and can create contact lists and diaries.
   - Manufacturing information placed on a network will allow suppliers to adjust production accordingly and reduce lead and delivery times.
   - Home-working made more effective by allowing access to shared information.
   - Help with customer service by providing information and individual details and transactions quickly.

3. CD ROM
   - Electronic data storage reduces the need for shelving and warehousing and provides quick access to information.
   - Easier to tailor presentations to a customer's needs with addition of sound and video.

4. Videoconferencing
   - Brings in outside expertise and allows for better communication for businesses based in isolated or rural setting.

5. Mobile telephone
   - Allows sales reps to work efficiently on the move and linked to a laptop computer enables access to records and data in different settings.

6. EDI
   - Speeds up payment of invoices by trading partners.
   - Can simplify paperwork of shipping, dispatch and money transfer.

7. Internet
   - Online recruitment finds a global pool of applicants.
   - Company Web site could have descriptions and prices of your products. Orders can also be placed.
   - Suppliers' stock levels and delivery times can be checked via Web sites.

- Sourcing cheaper or better goods and new suppliers becomes easier.
- Large companies are beginning to tender on the Web and expect responses in the same way.
- Research new export markets and overseas contacts.
- A company Web site will provide a global presence and attract overseas sales.

Growth of e-commerce

E-commerce has encouraged small businesses to enter the global market. Although in its infancy, there is no doubt that its current growth is set to continue. Given that there will be an estimated £3 billion spent on the Internet by the end of this year it should be given serious consideration by anyone starting out in business today – no matter how small that concern might be. If in doubt as to where to start, get help from either the government or from private consultants to formulate a needs assessment for your company and remember that marketing is only one area in which an ICT infrastructure can help.

Checklist: ICT questions

1. Consider your business needs and how electronic equipment can reduce costs and introduce efficiency.
2. Consider how your business might grow in the near future and the equipment you will need to accommodate expansion.
3. What areas of your business could benefit from ICT? Contact the ISI or eCentreuk for advice.
4. Consider the impact of marketing and selling on the Internet – do you have adequate administrative systems, distribution and warehousing to back it up?
5. Try and integrate your equipment into one infrastructure and don't duplicate functions with different equipment eg if your PC has a fax, do you need to buy a separate one (you will if you need to fax separate items that aren't generated from your PC unless you also have a scanner)?

6. Think about the speed and capacity of your equipment when purchasing and try to buy as high an entry specification as possible. This also applies to the modem.

7. Consider carefully the pros and cons of a free ISP or whether it is better to subscribe to a fuller service.

1.17 Legal Basics

Going to law is a process where the cure, in money terms, is often worse than the disease – which is why so many settlements are made out of court. Even seeking legal advice is an expensive business: £80 to £120 an hour is now the going rate, depending on where you are, and few legal bills come to less than this minimum, even for a short consultation. In complex disputes or where larger sums of money are involved, legal action may ultimately be the only course open. But at the more basic levels of trading law there are some straightforward principles laid down, though they are sometimes blurred by traditional tales – for instance, that a shopkeeper is obliged by law to sell anything he displays for sale. Knowing what the law actually says about this and other everyday trading transactions will help you to sort out minor disputes and, very often, save costly legal fees.

THE SALE OF GOODS ACT 1979

This Act and the more recent Sale and Supply of Goods Act 1994 place some clear but not unfair obligations on you as the seller once a contract has taken place, an event which occurs when goods have been exchanged for money. Nothing needs to be written or even said to make the contract legally binding and you cannot normally override it by putting up a notice saying things like 'No Refunds' or limiting your responsibilities in some other way. This is prohibited under the Unfair Contract Terms Act of 1977.

The Sale of Goods Act has three main provisions concerning what you sell.

1. The goods must be 'of satisfactory quality'. This means that they must be capable of doing what the buyer could reasonably expect them to do – for instance, an electric kettle should boil the water in it within a reasonable length of time.
2. The goods must be 'fit for any particular purpose' which you make known to the buyer. For instance, if you are asked whether a rucksack can carry 100 lb without the strap breaking and it fails to match up to your promise of performance, you will have broken your contract.
3. The goods must be 'as described'. If you sell a bicycle as having five speeds and it only has three, then again you are in breach of contract – as well as of the Trade Descriptions Act, if you do so knowingly.

But what happens if you yourself have been misled by the manufacturer from whom you bought the item in question? You cannot refer the buyer back to her: the Sale of Goods Act specifically places responsibility for compensating the buyer on the retailer, no matter from whom the retailer bought the goods in the first place.

Thus, if the goods fail on any of the three grounds shown above, you will have to take them back and issue a full refund, unless you can negotiate a partial refund, with the buyer keeping the goods about which he has complained. However, he need not accept such an offer, nor even a credit note. Furthermore, you may be obliged to pay any costs the buyer incurred in returning the goods, and even to compensate him if he had a justifiable reason to hire a replacement for the defective item; for instance, if he had to hire a ladder to do an urgent DIY job because the one you supplied was faulty.

The only let-out you have under the Act – which also covers secondhand goods – is if you warned the buyer about a specific fault, or if this was so obvious that he should have noticed it. In the case of the bike, he probably would have found it difficult to spot that a couple of the gears were not working, but he could reasonably be expected to notice a missing pedal.

THE SUPPLY OF GOODS AND SERVICES ACT 1982

This is essentially an extension of the Sales of Goods Act into the sphere of services. The point you have to watch out for is this: if you are offering a service, say, for repairs or some form of consultancy, the implied terms, which the Court will read into the arrangement whether they are written down or not, are: (1) that the supplier will carry out the service with reasonable care and skill; and (2) that it will be carried out in reasonable time and at reasonable cost.

A recent example of the Supply of Goods and Services Act in operation was when an architectural student carried out a small flat conversion job for a client. He neglected to obtain planning permission for some of the work and, even though he was not fully qualified at the time, it was held that, in offering his services, he should have known that this was a basic part of the service he had been offering.

Disclaiming responsibility for your actions under either of these Acts is not the answer; that would make you liable under the Unfair Terms in Consumer Contracts Regulations 1994.

THE CONSUMER PROTECTION ACT 1987

This is essentially a health and safety measure which says that where a defective product causes damage or injury, the supplier will be held liable unless he can show that not enough was known about its dangers at the time he supplied it.

OBLIGATION TO SELL

By law, all goods have to be priced but, contrary to some widely held beliefs, there is no obligation on you to sell goods on display for sale if you don't want to. For instance, an assistant in an antique shop might wrongly price a picture at £2.50 rather than £250. The intending buyer cannot force you to sell at that price,

Running Your Own Business

even though it is publicly displayed. However, once the goods have been sold at £2.50, even in error, a contract has taken place and cannot be revoked without the agreement of both parties.

This also applies when the buyer has paid a deposit and this has been accepted. Supposing she had paid £1 and offered to return with the balance, a bargain would have been made which you would be obliged to complete. It is, however, binding on both parties. If the buyer, having paid a deposit, decided to change her mind you would be within your rights in refusing to refund the money.

ESTIMATES AND QUOTATIONS

Self-employed people supplying services such as repairs are often asked for a quote or an estimate. How binding is the figure you give?

This is a grey area in which even the Office of Fair Trading finds it difficult to give legal ruling. They recommend, however, that a 'quote' should be a firm commitment to produce whatever the subject of the inquiry is at the price stated, whereas an 'estimate', while it should be a close guess, allows more leeway to depart from that figure. Therefore, if you are not sure how much a job is going to cost, you should describe your price as an estimate and say it is subject to revision. This may not, of course, satisfy the customer, in which case he would press you for a quote. If you really find it difficult to state a fixed sum because of unknown factors, you can either give some parameters (eg between £x and £y) or say that you will do £x-worth of work – which on present evidence is what you think it would take – but that you will notify the customer if that sum is likely to be exceeded to do the job properly. In general, though, an itemised firm quotation is the document that is least likely to produce disputes.

COMPLETION AND DELIVERY DATES

If you give a time for completing a job you will have to do it within that time – certainly if it is stated in writing.

232

In the case of delivery of goods ordered by customers the same is true. If you give a date you have to stick to it or the contract is broken and the customer can refuse the goods and even, in some cases, ask for compensation. Even if no date is given, you have to supply the article within a reasonable period of time, bearing in mind that what is reasonable in one case, such as making a dress, may not be reasonable in another – obtaining some ready-made article from a wholesaler, for example. The relevant law here is the Supply of Goods and Services Act 1982.

TRADING ASSOCIATIONS

In addition to legal obligations you may also belong to a trading association which imposes its own code of conduct. Such codes sometimes go beyond strict legal requirements, on the principle that 'the customer is always right'. This is not a bad principle to observe, within reason, whatever the legalities of the case. A reputation for fair dealing can be worth many times its cost in terms of advertising.

THE TRADE DESCRIPTIONS ACT 1968

Another piece of legislation you need to watch out for, especially in advertisements and brochures, is the Trade Descriptions Act. This makes it a criminal offence knowingly to make false or misleading claims, verbally or in writing, about any goods or services you are offering. That includes what is known as 'passing off' – using a brand name to which you are not entitled or implying an association with some better known product.

The notion of a trade description covers a wide range of characteristics, such as size, quantity, strength, method and place of manufacture, ingredients, testimonials from satisfied customers and claims that the goods or service are cheaper than the same bought elsewhere.

It is possible by cunning wording to stick to the letter of the law, but not its spirit. For instance, the words 'made with' some desirable substance or other may indicate that it was made with only a minute quantity of it. But on the whole it is better to stick to the truth, since a successful claim against you could result in a compensation award of up to £1000 – not to speak of loss of reputation.

THE DATA PROTECTION ACT 1984

This Act came in towards the end of 1985, with the object of protecting individuals from unauthorised use of personal data about them; for instance, by computer bureaux selling mailing lists to direct sales organisations. Registration under the Act had to be completed by May 1986. Though failure to register is a criminal offence, the indications are that very few small businesses have actually done so, other than those which are directly affected, such as computer bureaux. In theory, though, the obligation to register is quite widespread, because anyone with a word processor that can store personal data may be liable to register at a cost of £22.

Application forms and guidance notes are available from post offices. Essentially, data users have to disclose to the Registrar what lists they hold, how and where they obtained the details on them and for what purposes they intend to use them. They must also undertake not to disclose them to any unspecified third party, or to use them for any purposes other than the declared ones. However, data used for internal administrative purposes, such as payrolls, are exempt if they are used only for that function.

THE PRICE MARKING ORDER 1991

This is an EC Directive. It obliges you to state the price of goods offered for sale in writing.

> ### Checklist: legal basics
> 1. Find out about legislation that applies to your area of activity, and more generally to running a business of any kind.

2. If you are selling goods, make sure that they comply to the Sale of Goods Act and that you have made appropriate checks with your supplier that the goods are of suitable standard and 'as described'.
3. Be clear about the services you are offering and that you comply with the Supply of Goods and Services Act 1982.
4. Do not commit yourself to making a quote if you are unsure. An 'estimate' should be offered first, with a quote to follow once you have assessed costs etc.
5. Contact your trade association for codes of conduct and guidelines.
6. If you have personal data on individuals, collect forms from the post office to disclose this to the Registrar.

1.18 Pensions and Health Insurance

It is scarcely possible these days to open the financial pages of any newspaper without seeing at least one advertisement for self-employed pensions. It is also a fair bet that these are studied more closely by financial advisers than by the self-employed at whom they are aimed, unless of course the latter are nearing the age at which pensions begin to become of immediate interest – by which time it may be too late to do anything about it. The trouble is that the self-employed, by temperament, are more interested in risk than security and tend to place provisions for retirement rather low on their scale of priorities.

However, there are compelling reasons why you should take self-employed pensions seriously and find out what they involve, to outline which is the object of this chapter. In urging you to read it, we promise to avoid the mind-boggling pension jargon which generally sends readers of newspaper articles on the subject straight to the less demanding pastures of the sports or fashion pages.

STATE SCHEMES

Everyone in the UK is entitled to the basic state pension provided they have built up a record of National Insurance Contributions for a quarter of their working life (from age 16 through to state pension age). Contrary to popular belief, not everyone qualifies for the full state pension – only those with a record of contributions for nine-tenths of their working life. The self-employed should take particular care to ensure that they build up adequate contributions as they generally do not have a company pension to rely on when they retire. The second state pension is the top up scheme known as SERPS – the state earnings related pension scheme. The self-employed are not members of this scheme as the contributions to it are made from Class 1 National Insurance Contributions paid by employees (however if you were an employee in the past you may have built up some SERPS entitlement). Only a quarter of working people are members of SERPS, the rest have opted out (known as contracting out) either through a personal pension plan or their company pension scheme. If you have past SERPS entitlement check how much pension this will provide. If you also have earnings from employment and are under age 45 and a man, or under 40 and a woman, and earn at least £10–12,000, a year you should consider contracting out of SERPS and investing rebates in a personal pension plan (provided you are not a member of a company pension scheme). This is because the SERPS pension is being reduced and you'll be better off investing this cash to provide your own pension.

Stakeholder pensions are to be introduced in 2001 and are aimed at individuals who do not have an occupational pension. Although the plans should be cheaper and more flexible than personal pensions, the maximum contribution is only £3600 per annum. Some may see this as not enough.

TAX BENEFITS

Not being eligible for earnings-related benefit is in itself a reason why you should make additional arrangements as soon as you possibly can, but for the self-employed there is another compelling incentive. Investing in a pension scheme is probably the most tax-beneficial saving and investment vehicle available to you at this time. Here are some of its key features:

1. Tax relief is given on your contributions at your top rate of tax on earned income. This means that if you are paying tax at the top rate of 40 per cent you can get £1000 worth of contributions to your pension for an outlay of only £600.
2. Pension funds are in themselves tax exempt – unlike any company in whose shares you might invest. Thus your capital builds up considerably more quickly than it would in stocks and shares.
3. When you finally come to take your benefits – and you can take part of them as a lump sum and part as a regular pension payment (of which more later) the lump sum will not be liable to capital gains tax and the pension will be treated as earned income from a tax point of view, as distinct from investment income, which is regarded as 'unearned' and taxed much more severely.
4. Lump sum benefits arising in the event of your death are paid out to your dependants free of inheritance tax. This may enable you to build up pension funds to the extent where liability to inheritance tax is reduced quite drastically on other assets from which income has been siphoned to provide a pension.

The advantage of all this over various DIY efforts to build up a portfolio of stocks and shares – even if you are more knowledgeable about the stock market than most – should be obvious; you are contributing in that case out of taxed income, the resultant investment income is taxed at unearned rates and capital gains tax is payable on the profits you make from selling your holdings.

The convinced adherent of the DIY road may at this point say: 'Ah, but under my own provisions I can contribute as, when and how much I can afford and I am not obliged to make regular payments to a pension plan when it might be highly inconvenient for me to do so.' Pensions, however, are not like life insurance, though misguided sales reps sometimes try to make out that they are. You need not contribute a regular amount at all. You can pay a lump sum or a regular amount. In fact, you need not make a payment every year. There are even a number of plans now available under which you are entitled to borrow from your pension plan.

Age	Percentage of income qualifying for tax relief
36–45	20.0
46–50	25.0
51–55	30.0
56–60	35.0
61 and over	40.0

The only restriction that is put on you is imposed by the government and relates to tax benefits. In order for self-employed pensions not to become a vehicle for tax avoidance, the amount you can contribute to them is limited to 17.5 per cent of your income. You are, however, allowed to 'average out' your contributions over any six-year period to arrive at an overall percentage per year of 17.5 per cent.

There is also a further concession for older people making their own pension plans. Since an increasing number of self-employed people – and their financial advisers – have come to recognize the merits of these schemes, a great many companies have moved into the market for self-employed pensions. Under a fair amount of jargon and often confused lineage of print, the plans they offer boil down to the following options.

1. *Pension policy with profits.* In essence this is a method of investing in a life assurance company, who then use your money to invest in stocks, shares, government securities or whatever. As we said earlier, the advantage from your point of view is that pension funds are tax exempt, so the profits from their investments build up more quickly. These profits are used to build up, in turn, the pension fund you stand to get at the end of the period over which you can contribute. There is no time limit on this period, though obviously the more you do contribute the greater your benefits will be and vice versa; also, you can elect to retire any time between 50 and 75.

At retirement you can choose to have part of your pension paid as a lump sum and use it to buy an annuity. This could in some circumstances have a tax advantage over an ordinary pension, but the situation on it is quite complicated and you should seek professional advice in making your decision. What happens with an annuity, however, is that you can use it to buy an additional pension, the provider of which takes the risk that if you live to a ripe old age he might be out of pocket. Equally, you might die within six months, in which case the reverse would be true. The statistical probabilities of either of these extremes have been calculated by actuaries and the annuities on offer are based on their conclusions.

One important point about a conventional with-profits pension that often confuses people is that it is not really a form of life insurance. If you die before pensionable age, your dependants and your estate will not usually get back more than the value of the premiums you have paid, plus interest. The best way of insuring your life is through term assurance, of which more later.

2. *Unit linked pensions.* Unit linked policies are a variant of unit trust investment, where you make a regular monthly payment (or one outright purchase) to buy stocks and shares across a variety of investments through a fund, the managers of which are supposed to have a special skill in investing in the stock market.

Combining investment with a pension plan sounds extremely attractive and much more exciting than a conventional with-profits policy, and it is true that in some instances unit linked policies have shown a better return than their more staid rivals. However, as unit trust managers are at pains to warn you (usually in the small print), units can go down as well as up and if you get into one of the less successful unit trust funds – and there are quite wide variances in their performance – you may do less well than with a conventional policy.

There are also, of course, fluctuations in the stock market itself which affect the value of your holdings. Over a period of time these fluctuations should even themselves out – you can get more units for your money when the market is down, and fewer when share prices are high. The only problem is that if your policy terminates at a time when share prices are low, you will do worse than if you cash in on a boom. However, there is nothing to compel you to sell your holdings when they mature. Unless you desperately need the money you can keep it invested until times are better. Remember, though, since this policy is for your pension, you may not be able to delay using the funds for too long.

Most unit trust companies run a number of funds, invested in different types of shares and in different markets: for instance, there are funds that are invested in the US, Australia or Japan, or in specialist sectors such as mining or energy. If you find that the trust you are in is not performing as well as you had hoped (prices are quoted daily in the press), most trusts will allow you to switch from one fund to another at quite a modest administration charge.

3. _Unitized with profits._ This is a newer type of pension, which combines elements of with-profits and unit linked pensions. Your investment is given in terms of units (as with unit linked policies) but you also earn bonuses which, once added to your pension fund every year cannot be taken away or fall in value should the stock market perform badly (these bonuses are added to with-profits policies each year and on retirement).

4. _Term assurance._ While this is not a form of pension at all, it may be attractive to add term assurance to your pension policy for tax purposes. Term assurance is a way of insuring your life for a given period by paying an annual premium. The more you pay, the more you (or rather your dependants) get. If you do not die before the end of the fixed term (eg 20 years) nothing is paid out. As with any other form of insurance, your premiums are simply, if you like, a bet against some untoward event occurring.

There is one indirect but useful connection between pensions and term assurance. The tax people allow you a scheme under which you pay term assurance premiums along with your pension premiums, both of them being relieved of tax at your top earned income rate.

The one thing that all types of pension scheme have in common is that their sales forces are all eagerly competing for the self-employed person's notional dollar. They will be anxious to extol the virtues of their own schemes, to withhold any unfavourable information about them and to make no comparisons, which could be odious, with other schemes. Your best plan in making your selection is to work through a broker and to let her make the recommendation, but that does not mean that you can abdicate responsibility altogether. For one thing, in order for a broker to make the right selection of pension plans appropriate to your circumstances, you have to describe what your needs and constraints are:

1. Can you afford to make regular payments?
2. Does the irregular nature of your earnings mean that the occasional lump sum payment would be better?
3. Do you have any existing pension arrangements – eg from previous employment?
4. When do you want to retire?
5. What provision do you want to make for dependants?

Very likely the broker will come up with a mix of solutions – for instance, a small regular payment to a pension scheme, topped up by single premium payments. The suggestion may also be made that you should split your arrangements between a conventional with-profits policy and some sort of unit linked scheme; certainly you will be recommended to review your arrangements periodically to take care of inflation and possible changes in your circumstances.

Brokers have to be registered nowadays, so it is unlikely that you will be unlucky enough to land up with someone dishonest. Check that the person you are dealing with really is a *registered* broker – not a consultant, because anyone can call themselves that. Some very big household names among brokers are not, in fact, registered, but the majority are, although whoever you deal with, there are, as in other things in life, differences in the quality of what you get, which in this case is advice. It is as well to have a few checks at your elbow which will enable you to assess the value of the advice you are being given. For instance, national quality newspapers such as *The Daily Telegraph, The Guardian, The Independent* and the *Financial Times*, as well as some specialist publications such as *The Economist* and *Investors Chronicle*, publish occasional surveys of the pension business which include performance charts of the various unit funds, showing those at the top and bottom of the league table over one-, five- and ten-year periods. There are also tables of benefits offered by the various life companies showing what happens in each case if, for instance, you invest £500 a year over ten years. There are quite considerable differences between what you get for your money from the most to the least generous firms. If your broker is advising you to put your money in a scheme that appears to give you less than the best deal going, you should not commit yourself to it without talking to your accountant; but with brokers, as with many other professional advisers, the best recommendation is word of mouth from someone you can trust who can vouch for the ability of the person in question.

HEALTH INSURANCE

Running your own business requires stamina and good health. If you are unlucky enough to become ill it will be a priority to get back on your feet as quickly as possible. Private health insurance has become increasingly popular amongst the self-employed for this reason. There are four types of health insurance currently available on the market, as defined by a recent Office of Fair Trading report:

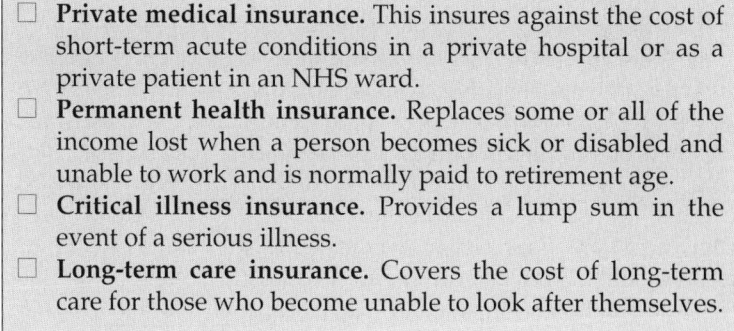

- ☐ **Private medical insurance.** This insures against the cost of short-term acute conditions in a private hospital or as a private patient in an NHS ward.
- ☐ **Permanent health insurance.** Replaces some or all of the income lost when a person becomes sick or disabled and unable to work and is normally paid to retirement age.
- ☐ **Critical illness insurance.** Provides a lump sum in the event of a serious illness.
- ☐ **Long-term care insurance.** Covers the cost of long-term care for those who become unable to look after themselves.

However, a recent Office of Fair Trading report has criticised the insurance industry for its lack of standardised products and complicated jargon. Indeed, it might well be worth getting independent advice before you commit yourself to purchasing a policy. It is also worth keeping an eye out for products specifically geared towards the self-employed, as there has recently been a launch of a combined health insurance policy which caters more closely to the needs of individuals working for themselves.

Checklist: pensions and health insurance

1. Review your current pension arrangements and assess whether or not they are adequate for retirement needs.

2. Discuss with your accountant the most tax-efficient way to invest in a pension scheme and with your broker about what kind of scheme is most appropriate.

3. Consider whether regular payment and/or one-off lump sum investments are best suited to your financial arrangements.

4. Check that you are receiving independent advice from a registered broker.

5. Examine surveys of pensions within the national press to ensure that you are receiving adequate advice from your broker.

6. Identify if it is speed, location or choice that you require within a private medical insurance policy – this will help determine which policy you will choose.

7. Check the qualifying period within a critical illness policy – many do not start to pay out until after an excess period of six weeks or three months. Could your business survive an absence of this length? If not, you will have to consider paying higher premiums.

Part Two:

Businesses Requiring Capital

2.1 Retailing

BUYING A SHOP

No book can answer all the questions or anticipate all the problems that buying a shop or starting a retail business entails, but it can warn you of the main reasons for failure:

☐ Paying an unrealistic price for the business.
☐ Lack of experience in the trade you enter.
☐ Cash flow problems caused by underestimating current costs.
☐ Failure to recognise the level of competition to the type of goods you sell or the service you offer (are you setting up a general food store next to a round-the-clock supermarket?).
☐ Choice of a bad location: away from the shopping centre, in a commercial area with little weekend trade, etc.

The character of areas and shopping precincts changes rapidly. The 'centre' of your town is perhaps moving, through lack of space, to an open-plan area with a multi-storey car park and a wide range of shopping units. Long-established shops in the 'older' part of town are often unable to survive, so be wary of being offered this type of business. There are wide variations in the desirability and potential profitability of even apparently similar retail businesses.

Ask where the business you have seen advertised is sited. Is it well positioned or far from the centre of trading activity? What is its reputation? Be sceptical of the seller's claims to a fund of 'goodwill' from long-standing customers. There is no guarantee that they exist or, if they do, that they will be as loyal to you. How much stock have you been offered as part of the purchase price? Does the shop need redecoration? What terms are you being offered: freehold or leasehold? What is the nature of the competition to your enterprise?

Such questions do not allow simple answers. These vary according to the type of business you intend to conduct. For example, a more specialised shop (selling, say, good-quality hi-fi or photographic equipment at competitive prices) does not need to be as central as a grocer's, butcher's or general goods store. Customers will hear about it and seek it out and, having been satisfied once, will return for accessories, improved equipment and advice.

Think, too, about general location and the composition of the local population: is it predominantly young or old, middle class or working class, close to sports facilities or not, and so on? Is there a seasonal trade that you might capture? Are there shops nearby that may attract certain types of people, whose custom you might aim to tap? Would you have to work special hours to fit in with the habits of your potential customers (by, for example, staying open until 7 or 7.30 pm in suburban residential areas)? Would those habits affect your trade adversely at certain times (low 'traffic' at weekends in business areas, for instance)?

In short, you must consider a whole range of locational factors before choosing to buy an established business or deciding *where* to start a new shop. Four rules:

☐ Talk to people who know the trade and the locality.
☐ Take the advice of an accountant and solicitor who will, respectively, assess the financial worth of the purchase and the legal commitments you will enter into.
☐ Do not buy the first shop offered to you unless *everyone* thinks it is an unmissable opportunity (and, even then, think again!).
☐ Always assume the seller is asking too much.

This is not sophisticated business thinking; it is plain common sense.

> 'Even if you have to borrow money, do not be under-capi-talised. Keep your shelves full and well stocked since this will attract customers ... Apart from fruit and veg, you will need to have five to seven times your weekly takings tied up in stock.'
>
> *George Thorpe, food retailer*

YOU AND YOUR BUSINESS

On a more personal level, can you and your family bear the strain of managing a shop: the hours of work, the tedium of filling in tax forms and keeping books, the problems of receiving early morning deliveries, the physical work that might be involved in taking and storing deliveries, the pressure of having always to be polite to the customers? (You might not wish to follow the dictum that the customer is always right, but would you survive? Small businesses depend on customers returning and on word-of-mouth promotion.)

Working hours are long, but made tolerable by a commitment to *your* business. You may grow to dislike VAT returns and diffi-cult customers and you will encounter a host of petty day-to-day administrative difficulties, but if you are serious about the move in the first place, you should survive these. But ask yourself: is my immediate family as dedicated to the project as I am? What is a challenge to you may be a burden to them. So, be as sensitive to their needs as you are to your own.

BUYING AN ESTABLISHED BUSINESS

Shops for sale are sometimes advertised in the local and national press and in some trade journals,* or you can consult a firm of business valuers and transfer agents. It is a good idea to write down the specific requirements that you are looking for: this will

---

* A full list of these is contained in *British Rate & Data* (*BRAD*), a monthly listing of all commercial periodical publications and newspapers, which should be avail-able in any reasonable business reference library.

not only help you to brief your agents and any other advisers such as your accountant and bank manager, but will also help you to clarify your ideas.

Shops are generally rented on a leasehold basis, and you should aim for a property with as long a lease as possible. In paying for the shop you will be buying the premises, fixtures and fittings, existing stock and 'goodwill'. How this price is arrived at depends on a number of factors, which you must analyse carefully before you commit yourself. *Stock* is generally valued for business sale purposes at current market cost price, and an independent valuation of the stock is desirable. *Fixtures and fittings* should also be independently valued, and an inventory of these should be made and attached to the contract of sale. *Goodwill* is a nebulous concept to which an exact value cannot be attached. Obviously, the more the shop relies on regular, established customers, the higher the value of the goodwill; conversely, the more it relies on casual, passing trade, the lower the goodwill value. The price of a shop will also to a large extent depend on the potential of the local area. You will need to make a careful assessment of factors such as:

1. Competition. Do not make the mistake of thinking that the absence of a nearby competitor *necessarily* guarantees success. A shop that has done reasonably well in the face of nearby competition is a safer bet than a shop with a similar record which has had a virtual monopoly of local trade. There is always a danger that if there is no competition, someone else may move in after you. Another common mistake is to see only shops of the same trade as competition. Indirectly, all other traders in the area are competition, since all are competing for a share of the consumers' spending power.
2. Nearness to railway stations, bus stops, etc: this may substantially increase the flow of passing trade. A map may help to clarify the exact potential of the location.
3. Any further local development plans – check with the local authority.

It is important that you and your accountant study the books thoroughly. In particular, examine the trend of the profit and loss account over the past few years to determine whether the business is improving. Another important point to note is whether the previous trader has been paying himself a salary, or whether this has to be deducted from the net profit figure.

> 'Location, potential competition and overheads are the three key points to watch. If you're buying an existing store, scrutinise the accounts minutely. Is it possible to run it with one less member of staff, for example? Are home deliveries being made? These can be very, very expensive. Don't try to compete on prices with the big boys – you'll lose! Stock lots of lines and if need be sell, say, sugar at a loss knowing you've got a good margin on shampoo. There's no guarantee that goodwill will pass over to you on completion of the sale – your face might not fit and there's little allegiance nowadays from customers.'
>
> *Owner of general goods shop*

STARTING FROM SCRATCH

You may want to take over premises which have previously been used for other purposes, in which case you should look closely at the previous owner's reasons for closing down and determine to what extent the same factors will affect you, even though you are engaged in a different trade. If you are going to use them for another type of business, you must get planning permission first. Or you may want to rent newly built premises, in which case you will probably have to pay a premium. The premium is based on the potential of the area, but try to get an *exact* idea of what that potential is: the number of new flats being built nearby, for example. In general, the premium should be lower than the goodwill price you would pay for a going concern, since it only indicates potential, not a record of success.

LEGAL OBLIGATIONS

These fall into four categories: employment legislation (see Chapter 1.13). Check the ages of your employees; ensure that they are taxed, and that you pay your share of their National Insurance contributions; cover them regarding pensions and superannuation; know where they stand in relation to the Employment Protection Act.

Second, safety, security and planning. You should insure your premises and stock, and cover yourself against liability, including liability for defective goods (potentially liability will vary widely depending on the goods you sell and the services you offer). In the case of a food shop, you must satisfy a health inspector, and other types of premises will have to be passed fit by a fire officer. Check these and local planning laws before you start trading. The quickest way to find out which of these laws apply to you is to contact your local Shops Act Inspector. She will also provide details of by-laws on opening hours, Sunday trading, pavement displays, etc.

Third, fair trading. Know and follow the provisions of the Consumer Credit Act and the Trade Descriptions Act. There are strict rules on how you display prices, on recommended prices and 'special ' offers, on the giving of guarantees, on the rates of hire-purchase you can offer and the other types of credit you make available, and so on. Again, cover yourself against expensive litigation by going through existing legislation with a solicitor, looking at standard practice in businesses similar to your own, and taking advice from the local Weights and Measures Inspector.

Finally, be aware of your standing under the Sale of Goods Act. When you sell something, the merchandise you sell should be in good condition and fit for its stated purpose. If it is not, your customer is entitled to a suitable replacement or a refund. When you provide a service, under contract law it should be up to the required standard; if it is not, the customer can claim compensation. The Supply of Goods and Services Act 1982 brings the sale of goods and the provision of services into line and makes all retailers responsible for the product or service they provide. You must also be aware of recent legislation that makes it illegal to trade in imperial measurements.

KEEPING ACCOUNTS

A great deal of bookwork will be inevitable: keeping count of stock levels and daily sales (for personal use and for VAT purposes); an elementary statistical breakdown of what is selling; keeping tabs on credit customers, orders, returned goods, etc. Your accountant and bank manager will wish to see comprehensive and up-to-date accounts to check your progress. See Chapter 1.7 for an introduction to simple accounting, but be warned: for anything more than day-to-day bookkeeping it is worth using a qualified accountant.

LEASING

Leases are written in legal jargon and for that reason the vendor is sometimes apt to sign without really understanding what the lease says. This is a great mistake, and if you cannot follow the wording or are unclear about anything, you should ask your solicitor to explain it to you. Look out particularly for restrictive covenants that prevent you from transferring the lease to a third party or from carrying on certain trades and professions at those premises.

SECURITY

Never leave cash lying about. If there is a lot of money in the till, take out a round sum in notes and leave a chit in the till to remind yourself where it is. Watch out for shoplifters, and ensure against them as far as possible by not leaving small, valuable items in easily accessible positions. Do not leave customers or visitors unattended. Remember that you must be insured right from the start, even before you have opened up for business. The Home Office produces a pamphlet on theft by staff, a danger which must not be overlooked. Consult your local crime prevention officer, who will advise you on ways to combat both dangers.

STOCK

It is sensible to buy stock from a wholesaler, or cash and carry, or from a manufacturers' agent, since you will generally need frequent deliveries of small quantities of goods. Have as few sources of supply as possible, to cut down your workload. There are a few exceptions to this. In the case of cigarettes, for example, it is better to deal direct with the manufacturer.

Make sure you know at all times what your stock levels are, and devise a system whereby you know when to reorder, before stocks run too low. The stock should be cleaned and dusted regularly and any stock that remains unsold over a long period should be discarded. Stock-taking should be carried out regularly, depending on the type of business in which you are engaged.

LAYOUT AND DISPLAY

Cleanliness and hygiene are, of course, absolute musts. Layout too, will be important. Make the interior of the shop as attractive as you can: displays, however small, should have a focal point, and should be changed frequently. Allow space for your customers to move and, if necessary, push prams, and make sure that they have access to all the goods on your shelves. Think, also, about your window displays: manufacturers will often supply signs and special display items which may improve the look of your shop.

Useful information

National Association of Shopkeepers, Lynch House, 91 Mansfield Street, Nottingham NG1 3FN. Tel. 0115 947 5046.

Buying a Shop, Kogan Page.

2.2 Farming and Market Gardening

The 'back to the land' movement has been quite fashionable in recent years, with all kinds of people giving up their jobs and homes in cities to live on smallholdings (communal or otherwise) where they try to be completely self-sufficient. Others, more commercially minded, may take up market gardening, which gives them a pleasant life in the country while they sell the fruits of their labours to others. Some more conventional souls may simply decide to buy a farm and rear cattle, grow corn or keep pigs or poultry.

In all cases, the romantic glow soon disappears. There are two essentials for any of these occupations, neither of them romantic: capital and the capacity for hard work. Take advice from professional bodies such as the Ministry of Agriculture, Fisheries and Food's Advisory Service or the local county office of the National Farmers' Union. The local authority is responsible for agricultural education and you should make inquiries about courses that might be available in your area. The soaring costs of fuel and animal foodstuffs have already put many market gardeners and farmers out of business, so it is obviously essential to go into the finances of the operation very thoroughly before making a decision.

It is also essential to have the complete support of your family. This can be a very hard life, getting up early in all weathers to feed animals, breaking your back hoeing and weeding, and you have to be extremely keen and enthusiastic to take it on. If your nearest and dearest are not equally enthusiastic, forget it, for you are going to need their active help, since labour is both expensive and hard to come by.

FARMING

Farming has become a technological occupation, requiring all kinds of special skills and knowledge. Unless you can convince a bank that you have this know-how (and some business experience) you are unlikely to get your money. Long-term loans for the purchase of land are available from the Agricultural Mortgage Corporation Ltd but, here again, properly prepared budgets and a realistic and comprehensive proposal will be required if the application is to be successful.

Now a highly risky occupation, farming gives only a 3 to 4 per cent return on the land. The failure rate is very high, and to take it up with little or no experience almost guarantees failure. Unless you know about fertilisers, pesticides, animal husbandry and farm machinery, you are likely to make some expensive mistakes, and remember that two bad years could wipe you out financially. The farmers who are most successful are those who start young, probably in a family-owned business. By the time they take over, they have acquired the necessary experience, usually backed up these days with a course at one of the agricultural colleges. You should not contemplate farming without some practical experience, or a degree or diploma from an agricultural college, or preferably both.

Another idea which is very popular with the 'get-away-from-it-all' brigade is to buy a smallholding and try to be entirely self-sufficient, perhaps even setting up a commune. It is an attractive idea, and the initial cost need not be great, but be warned: this is subsistence farming and you will find yourself working as hard as the American pioneers did. Also, even on a commune you may need a tractor and, for that, you are going to need money. You really need to be dedicated or rich (preferably both).

If the foregoing has not deterred you, get some professional advice, either from ADAS (the Agricultural Development Advisory Service of the MAFF) or from your local agricultural college or institute. There are also various farm management consultants and land agency firms who will (for a fee) give advice on what to do.

Even running a smallholding will demand considerable capital and expertise, as well as determination and immense hard work.

> 'You must start with sufficient capital to carry you through the first year, since you will almost certainly make nothing at all until your second year. All the self-employed work long hours but running a smallholding involves particularly long hours – weekends don't exist.'
>
> _Pat Burke, smallholding owner_

MARKET GARDENING

Unless you take over an established business, the main problems for the would-be market gardener are acquiring the necessary land and a greenhouse. You may be lucky enough to own a suitable piece of land already, or a garden big enough (two or three acres) to be worked commercially. However, if you have to purchase land the price of this will depend on the area, quality of soil and drainage, previous history and needs of use. This can cost anything between £1500 and £5000 per acre. A greenhouse is the other big expense. It is a vital piece of equipment, enabling you to grow tomatoes, bedding plants, pot plants for the winter months and seedlings for early vegetables. You can do without one, but you must then make enough money in the spring and summer to make up for the lean winter months when you have virtually nothing to offer except a few winter vegetables. You also have to make provision for the cost of heating a greenhouse: price increases in fuel have sent the cost sky-high, so you must make sure that every inch of space is working for you, if your profits are not going literally to disappear in smoke. You can expect to pay for a new, modern, glasshouse shell the minimum of £100,000 pro rata. The smaller the house the higher rate the cost per square metre.

If you are not a trained horticulturalist, it is a good idea to employ someone who is, or who has at least had practical experience of running a big garden and greenhouse. One full-time helper is probably all you will be able to afford in the early years. Seasonal help picking tomatoes, strawberries, beans, etc costs about £3.60 an hour, and is often difficult to find. You (and your family) must be prepared to work long hours and turn your hand to anything. On the other hand, there is a growing trend towards advertising 'pick your own' facilities during peak seasons. The amount people are willing to pay for the privilege of picking their own fruit compares favourably with the wholesale prices you would be able to obtain.

For general information, particularly on the economics of growing produce, contact the National Farmers' Union, which has a very good horticultural section. Another excellent source of information on what crops to grow, soil tests, etc is the Agricultural Development Advisory Service of the Ministry of Agriculture (ADAS).

One basic decision to be made, once you have decided on your crops, is how you are going to market your produce. If you are on a busy main road you may decide to rely heavily on local advertising and passing trade from tourists, etc, sending the surplus to the local market, or even taking a stall in the local market yourself. You can also send your produce to one of the big central markets, but you then have to pay a fee to the auctioneer, as well as transport costs.

ALTERNATIVE RURAL BUSINESSES

The recent problems in farming have seen many people previously employed in the sector looking for new opportunities within a rural context. Indeed, if one wanted to find evidence of how flexible and imaginative the self-employed can be, there are many examples in the industries that have sprung up in rural areas supporting, or in some cases replacing, the income lost from traditional farming. Some have turned to organic farming to find new markets, while others have found more unusual avenues. However, it is worth remembering if you are new to this sector, and to a rural environment, that conditions are often extremely hard.

Lesley Stimson started her angora farm with no previous experience of handling livestock apart from keeping a horse and pets. She now has a herd of 28 goats from which she makes angora products.

> 'It's not a 9-5 job. With animals, if it's cold at night you still have to go out at 10 o'clock and top up the water buckets. You're always here and you can't go away very easily if you have animals.'
>
> _Lesley Stimson, Silvermore Mohair_

An ex-teacher, she has found advice from the National Farmer's Union useful with help on matters such as insurance, and interestingly, she says that the Inland Revenue was particularly helpful.

> 'The tax inspector was extremely good. I put all my cards on the table and it was him who advised me not to be self-employed and to be in a partnership. It is important to make an appointment with the Inland Revenue and to go to them with your plans and books and they will help you.'
>
> _Lesley Stimson, Silvermore Mohair_

Business in a rural environment can be found if you look for obvious gaps in the market. That's what Gay Russell, Farm Administrator, did when she set up her business nine years ago.

'My business sense said, what can you do in East Anglia? What goes on here and what skills have you got that can be utilised here? We live in a very isolated position and this has always been a predominantly agricultural area. I'm used to working on my own and I wanted to be self-employed. I need to be able to choose my own times of working when I work and how much I do to fit in with the other things in my life.'

Gay Russell, Farm Administrator

Working as a sole trader the first thing she did was to join the local branch of her professional association the Institute of Agricultural Secretaries and Administrators. Conferences, seminars and continuous professional development are offered by the Institute; with half-day workshops on accountancy, VAT and other business issues. Marketing her services was also something she considered but she found that in an occupation where confidentiality was important it was word of mouth that helped her pick up work.

'At first I did put a few postcards around which were useless. Word of mouth worked best because it is quite a personalised job and people are very worried about confidentiality so to be recommended is much the best plan so that they can feel safe that their records and things will be secure. Being a member of a professional association also helps.'

Gay Russell, Farm Administrator

Her professional institute helped, as did a local government sponsored organisation, MENTA. This involved local professionals giving help to start-ups with business plans, marketing and sales lectures, promotions and packaging.

These are just two examples of innovative enterprise in areas where traditional forms of industry are diminishing. The National Farmers Union's Countryside Division is particularly helpful for alternative rural businesses and can offer good advice and help.

_____

260

Useful information

Agricultural Development Advisory Service, Oxford Spires, The Boulevard, Kidlington, Oxon OX5 1NZ. Tel. 01865 842742. Web: www.adas.co.uk.

Agricultural Mortgage Corporation Ltd, AMC House, Chantry Street, Andover, Hampshire, SP10 1DD. Tel. 01264 334344.

Royal Horticultural Society, 14–15 Belgrave Square, London SW1X 8PS. Tel. 020 7245 6943. Web: http://www.horticulture.demon.co.uk.

National Farmers' Union, Agricultural House, Knightsbridge, London SW1X 7NJ. Tel. 020 7331 7200. Web: http://www.nfu.org.uk.

2.3 | Hotels, Catering and Entertainment

Hotels, pubs, clubs and the range of independently owned eating places, from simple corner-shop cafés to long-established, expensive restaurants, constitute a vast business. There are over 30,000 hotels and large guest houses and a vast number of pubs and clubs in the UK, and in employment terms, catering is one of the biggest industries there. The range of opportunities and business options is so wide that we can barely scratch the surface, but an outline of each area will be given and some general conclusions drawn.

THE BUSINESS

What is true of running a shop, that you need unstinting energy and commitment, is even truer in this field. Your hours will be long and irregular. You are likely to have to work 365 days a year. You may have to deal with dissatisfied and difficult customers. There is a mountain of paperwork to monitor and national and local regulations to understand and abide by. Your family, which is in any case likely to be directly involved in the running of your hotel, restaurant or café, should be as committed to succeeding as you are.

Offsetting these disadvantages, these areas, particularly owning a restaurant or hotel on which you can stamp your personality and deal very closely with your customers, have many attractions. Indeed, perhaps too many: new restaurants open with great frequency but often quickly collapse because of poor planning, bad management, lack of finance, or a simple lack of realism about the scope for *that* type of restaurant in *that* locality.

LOCATION

As in retailing, location is crucial. Decide what sort of operation you wish to conduct and then look for the premises. If you want to start a hotel or guest house, look for an expanding inland tourist spot or popular seaside resort. In the latter, think about the problems of surviving the winter, with only limited and erratic custom. Ask yourself what type of visitor the place attracts and who might be attracted by price reductions out of season (pensioners or disabled people perhaps). Understand the character of the area in which your business will be sited, and have some idea *whose* needs you will cater for. This applies as much to services as to manufacturing firms, and is crucial when you decide how to market that service.

GETTING PLANNING PERMISSION

This is more difficult than you might think. Local authorities will want details not only of what you intend to do with the premises but of structural changes you intend to make, of the effect the development will have on other properties, of the safety factors involved, of the parking facilities available for your customers, and so on. You will have to submit detailed plans, and will probably need to consult a lawyer and a surveyor. Even then your application may not succeed, and you will have bought a good deal of expensive legal advice with no return. Remember that restaurants and clubs may be noisy, keep long hours and attract a large number of patrons – local authorities are naturally anxious to regulate these developments, and your application may therefore be lengthy and will need to be well planned and properly researched.

RESTAURANTS

New restaurants open every week, particularly in the London area. But almost as many close, and only the gifted and the adaptable survive. Establishing a restaurant is extremely expensive, particularly when you have to convert premises (as is usually the case). A good idea is not sufficient; you also need diligence and, above all, *money*. In a period of tight money and high interest rates, financial backing for enterprises as doubtful as restaurants is in short supply.

There are basically two kinds of people who open a restaurant – the gifted amateur or professional cook, and the 'ideas person' who knows how to fulfil a taste and buys premises and finds the staff to meet that need (many of the 'in places' in London are now more rated for décor, music and clientele than for their cuisine). The main problem for the amateur or professional is likely to be how to maintain standards without wasting an enormous amount of food and losing money. One answer is to have a *small* choice of dishes which are changed regularly. You will have to spend quite a lot of time finding the best sources locally for fresh meat, fish and vegetables, since your reputation depends on it. The restaurateur who has a speciality (such as steaks) and sticks to it will find life a lot simpler.

Where your restaurant is located is obviously essential. If it is in the centre of town, well and good. If not, you must set out advertising, make sure your friends spread the word around, find an eye-catching décor and try to get yourself written up in the local paper. If you are sufficiently confident, you could try writing to the restaurant critics on some of the big magazines (such as *Harpers & Queen*) or newspapers.

If your restaurant is quite small, you will probably find it more economical in the long run to be as mechanised as possible with chip machines, dishwashers, freezers, etc, rather than hiring a lot of expensive, possibly unreliable, staff. Costing can be quite difficult, with the rising price of food, but beware of undercharging. There is a temptation to court trade with low prices, but you will soon find it impossible to keep up standards. Moreover, do not undercharge when you first open simply to attract customers; when your prices rise they will see through your scheme and look elsewhere. Charge the going rate: decent food, pleasant surround-ings, efficient and friendly service and a reasonable location should guarantee some degree of success.

It is a good idea, too, to realise your limitations and not try to be grander than you are – if you are basically steak and chips there is no point in trying to produce cordon bleu menus: you will soon be found out!

We spoke to a restaurateur, who points to seven problem areas:

1. Wastage.
2. Overheads – heating and lighting cost £80 per week for a 30-seat restaurant!
3. Payment of VAT.
4. Establishing good and appropriate décor.
5. The need to change the menu – don't let yourself or your customers get bored with it.
6. Maintaining your profit margins.
7. Coping with fluctuations in demand – no customers one night, 50 the next!

CAFÉS, SNACK BARS, ETC

The large restaurant has very different problems from the small, unpretentious café. The former provides particular foods with (one hopes) a distinctive touch, and will seek to build up a clientele. It may encounter problems in employing staff, dealing with alcohol licensing, regulations on opening hours, fire precautions, and so on. Moreover, it may be vulnerable to economic downturns and changing consumer tastes. By contrast, the café offers a simple service to the local workforce and others at a reasonable price. Fads of taste and the vagaries of economics count for little.

Owning a café is more closely allied to general retailing than to being a restaurateur. True, you must be able to prepare a reason-ably wide range of good food cheaply, quickly, efficiently and hygienically. But this should not be beyond the capabilities of the average person.

Reread the retailing section: location will be important and your business must be located in heavy 'traffic' areas. Recognise that each day will have peaks and troughs – a rush at noon to 2 pm perhaps? Can you cope and, if you can, will you then be overstaffed for the rest of the day?

Think carefully about why you have chosen the location and what will make your café different from any other in the area. For example, the owner of an Internet café in a small town in the Peak District saw the chance to marry two needs in her new venture:

> 'There was a gap in the market in the sense that New Mills was crying out for another café. Also, the Internet was just emerging as a new technology. The idea at the time was to combine a beautiful location with the technology, training and accessibility necessary to enable teleworking, or working from home.'
>
> *Eleanor Chronnell, Peak Art Cyber Café, New Mills*

However, her vision was not always shared by the people she went to for advice and help:

> 'Business Link High Peak has been the most helpful in terms of information both at the setting-up stage and with ongoing advice. I also have a very good accountant, and, of necessity, a bank manager! The banks were probably the least helpful, and asked useless questions like 'What is the Internet?' and 'Why will people use it?' Little foresight and no leeway whatsoever!'
>
> *Eleanor Chronnell, Peak Art Cyber Café, New Mills*

Whatever makes your café stand out from the crowd, uniform legislation applies to the whole sector without exceptions. For example, your business must be covered by health and safety regulations and must be passed by a food inspector and a fire officer. Regulations on bookkeeping and VAT returns apply to you with equal force as to any other retail business.

THE HOTEL BUSINESS

You must choose your hotel or guest house with great care. It is a big investment to make, so be sure to examine the following points:

The area

What is the competition like? Are there any plans for redevelopment locally which might involve one of the big hotel groups? Is it on a main road or tourist route, or is it hidden in the back streets or down a country lane? Does the area as a whole seem to be coming up in the world, or going down?

The customers

Ideally, you want to attract a variety of clientele, so that you are fairly busy all year round. Seaside hotels are full up for most of the summer, but virtually deserted in the winter: are you going to make enough profit to cover those lean winter months? Other hotels in industrial or commercial areas will find that they are full of business travellers during the week, but that the weekends are very quiet. The most successful hotels are those which have a good mix of commercial, holiday, conference and banqueting business. Study the accounts if you can and see what the pattern of business is.

The fabric

What state is your hotel in? You must find out how much renovating or decorating needs to be done and how much this is going to cost. What are the maintenance costs likely to be?

The law

There are a number of laws that the hotelier is subject to, particularly health and safety legislation. Insure your property and protect yourself against liability; make sure you meet the necessary safety levels for fireproofing and hygiene, or your insurance may be worthless. Another important set of regulations, if you are opening a new hotel, covers licensing. There are various guides to the licensing laws, but if you have to apply for a new licence it is wise to do it through a solicitor.

Also very important is the Fire Precautions Act of 1971. Every hotel, if it sleeps more than six people, must have a fire certificate from the local fire authority. When buying a going concern, find out if it has a fire certificate, or if an application for one has been made (if not, the hotel is being run illegally). If the fire authority has already inspected the building, check on the cost of any alterations required to bring the premises into line with the Act.

Staff

Good staff are obviously essential for the smooth and efficient running of a hotel, but they are very difficult to come by. This is an industry with a very high staff turnover, especially among unskilled staff, and you must expect to spend a lot of time interviewing, supervising and training. Everyone in the business agrees that it pays to take your time (however inconvenient) and select staff very carefully, rather than always employing the first person you see because you are busy.

Goodwill

Does the hotel you are considering buying have a good reputation? Will regular visitors return even though the hotel has changed ownership?

Past performance and potential

How has it operated in the past: could you improve on it? What is the sleeping capacity? Could it be increased without reducing standards? Can seasonal fluctuations be reduced by good marketing? How great are staff expenses and other overheads as a proportion of turnover? What is the hotel's net profit as a percentage of turnover?

PUBS

The following section refers to brewery tenants, not to pub managers (who are not self-employed) or to the owners of free houses, which are now so few and far between as to make the possibility of finding a vacant one very unlikely.

Tenants rent their pubs from the brewery company, paying an agreed sum to the outgoing tenant for fittings, equipment and stock. They agree to buy their beer from the brewery, and generally cannot buy stock (even of items other than liquor) from any other source without the brewery's permission. They keep their own profits and are responsible for their own losses, the brewery receiving only the rent on the premises and the guaranteed outlet for its product.

There are more applications from prospective tenants than there are tenancies available, so the breweries are able to 'pick and choose' to some extent. The qualities they look for in a prospective tenant are:

1. Sufficient capital resources to purchase fittings, equipment and stock in hand, to cover immediate running expenses, and to provide a sufficient reserve to cover the tenant in the event of a temporary reduction in trade.
2. A preference for married tenants. Running a pub is very much a family affair, and your spouse's experience and attitude can be a decisive factor.
3. Good health, since running a pub involves hard physical work and long hours.
4. Some managerial experience, in any trade – this would count in the applicant's favour, though it is not strictly necessary. Similarly, experience or training in the liquor trade would be useful, and though not a mandatory requirement it would be useful from your point of view to have experienced the trade in various capacities first.

> 'Watch the optics, the fiddles and the free drinks to friends. Watch that the brewers don't send you lines you don't want. Don't commit yourself to loans and brewers' discounts – there'll be conditions in the fine print you won't like. The Weights and Measures boys will be calling often to check your measures and make sure you have price notices and age warnings up.'
>
> *Publican*

Tenancy agreements

Most breweries have a standard form of agreement to be signed by the tenant. The procedure for taking over the fittings, furniture and equipment is the only area in which there may be a substantial difference between breweries: some require the new tenant to buy these items from the outgoing tenant, while in other cases they remain the property of the brewery and the tenant lodges a deposit, returnable when the tenancy is given up. Other items covered in the tenancy agreement include rent (usually paid quarterly), the term of the tenancy, responsibility for repairs, a requirement that the tenant must take out employees' and public liability insurance, the terms on which the stock is purchased, the brewery company's right of access to the premises, requirements connected with transfer of the licence, and terms on which the tenancy can be terminated.

Licences

The tenant usually takes over premises that are already licensed, so you have to negotiate the transfer of the licence from the outgoing tenant to yourself. It is advisable to be represented by a solicitor in your application for transfer of the licence.

Training

If you are accepted by a brewery for a tenancy, and neither you nor your spouse has any experience of the trade, it is likely that both of you will be asked to attend a short residential course, run by the brewery company and lasting from one to two weeks. While you are waiting for a suitable tenancy, or applying to different breweries, it is advisable, if you have no experience, to work part-time in a pub. This will give you some experience, and will help you to decide whether you are really suited to what is in fact a very arduous job.

OTHER OPPORTUNITIES

It is possible to run clubs, cinemas, theatres and so on independently. Indeed, the attractions for the music lover or cinema buff are considerable, as it seems to be possible to mix business with pleasure. But base any decision on *business* sense, not on a romantic notion of making your leisure interest pay. Can the town support another cinema, particularly if you intend to show nothing but *avant garde* and experimental films? (Whether you want to show more obscure films or not, if the major companies have tied up the distribution of the money-spinning movies you may have no option!)

You will face the same problems as the hotelier and restaurateur in choosing the right location, employing staff, perhaps getting restrictions on opening hours lifted, obtaining a licence to serve alcohol and meeting fire regulations.* (Some of these problems can be circumvented if you make your institution a private club, admitting members only at some sort of fee, though future legislation may close this loophole.) And do not forget the less well-known legislation on health, hygiene, noise abatement, etc, which may involve you in short-term inconvenience or, worse, long-term and expensive rounds of litigation.

---

* This could be extremely expensive if alterations to a club or cinema have to be made to comply with regulations. Consider this when you buy a property which you hope to convert, and check that an established business has a fire certificate.

WHICH BUSINESS?

Whatever type of service you provide, you will need sound financial backing, commercial acumen, the ability to offer something distinctive and market it accordingly, and patience in choosing the right opening. Fix on a 'target' population: advertise in newspapers and periodicals which they are likely to read, and be prepared for an initial struggle while you attempt to build up the business. The business field you choose to enter should be one in which you have some expertise, something distinctive to offer and a practical marketing strategy. But, even then, you will need resilience and the ability to work hard for long periods.

Useful information

British Institute of Innkeeping, Wessex House, 24 Park Street, Camberley, Surrey, GU15 3PL. Tel. 01276 684449. Web site: www.barzone.co.uk.

Careers Information Service, Hotel and Catering Training Company, International House, High Street, London W5 5DB. Tel. 020 8579 2400. Web site: www.htf.org.uk.

Hotel and Management International Management Association, 191 Trinity Road, London SW17 7HN. Tel. 020 8672 4251. Web site: www.hcima.org.uk/.

Brewers and Licensed Retailers Association, 42 Portman Square, London W1H 0BB. Tel. 020 7486 4831. Web site: www.blra.co.uk.

Careers in Catering and Management, Kogan Page
Guide to Careers in the Catering, Travel and Leisure Industries, Kogan Page
The Publican's Handbook, Kogan Page

2.4 Construction, Building and Maintenance Services

Builders, carpenters, plumbers and electricians are in constant demand. Established firms charge high labour rates, and people qualified in these trades can obtain a steady income by taking on extra work at reasonable rates. Alternatively, if you are more ambitious, you may start a building or redecoration company. You will need some capital, the necessary equipment, some means of transport, and a rudimentary administrative system – to take commissions for work, send invoices, check payments, keep tabs on costs, etc.

You may also need a tax exemption certificate, which customers (such as the local authorities) will require to ensure that you are a Schedule D taxpayer. If you work solely for private householders, small shops, etc, you will not need this certificate. But if you work for a main contractor, local authority or government department, you will have 30 per cent of all bills (except the cost of materials and VAT) automatically deducted by them, unless you have this certificate.

The Inland Revenue publishes a guide on how to apply for and use these certificates. If you are refused a certificate – and without one you will find work difficult to get – you can appeal within 28 days to the local General Commissioners.

TRAINING

The orthodox training for these trades is by entering into apprenticeship after leaving school, but it is now sometimes possible for older people to learn these skills at government training centres (details from your local employment office).

Much of the work available in private households consists either of very small jobs, such as putting up shelves or wallpapering, or conversion work, for which you must take into account building regulations and you or the house owner should get planning permission if applicable. You will find that the wider the range of skills you can offer, the more you will be in demand, since one job might involve both carpentry and decorating, for example.

It is advisable to work with a partner, since you will often need help with lifting, measurement, etc. You will also find that it is invaluable to have contacts who specialise in other, related trades, since you will often find that you cannot complete a job without the help of, say, an electrician. Contacts will also help you to find work since they will get in touch with you to finish jobs that they themselves cannot complete.

THE BUILDING REGULATIONS

Major structural changes must conform with national and local building regulations. If in doubt, consult your local authority (ask for the District Surveyor or Building Inspector).

Planning permission needs to be granted for external extensions exceeding 1300 cubic feet. If the building you are working on is listed as being of historic interest there may be regulations against changing its external appearance – again, check with the local authority. These problems concern the person who commissioned the work more than they affect you, but it is as well to guard yourself against liability.

HOW TO GET WORK

As explained above, contacts in related trades are invaluable. You might also obtain subcontracted work from small building firms.

Landlords and property agents are useful people to cultivate, as they often provide a great deal of maintenance and conversion work. You may also wish to advertise in the local press. But beware of making claims which you cannot support: do not, for example, say that you are a master builder if you hold no such certificate.

Sources of information

1. The Department of the Environment publishes a leaflet called *How To Find Out: Getting the Best from Building Information Services*, listing 80 important information sources for the construction industry. They also publish free leaflets on a wide range of subjects such as paint, water supply, mortar and rendering which may be of interest. Contact the Department of the Environment's free publication line on 0870 122 6236 and ask for leaflets to be sent to you covering the subject areas you require.

2. The Building Centre is at 26 Store Street, London WC1E 7BS (tel: 020 7637 1022). There is a bookshop and displays.

3. The Building Research Establishment is the largest and most comprehensive source of technical advice available to the construction industry. It operates from Watford.

PAINTING, DECORATING, PLUMBING AND ELECTRICAL WORK

These are areas which attract numerous 'cowboys' offering little or no expertise and a generally poor service. Fortunately, because continued custom depends so much on word of mouth, the rogues tend to fall by the wayside and only those offering a professional service survive. If you are experienced in one of these areas, try it for a while on a part-time basis and, if you have a steady stream of jobs and apparently satisfied customers, enter the profession full-time.

You will probably have been employed with a firm in this capacity and may at first worry about days (or weeks) without work and a long-term shortage of orders. But you must learn to live with the downturns, and price your work for jobs accordingly. These services are always in demand, and if you do a competent job at a competitive price you will survive. Word of mouth will win you most orders but, if you can cope with additional work, go out and look for it: put ads in the windows of local shops, in local newspapers and in the *Yellow Pages*.

'It's silly to start with no work in hand so make sure you have sufficient work before you take the plunge. By "sufficient" I don't mean bits and pieces but solid full-time jobs. Recommendation is better than advertising, and do a good job for a fair price.'

Painter and decorator

Useful information

Federation of Master Builders, 14–15 Great James Street, London WC1N 3DP. Tel. 020 7242 7583. Web: www.fmb.org.uk Construction Industry Training Board, Bircham Newton, King's Lynn, Norfolk PE31 6RH. Tel. 01485 577577, Web: www.citb.org.co.uk

Appendices

Useful Information

SECTOR INFORMATION FOR LOW INVESTMENT, PART-TIME AND FREELANCE OPPORTUNITIES

This is not an exhaustive list. However, it is an indicator of the range of opportunities available to people who want to work for themselves. Where possible details of trade associations and other sources of useful information are included. Information on training, qualifications and industry codes of conduct can generally be obtained from these sources. Further information can be obtained from *The A-Z of Careers and Jobs*, Kogan Page.

ACUPUNCTURIST

The British Acupuncture Council, 206 Latimer Road; tel: 020 8964 0222; Web site: www.info@acupuncture.org.uk
Working in Complementary and Alternative Medicine, Kogan Page.

AERIAL ERECTOR

Confederation of Aerial Industries Ltd (CAI), Fulton House Business Centre, Fulton Road, Wembley Park, Middlesex HA9 0TF; tel: 020 8902 8998.

ANTIQUE DEALER

British Antique Dealer's Association, 20 Rutland Gate, London SW7 1BD; tel: 020 7589 4128; Web site: www.bada.org

ART THERAPY

The British Association of Art Therapists, 11a Richmond Road, Brighton, East Sussex BN2 3RL.
Careers in Art and Design, Kogan Page.

BEAUTICIAN

British Association of Beauty Therapy and Cosmetology, Parabola House, Parabola Road, Cheltenham, Glos GL50 3AD; tel: 01242 570284.
International Health and Beauty Council, 46 Aldwick Road, Bognor Regis, West Susse PO21 2PN; tel: 01243 842064.
Careers in Hairdressing and Beauty Therapy, Kogan Page.

BLACKSMITH

The Farriers Registration Council, Sefton House, Adam Court, Newark Road, Peterborough PE1 5PP; tel: 01733 319911.
Herefordshire College of Technology, Folly Lane, Hereford HR1 1LS; tel: 01432 352235; Web site: www.hereford-tech.ac.uk
National Association of Farriers, Blacksmiths and Agricultural Engineers, Avenue R, Seventh Street, NAC, Stoneleigh, Kenilworth CV8 2LG; tel: 024 76 696595.

BOAT BUILDER

British Marine Industries Federation, Meadlake Place, Thorpe Lea Road, Egham, Surrey TW20 8HE; tel: 01784 473377; Web site: www.bmif.co.uk

BOOKSELLER

Booksellers Association of Great Britain and Ireland, Minster House, 272 Vauxhall Bridge Road, London SW1V 1BA; tel: 020 7834 5477; Web site: www.booksellers.org.uk

CARPENTER AND BENCH JOINER

Construction Industry Training Board, Bircham Newton, King's Lynn, Norfolk PE31 6RH; tel: 01485 577577; Web site: www.citb.org.uk
Institute of Carpenters, Central Office, 35 Hayworth Road, Sandiacre, Nottingham NG10 5LL; tel: 0115 9490641; Web site: www.central-office.co.uk
Practical Guide to _Woodworking Careers and Educational Facilities_, Guild of Master Craftsmen.

CARPET FITTER

National Institute of Carpet Fitters, 4D St Mary's Place, The Lace Market, Nottingham NG1 1PH; tel: 0115 958 3077; Web site: www.carpetinfo.co.uk

COMPUTERS/IT CONSULTANT

Association of Computer Professionals, 204 Barnett Wood Lane, Ashtead Surrey KT21 2DB; tel: 01372 273442.
British Computer Society, 1 Sanford Street, Swindon, Wiltshire SN1 1HJ; tel: 01793 417 417; Web site: www.bcs.org.uk
Freelance Informer, Reed Publications, 01753 567567.

CONFERENCE ORGANISING

The Association of Conferences and Events, ACE International, Riverside House, High Street, Huntingdon, Cambs PE18 6SG; tel: 01480 457595; Web site: www.martex.co.uk/ace

CONSERVATION (HISTORICAL)

Association of British Picture Restorers, Station Avenue, Kew, Richmond TW9 3QA; tel: 020 8948 5644; Web site: www.members.aol.com/abprlondon/abpr.htm
The Conservation Unit, Museum and Galleries Commission, 16 Queen Anne's Gate, London SW1H 9AA; tel: 020 7233 4200.
Institute of Paper Conservation, Leigh Lodge, Leigh, Worcester WR6 5LB; tel: 01886 832323; Web site: www.palimpsest.stanford.edu/ipc
Museums Association, 42 Clerkenwell Close, London EC1R 0PA; tel: 020 7608 2933; Web site: www.museumsassociation.org
Historic Scotland, Longmore House, Salsibury Place, Edinburgh EH9 1SH; tel: 0131 668 8600; Web site: www.historic-scotland.gov.uk
Scottish Society for Conservation and Restoration, The Glasite Meeting House, 33 Barony Street, Edinburgh EH3 6NX; tel: 0131 556 8417; Web site: www.sscr.demon.co.uk
Society of Archivists, 40 Northampton Road, London EC1R 0HB; tel: 020 7278 8630; Web site:www.archives.org.uk

COOKING

Careers Information Service, Hotel and Catering Training Company, International House, High Street, London W5 5DB; tel: 020 8579 2400; Web site: www.htf.org.uk
The Catering Management Handbook, Kogan Page.

DESIGNER

Chartered Society of Designers, 32-38 Saffron Hill, London EC1N 8SH; tel: 020 7831 9777.
Design Council, 34 Bow Street, London, WC2E; tel: 020 7420 5200; Web site: www.design-council.org.uk
Careers in Art and Design, Kogan Page.

DETECTIVE/PRIVATE INVESTIGATOR

Association of British Investigators, ABI House, 10 Bonner Hill Road, Kingston-Upon-Thames, Surrey KT1 3EP; tel: 020 8546 3368.

DISC JOCKEY

Phonographic Performance Ltd, 14-22 Ganton Street, London W1V 1LB; tel: 020 7437 0311.

DOG GROOMER

British Dog Groomers Association, Bedford Business Centre, 170 Mile Road, Bedford MK42 9TW; tel: 01234 273933; Web site: www.petcare.org.uk

DRAMA THERAPIST

British Association for Dramatherapists, 41 Broomhouse Lane, London SW6 3DP; tel: 020 7731 0160.

DRIVING INSTRUCTOR

Driving Instructor's Association, Safety House, Beddington Farm Road, Croydon CR0 4XZ; tel: 020 8665 5151.
Registrar of Approved Driving Instructors, Driving Standards Agency, Stanley House, 56 Talbot Street, Nottingham NG1 5GU; tel: 0115 901 2500.
The Driving Instructor's Handbook, Kogan Page.

EDITING

The Society of Freelance Editors and Proofreaders, Mermaid House, 1 Mermaid Court, London EC1 1HR; tel: 020 7403 5141; Web site:www.sfep.demon.co.uk

ESTATE AGENT

The Incorporated Society of Valuers and Auctioneers, 3 Cadogan Gate, London SW1X 0AS; tel: 020 7235 2282; Web site: www.isva.co.uk
The National Association of Estate Agents, Arbon House, 21 Jury Street, Warwick CV34 4EH; tel: 01926 496800; Web site:www. propertylive.co.uk

FILM PRODUCTION

Broadcasting, Entertainment, Cinematograph and Theatre Union (BECTU), 111 Wardour Street, London W1V 4AY; tel: 020 7437 8506; Web site: www.bectu.org.uk
FT2 (Film and Television Freelance Training), Fourth Floor, Warwick House, 9 Warwick Street, London W1R 5RA; tel: 020 7734 5141; Web site:www.FT2.org.uk

FLORIST

Floristry Training Council, Roebuck House, Hampstead Norreys Road, Hermitage, Thatcham, Berkshire RG18 9RX; tel: 01635 200465.

GARDENER

Institute of Horticulture, Askham Bryan College of Agriculture and Horticulture, Askham Bryan, York YO2 3PR; tel: 01904 772277; Web site:www.askham-bryan.ac.uk

Royal Horticultural Society, 14-15 Belgrave Square, London SW1X 8PS; tel: 020 7245 6943; Web site:www.horticulture. demon.co.uk
Careers Working Outdoors, Kogan Page.

GENEALOGIST

The Society of Genealogists, 14 Charterhouse Buildings, Goswell Road, London EC1M 7BA; tel: 020 7251 8799; Web site: HYPER-LINK http://www.sog.org.uk

GLAZIER

Construction Industry Training Board, Bircham Newton, King's Lynn, Norfolk PE31 6RH; tel: 01553 776677. Web site: HYPER-LINK http://www.citb.org.uk

HAIRDRESSER

Hairdressing Training Board, 3 Chequer Road, Doncaster DN1 2AA; tel: 01302 380000.
National Hairdressers' Federation, 11 Goldington Road, Bedford MK40 3JY; tel: 01234 360332.
Careers in Hairdressing and Beauty Therapy, Kogan Page.
Running Your Own Hairdressing Salon, Kogan Page.

HOMEOPATH

British School of Homeopathy, 23 Sarum Avenue, Melksham, Wiltshire SN12 6BN; tel: 01225 790051.
Society of Homeopaths, 2 Artizan Road, Northampton NN1 4HU; tel: 01604 621400; Web site: www.homeopathy.org.uk

HORTICULTURIST

See 'Gardener'.

ILLUSTRATOR

The Association of Illustrators, 1 Colville Place, London W1P 1HN; tel: 020 7733 5844.
Careers in Art and Design, Kogan Page.

INDEXER

Society of Indexers, Mermaid House, 1 Mermaid Court, London SE1 1HR; tel: 020 7403 4947.

INTERIOR DECORATOR/DESIGNER

Interior Designers and Decorators Association, 1-4 Chelsea Harbour Design Centre, Lots Road, London SW10 0XE; tel: 020 7349 0800; Web site:www.idda.co.uk
Chartered Society of Designers, 32-38 Saffron Hill, London EC1N 8SH; tel: 020 7831 9777.

INTERPRETER

Institute of Linguists, 24A Highbury Grove, London N5 2DQ; tel: 020 7359 7445.
Institute of Translation and Interpreting, 377 City Road, London, EC1V 1NA; tel: 020 7713 7600; Web site:www.iti.org.uk
Careers Using Languages, Kogan Page.

JEWELLERY

British Jewellers' Association, 10 Vyse Street, Birmingham B18 6LT; tel: 0121 237 1109; Web site: www.bja.org.uk
National Association of Goldsmiths, 78a Luke Street, London EC2A 4PY; tel: 020 7613 4445; Web site: www.jewellers.org

JOURNALIST

Chartered Institute of Journalists, 2 Dock Offices, Surrey Quays Road, London SE16 2XU; tel: 020 7252 1187; Web site: www.cioj.dircom.co.uk
National Council for the Training of Journalists, Latton Bush Centre, Southern Way, Harlow, Essex CM18 7BL; tel: 01279 430009; Web site:www.itecharlow.co.uk/nctj

LANDSCAPE ARCHITECT

The Landscape Institute, 6-7 Barnard Mews, London SW11 1QU; tel: 020 7738 9166; Web site: www.l-i.org.uk
Careers Working Outside, Kogan Page.

MANAGEMENT CONSULTANT

Institute of Management Consultants, 5th Floor, 32-33 Hatton Garden, London EC1N 8DL; tel: 020 7242 2140; Web site: www.imc.co.uk
Management Consultants Association, 11 West Halkin Street, London SW1X 8JL; tel: 020 7235 3897; Web site: www.mca.org.uk

MARKET RESEARCH

Market Research Society, 15 Northburgh Street, London EC1V 0AH; tel: 020 7490 4911.

MASSEUR

The Northern Institute of Massage, 100 Waterloo Road, Blackpool FY4 1AW; tel: 01253 403548.

MUSICIAN

Incorporated Society of Musicians, 10 Stratford Place, London W1N 9AE; tel: 020 7629 4413; Web site:www.ism.org
Musicians' Union, 60-62 Clapham Road, London SW9 0JJ; tel: 020 7582 5566; Web site:www.musiciansunion.org.uk

MUSIC THERAPIST

British Society for Music Therapy, 25 Rosslyn Avenue, East Barnet, Hertfordshire EN4 8DH.

NATUROPATH

The British College of Naturopathy and Osteopathy, Frazer House, 6 Netherhall Gardens, London NW3 5RR; tel: 020 7435 6464; Web site: www.bcno.org.uk

OFFICE SKILLS

Institute of Qualified Private Secretaries, First Floor, 6 Bridge Avenue, Maidenhead FL6 1RR; tel: 01628 625007; Web site: www.iqps.org

OSTEOPATH

See 'Naturopath'
Working in Complementary and Alternative Medicine, Kogan Page.

PHOTOGRAPHER

Association of Photographers Ltd, 81 Leonard Street, London EC2
4QS; tel: 020 7739 6669; Web site: www.aophoto.co.uk
British Institute of Professional Photography, Fox Talbot House,
Amwell End, Ware, Hertfordshire SG12 9HN; tel: 01920 464011;
Web site: www.bipp.com
The National Council for the Training of Journalists – see
'Journalist'

PIANO TUNER

Pianoforte Tuners' Association, c/o 10 Reculver Road, Herne Bay,
Kent CT6 6LD; tel: 01227 368808.

PLAYGROUP LEADER

Pre-School Playgroups Alliance, 69 King's Cross Road, London
WC1X 9LL; tel: 020 7833 0991.

PLUMBER

Institute of Plumbing, 64 Station Lane, Hornchurch, Essex RM12
6NB; tel: 01708 472791; Web site: www.plumbers.org.uk

POTTER

Crafts Council, 44a Pentonville Road, London N1 9BY; tel: 020
7278 7700; Web site:www.craftscouncil.org.uk
Contemporary Ceramics Association, 4 Marlborough Court,
London W1V 1PJ; tel: 020 7437 7605.

RIDING INSTRUCTOR

The British Horse Society, British Equestrian Centre, Stoneleigh, Kenilworth, Warwickshire CV8 2LR; tel: 01926 707700; Web site: HYPERLINK http://www.bhs.org.uk

SELLING

The Direct Selling Association, 29 Floral Street, London WC2B 9DP; tel: 020 7497 1234; Web site:www.dsa.org.uk

SPORTS COACH/PERSONAL TRAINER

Sports England, 16 Upper Woburn Place, London WC1H 0QP; tel: 020 7273 1500; Web site:www.english.sport.gov.uk
The Scottish Sports Council, Caledonia House, South Gyle, Edinburgh EH12 9DQ; tel: 0131 317 7200; Web site:www.ssc. org.uk
Careers in Sport, Kogan Page.

STEEPLEJACK

National Federation of Master Steeplejacks and Lightning Conductor Engineers, 4D St Mary's Place, The Lace Market, Nottingham NG1 1PH; tel: 0115 955 8818; Web site: www. nfmslce.co.uk

STONEMASON

Building Crafts College, 153 Great Tichfield Street, London W1P 7FR; tel: 020 7636 0480; Web site: www.TheCarpentersCompany. co.uk

TAXI DRIVER

Licensed Taxi Drivers Association, 9-11 Woodfield Road, London W9 2BA; tel: 020 7286 1046.

THATCHER

National Council of Master Thatchers Association, Thatcher's Rest, Levens Green Great Munden, Nr Ware, Hertfordshire SG11 1HD.

TOUR OPERATOR

Institute of Travel and Tourism, 113 Victoria Street, St Albans, Hertfordshire AL1 3TJ; tel: 01727 854395.

TRANSLATOR

See 'Interpreter'.
Careers Using Languages, Kogan Page.

UPHOLSTERER

London Guildhall University, Old Castle Street, London E1 7NT; tel: 020 7320 1000.

WINE TRADE

Wine and Spirit Education Trust, Five Kings House, 1 Queen Street Place, London EC4R 3AJ; tel: 020 7236 3551; Web site: www.wset.co.uk

WRITER

See 'Journalist'

Institute of Scientific and Technical Communicators, Kings Court, 2-16 Goodge Street, London W1P 1FF; tel: 020 7436 4425; Web site: www.istc.org.uk/istc

Society of Authors, 84 Drayton Gardens, London SW10 9SB; tel: 020 7373 6642; Web site: www.writer.org.uk/society

USEFUL CONTACTS

Government

The Adjudicator's Office
(For complaints against rulings by Customs and Excise)
Haymarket House
28 Haymarket
London SW1Y 4SP
Tel: 020 7930 2292
Web site:www.open.gov.uk/adjoff/aodemo1.htm

Business Links
Signpost Line: 08457 567765
freephone 0800 500200.

CCTA Government Information Service
A gateway to all Government Department Web sites:www.open.gov.uk

Central Office of Information
Web site: www.coi.gov.uk

Customs and Excise
New King's Beam House
22 Upper Ground
London SE1 9JP
Tel: 020 7620 1313
Web site: www.open.gov.uk/customs

The Data Protection Registrar
Wycliffe House
Wilmslow
Cheshire, SK9 5AF;
Tel: 01625 535777
Web site:
www.dpr.gov.uk

Department for Education and Employment
Sanctuary Buildings
Great Smith Street
London SW1P 3BT
Tel: 020 7925 5000
Web site: www.dfee.gov.uk

Department of the Environment, Transport and the Regions
Eland House
Bressenden Place
London SW1E 5DU
Tel: 020 7944 3000
Web site: www.detr.gov.uk

Department of Trade and Industry
Enquiries: 1 Victoria Street
London SW1H 0ET
Tel: 020 7215 5000.

Small Firms and Business Link Division: level 2,
DTI St Mary's House
c/o Department for Education and Employment
Moorfoot
Sheffield S14PQ
Tel: 0114 270 1356;
Web site: www.dti.gov.uk

Exports Credits Guarantee Department (ECGD)
PO Box 2200
2 Exchange Tower
Harbour Exchange Square
London E14 9GS
Tel: 020 7512 7421;
Web site: www.open.gov.uk/ecgd

Her Majesty's Treasury
The Public Enquiries Unit
Room 110/2
Treasury Chambers
Parliament Street
London SW1P 3AG
Tel: 020 7270 4558;
Web site: www.hm-treasury.gov.uk

Inland Revenue
The Inland Revenue has a number of helplines for enquiries, a listing of which can be found on its Web site at www.inlandrevenue.gov.uk

Office of Fair Trading
Field House
Breams Buildings
London EC4A 1PR
Tel: 020 7 211 8000
Web site: www.oft.gov.uk

Office for National Statistics
1 Drummond Gate
London SW1V 2QQ
Tel: 020 7533 6207;
Web site: www.ons.gov.uk

Rural Development Commission
141 Castle Street
Salisbury SP1 3TP
Tel: 01722 336255;
Web site: www.argonet.co.uk

Training and Enterprise Councils (TECs) and Local Enterprise Companies
List obtained from: Small Firms and
Business Link Division
Level 2
Department of Trade and Industry
St Mary's House
c/o Moorfoot
Sheffield S1 4PQ
Tel: 0114 270 1356;
Web site: www.tec.co.uk

Government Offices for the Regions

Four departments (Employment, Trade and Industry, Environment and Transport) have been organised into integrated offices known as Government Offices (GOs for the Regions.

Government Office for the East
Building A
Westbrook Centre
Milton Road
Cambridge CB4 1YG
Tel: 01223 346700;
Web site: www.go-east.gov.uk

Government Office for the East Midlands
The Belgrave Centre
Stanley Place
Talbot Street
Nottingham NG1 5GG
Tel: 0115 9719971.
Web site: www.go-em.gov.uk

Government Office for London
157-161 Millbank
London SW1P 4RK
Tel: 020 7217 3222
Web site: www.open.gov.uk/glondon

Government Office for the North East
Wellbar House
Gallowgate
Newcastle Upon Tyne NE1 4TX
Tel: 0191 201 3300

Government Office for the North West
Sunley Tower
Piccadilly Plaza
Manchester M1 4BE
Tel: 0161 952 4000
Web site: www.go.nw.gov.uk

Government Office for the South East
Bridge House
1 Walnut Tree Close
Guildford GU1 4GQ
Tel: 01483 882 255
Web site: www.go-se.gov.uk

Government Office for the South West
The Pithay,
Bristol BS1 2PB
Tel: 0117 927 2666
Web site: www.gosw.gov.uk/gosw

Mast House, Shepherds Wharf,
24 Sutton Road
Plymouth PL4 OHJ
Tel: 01752 221 891

294

**Government Office for the West
Midlands**
77 Paradise Circus
Queensway
Birmingham B1 2DT
Tel: 0121 212 5050
Web site: www.go-wm.gov.uk

**Government Office for Yorkshire and
Humberside**
25 Queen Street
Leeds LS1 2TW
Tel: 0113 244 3171
Web site: www.goyh.gov.uk

Government Office for
Northern Ireland

**Department of Economic
Development (DED)**
Netherleigh
Massey Avenue
Belfast BT4 2TP
Tel: 028 905299000.
Web site: www.nics.gov.uk/ni-
direct/ded/

Government Office for
Scotland

Scotland Office
1 Melville Crescent
Edinburgh EH3
Tel: 0207 2706754
Web site: www.scotland.gov.uk

Government Office for Wales

Welsh Office
Industry Department
Crown Building
Cathays Park
Cardiff CF1 3NQ
Tel: 029 20825111
Web site: www.wales.gov.uk

Start-up advice
England and Wales

Local Enterprise Agencies
Business in the Community
44 Baker Street
London W1M 1DH
Tel: 020 7224 1600
Web site: www.bitc.org.uk

The National Assembly for Wales
Industry and Training Department,
Cathays Park
Cardiff CF1 3NQ
Tel: 029 20825111
Web site: www.wales.gov.uk

Welsh Development Agency
Principality House
Friary
Cardiff
South Glamorgan CF1 4AE
Tel: 0845 775577
Web site: www.wda.co.uk

Scotland

Highlands and Islands Enterprise
Bridge House
20 Bridge Street
Inverness IV1 1QR
Tel: 01463 234171
Web site: www.hie.co.uk

Scottish Business in the Community
30 Hanover Street
Edinburgh EH2 2DR
Tel: 0131 220 3001.

Scottish Enterprise
120 Bothwell Street
Glasgow G2 7JP
Tel: 0141 248 2700
Web site: www.scotant.co.uk

The Office of the Scottish Executive
Education and Industry Department
Meridian Court
Cadogan Street
Glasgow G2 6AT
Tel: 0141 248 2855
Web site: www.scotland.gov.uk

Northern Ireland

Industrial Development Board for Northern Ireland
IDB House
64 Chichester Street
Belfast BT1 4JX
Tel: 028 90233233
Web site: www.aexandre.nics.gov.uk/idb

Local Enterprise Development Unit (LEDU)
LEDU House
Upper Galway
Belfast BT8 6TB
Tel: 028 90491031
Web site: www.ledu-ni.gov.uk

National associations representing small firms

Association of British Chambers of Commerce
9 Tufton Street
London SW1P 3QB
Tel: 020 7565 2000
Web site: www.britishchambers.org.uk

Association of Independent Business
Independence House
26 Addison Place
London W11 4RJ
Tel: 020 7371 1299

British Franchise Association
Thames View
Newton Road
Henley on Thames
Oxfordshire RG9 1HG
Tel: 01491 578049
Web site: www.british-franchise.org.uk

Confederation of British Industry (CBI)
Centre Point
103 New Oxford Street
London WC1A 1DU
Tel: 020 7379 7400
Web site: www.cbi.org.uk

Federation of Small Businesses Ltd
32 Orchard Road
Lytham St Annes
Lancs FY8 1NY
Tel: 01253 72091
Web site: www.fsb.org.uk

The Forum of Private Business Ltd
Ruskin Chambers
Drury Lane
Knutsford
Cheshire WA16 6HA
Tel: 01565 634467
Web site: www.fpb.co.uk

The Industrial Society
Peter Runge House
3 Carlton House Terrace
London SW1Y 5DG
Tel: 020 7839 4300
Web site: www.indsoc.co.uk

Smaller Firms Council (CBI)
Centre Point
103 New Oxford Street
London WC1A 1DU
Tel: 020 7379 7400
Web site: www.cbi.org.uk

Forming a company

Companies Limited/Rapid Refunds
376 Euston Road
London NW1 3BL
Tel: 020 7383 2323
Web site: www.limited-companies.co.uk
To buy an off-the-shelf company.

**Industrial Common Ownership
Movement (ICOM)**
Vassalli House
20 Central Road
Leeds LS1 6DE
Tel: 0113 246 1737.
Advice on setting up worker co-operatives.

The Institute of Business Advisers
PO Box 8
Harrogate
North Yorkshire, HG2 8XB
Tel: 01423 879208
Web site: www.iba.org.uk

The Institute of Directors
116 Pall Mall
London SW1Y 5ED
Tel: 020 78398 1233
Web site: www.iod.co.uk

Lawyers for Your Business
Law Society
113 Chancery Lane
London WC2A 1P
Tel: 020 7320 5764
Web site:www.lfyb.lawsociety.org.uk

The Patent Office
Cardiff Road
Newport
Gwent NP9 1RH
Tel: 01633 814000
Web site: www.patent.gov.uk

Registrar of Companies
Companies Registration Office
Crown Way
Maindy
Cardiff CF4 3UZ
Tel: 029 2038 8588
Web site: www.companies-house.gov.uk

For Scotland:
37 Castle Terrace
Edinburgh EH2 3DJ
Tel: 0131 535 5800

For London:
Companies Registration Office
55 City Road
London EC1Y 1BB
Tel: 020 7253 9393.

Banks

**Barclays Bank plc Small Business
Services**
PO Box 120
Longwood Close
Westwood Business Park
Coventry CV4 8JN
Tel: 024 76 694242
Web site: www.barclays.co.uk

HSBC plc Business Unit
6th Floor
Watlin Court
44-57 Cannon Street
London EC4M 5SQ
Tel: 020 7260 8711
Web site: www.banking.hsbc.co.uk

**Lloyds Bank plc, Small Business
Advice**
PO Box 112
Canons House
Canons Way
Bristol BS99 7LB
Tel: 0117 9433433
Web site: www.lloydstsb.co.uk

**National Westminster Bank plc,
Small Businesses Service**
Level 10 Drapers Gardens
12 Throgmorton Avenue
London EC2N 2DL
Tel: 020 7920 5555
Web site: www.natwest.co.uk

Raising capital

**Association of British Credit Unions
Ltd**
Holyoake House
Hanover Street
Manchester M60 0AS
Tel: 0161 832 3694

**British Insurance and Investment
Brokers Association**
BIIBA House
14 Bevis Marks
London EC3A 7NT
Tel: 020 7623 9043

British Venture Capital Association
Essex House
12-13 Essex Street
London WC2R 3AA
Tel: 020 7240 3846
Web site: www.bveg.co.uk

European Grants Ltd
94 Alfred Gelder Street
Hull HU1 2AL
Tel: 01482 211912
Web site: www.europeangrants.com

Factors and Discounters Association
Boston House
The Little Green
Richmond
Surrey TW9 1QE
Tel: 020 8332 9955
Web site: www.factors.org.uk

Finance and Leasing Association
Imperial House
15-19 Kings Way
London WC2B 6UN
Tel: 020 7836 6511
Web site: www.fig-org.uk

Institute of Patentees and Investors
Suite 505a
Triumph House
189 Regent Street
London W1R 7WF
Tel: 020 7434 1818

**Local Investment Networking Co
(LINC)**
London Enterprise Agency
4 Snow Hill
London EC1A 2BS
Tel: 020 7236 3000

The Prince's Youth Business Trust
18 Park Square East
London NW1 4LH
Tel: 020 7543 1234
Web site: www.princes-trust.org.uk

3I plc
9 Waterloo Road
London SE1 8XP
Tel: 020 7928 3131
Web site: www.3i.com/

Venture Capital Report Ltd
Magdalen Centre
Oxford Science Park
Oxford OX4 4GA
Tel: 01865 784411
Web site: www.vcr1978.com

Managing finance

Chartered Accountants Directory
Datacomp
4 Houldsworth Square
Reddish
Stockport
Cheshire SK5 7AF
Tel: 0161 442 5233
Web site: www.chartered-accountants.
co.uk

**Chartered Association of Certified
Accountants**
29 Lincoln's Inn Fields
London WC2
Tel: 020 7242 6855
Web site: www.acca.co.uk

Chartered Institute of Taxation
12 Upper Belgrave Street
London SW1X 8BB
Tel: 020 7235 2562
Web site: www.tax.org.uk

Institute of Chartered Accountants in England and Wales
PO Box 433
Chartered Accountants Hall
Moorgate Place
London EC2P 2BJ
Tel: 020 7920 8100
Web site: www.iacaew.co.uk

Institute of Chartered Accountants of Scotland
27 Queen Street
Edinburgh EH2 1LA
Tel: 0131 225 5673
Web site: www.cas.org-uk

Institute of Company Accountants
40 Tyndales Road
Clifton
Bristol BS8 1PL
Tel: 0117 973 8261

The International Association of Book-keepers
Burford House
London Road
Sevenoaks
Kent TN13 1AS
Tel: 01732 458080
Web site: www.iab.org.uk

Marketing and Sales

The Advertising Association
Abford House
15 Wilton Road
London SW1V 1NJ
Tel: 020 7828 2771
Web site: www.adassfoc.org.uk

British Safety Council
70 Chancellor's Road
London W6 9RS
Tel: 020 8741 1231
Web site:
www.britishsafetycouncil.org

British Standards Institution
389 Chiswick High Road
London W4 4AL
Tel: 020 8996 9000
Web site: www.bsi.org.uk

Chartered Institute of Marketing
Moor Hall
Cookham
Maidenhead
Berkshire SL6 9QH
Tel: 01628 457 500
Web site: www.cmi.co.uk

Direct Marketing Association UK Ltd
Haymarket House
1 Oxendon Street
London SW1Y 4EE
Tel: 020 7321 2525
Web site: www.dma.org.uk

Institute of Direct Marketing
1 Park Road
Teddington
Middlesex TW11 0AR
Tel: 020 8977 5705
Web site: www.theidm.com

Institute of Public Relations
The Old Trading House
15 Northburgh Street
London EC1V 0PR
Tel: 020 7253 5151
Web site: www.ipr.org.uk

Market Research Society
15 Northburgh Street
London EC1V 0AH
Tel: 020 7490 4911
Web site: www.mrs.org.uk

Marketing Society
St George's House,
3-5 Pepys Road
London SW20 8NJ
Tel: 020 8879 3464
Web site: www.marketing-society.org.uk

Appendices _____

Export

Association of British Chambers of Commerce
Export Marketing Research Scheme
4 Westwood House
Westwood Business Park
Coventry CV4 8HS
Tel: 024 76694484
Web site: www.britishchambers.org.
uk/exportzone

British Exporters Association
Broadway House
Tothill Street
London SW1H 9NQ
Tel: 020 7 222 5419
Web site: www.bexa.co.uk

British International Freight Association
Redfem House
Browells Lane
Feltham
Middlesex TW13 7EP
Te: 020 8844 2266
Web site:www.bifa.co.org

Commission of the European Communities
Jean Monet House
8 Storey's Gate
London SW1P 3AT
Tel: 020 7 973 1992

Department of Trade and Industry
Export Control Enquiry Unit,
Kingsgate House
66-74 Victoria Street
London SW1E 6SW
Tel: 020 7215 5444,
Web site: www.dti.gov.uk

European Commission
European Information Centres
8 Storey's Gate
London SW1P 3AT
Tel: 020 7973 1992

Export Credits Guarantee Department
2 Exchange Tower
PO Box 2200
Harbour Exchange Square
London E14 9GS
Tel: 020 7 512 7000
Web site: www.open.gov.uk/ecqd

Institute of Export
64 Clifton Street
London EC2A 4HB
Tel: 020 7247 9812
Web site: www.export.org.uk

London Chamber of Commerce and Industry
33 Queen Street
London EC4R 1AP
Tel: 020 7248 444
Web site: www.londonchamber.co.uk

Simpler Trade Procedures Board
Venture House
29 Glasshouse Street
London W1R 5RG
Tel: 020 7 287 3525

Technical Help for Exporters
British Standards Institution
389 Chiswick High Road
London W4 4AL
Tel: 020 8996 9000
Web site: www.bsi.org.uk

Trade Indemnity plc
12-34 Great Eastern Street
London EC2A 3AX
Tel: 020 7739 4311

TradeUK
Web site: www.tradeuk.com
Online advice on export issues and e-commerce.

Labour relations and personnel management

Advisory, Conciliation and Arbitration Service (ACAS)
Brandon House
180 Borough High Street
London SE1 1LW
Tel: 020 7 210 3000.
Web site: www.acas.org.uk

Health and Safety Executive
Rose Court
2 Southwark Bridge
London SE1 GHS
Tel: 020 7717 6000

Institute of Personnel and Development
IPD House
35 Camp Road
Wimbledon
London SW19 4UX
Tel: 020 8 971 9000
Web site: www.ipd.co.uk

The Institute of Management
Small Firms Information Service,
Management House
Cottingham Road
Corby
Northants NN17 7IT
Tel: 01536 204222
Web site: www.inst-mqt.org.uk

The Institute of Management Consultants
5th Floor
32-33 Hatton Garden
London EC1N 8DL
Tel: 020 8971 9000
Web site: www.imc.co.uk

Premises

English Partnership
St George's House
Kingsway
Team Valley
Gateshead
Tyne and Wear NE11 0NA
Tel: 0191 487 8941
Web site: www.englishpartnerships.co.uk

Estates Today
Web site: www.estatestoday.co.uk
Online commercial estate agent.

Royal Institution of Chartered Surveyors
12 Great George Street
Parliament Square
London SW1P 3AD
Tel: 020 7222 7000
Web site: www.rics.org

Information and communication technologies

British Telecom
Web:www.britishtelecom.co.uk
Advice on communications and information technologies for business.

eCentreuk
www.eca.org.uk

Exploit
Website : www.exploit.exploit.com
SubmitIt
Web site:www.submitit.com
These companies will submit your web site address to online search engines.

Information Society Initiative
For IT advice and support centres
Web site: www.isi.gov.uk

Internet Link Exchange
Web:www.linkexchange.com
Exchange advertising banner with
other sites.

Liszt
Web site: www.liszt.com
Description of most mailing lists and
joining details.

Nominet
To register Internet name
Web site:www.nic.uk

Technologies for Training
Web: www.tft.co.uk
Gateway to IT help with links to
numerous organisations working in IT.

WebCounter
www.digits.com
Adds visitor counter to your Web site.

FURTHER SOURCES OF INFORMATION

Specialist libraries

Business Information Service
British Library
Lloyds Bank Business Line
25 Southampton Buildings
London WC2A 1AW
Tel: 020 7412 7454/9799

Business Statistics Office
Government Buildings Cardiff Road
Newport
Gwent NP9 1XG
Tel: 01633 815696.
Website: www.ons.gov.uk

**Chartered Institute of Marketing
Library**
Moor Hall
Cookham
Maidenhead
Berkshire SL6 9QH
Tel: 0628 427 500.

**Department of Trade and Industry
Library**
Information and Library Centre
1 Victoria Street
London SW1H 0ET
Tel: 020 7215 5006/7

**Export Market Information Centre
Library**
Kingsgate House
66-74 Victoria Street
London SW1E 6SW
Tel: 020 7215 5444

**Frobisher Crescent Library at City
University**
Barbican
London EC2Y 8HB
Tel: 020 7477 8787
Web site: www.city.ac.uk

Institute of Management Library
Management House
Cottingham Road
Corby
Northants NN17 1TT
Tel: 01536 204222

London Business School Library
Sussex Place
Regents Park
London NW1 4SA
Tel: 020 7262 5050
Web site: www.lbs.lon.ac.uk/library

London Guildhall University
School of Business Studies
84 Moorgate
London EC2M 6SQ
Tel: 020 7320 1000

**Monopolies and Mergers
Commission Library**
New Court
48 Carey Street
London WC2A 2JT
Tel: 020 7324 1467

Office of Fair Trading Library
Field House
15-25 Bream's Buildings
London EC4A 1PR
Tel: 020 7242 2858.

Web sites of interest

DTI
Web site: www.dti.gov.uk
Good links to government-sponsored schemes.

Electronic Telegraph
Web site: www.telegraph.co.uk
Access to full text of _Daily Telegraph_ and directory listing of British business.

Enterprise Zone
Web site: www.enterprise-zone.org.uk
Extremely useful resource with useful links for Start-ups.

Financial Times
Web site: www.ft.com
Business directory and up-to-date financial information.

Keele University Management Web Resources Database
Web site: www.keele.ac.uk
Well resourced database of business and management Web sites with good links.

Kogan Page
Web site: www.kogan-page.co.uk
Extensive list of publications for start-ups and SMEs.

Strathclyde University Business Information Sources on the Internet
Web site: www.dis.strath.ac.uk
Thoroughly recommended Web site with extensive listings of sites and general sources of business information.

WhoWhere
Web site: www.whowhere.com
E-mail address, telephone number and street address directory.

Yahoo
Web site: www.yahoo.com
Search engine with extensive business directory.

Yell
Web: www.yell.co.uk
Online version of the _Yellow Pages_.

303

Select Bibliography

PART ONE

Accounting for Non-Accountants, 4th edition, Graham Mott (Kogan Page)
The Allied Dunbar Tax Guide, W I Sinclair (Longman, published annually)
Be Your Own Boss!, David McMullan (Kogan Page)
Be Your Own PR Man, Michael Bland (Kogan Page)
The Business Property Handbook (Royal Institution of Chartered Surveyors)
Croner's Reference Book for Exporters (Croner Publications Ltd)
Croner's Reference Book for the Self-employed and Smaller Business (Croner Publications Ltd)
Directory of Enterprise Agencies (Business in the Community)
Doing Business on the Internet, Simon Collin (Kogan Page)
Fair Deal: A Shopper's Guide (Office of Fair Trading)
Forming a Limited Company, 4th edition, Patricia Clayton (Kogan Page)
Going Freelance, 5th edition, Godfrey Golzen (Kogan Page)
A Guide to Franchising, Martin Mendelsohn (Cassell)
A Guide to Sources of Finance for SMEs, Michael Brand (Kogan Page)
Looking Ahead: A Guide to Retirement, Fred Kemp and Bernard Buttle (Springfield)
Management of Trade Credit, T G Hutson and J Butterworth (Gower Press)
Managing for Results, Peter F Drucker (Pan Books)
Getting Started in Export, Roger Bennett (Kogan Page)
Getting Started in Importing, John R Wilson (Kogan Page)
Self-Employment in the United Kingdom, Nigel Meager (Institute of Employment Studies)
The Small Business Casebook, Sue Birley (Macmillan Press)
The Small Business Guide, 4th edition, C Barrow (BBC Publications)
Small Business Guide, S Williams (Penguin)
Your Home Office, Peter Chatterton (Kogan Page)

Many of the pamphlets produced by the Department of Trade and Industry, the Department of Social Security, the Inland Revenue, the

Department for Education and Employment and the Department of the Environment will also be of value.

Also, a useful magazine is _Home Run_, Cribau Mill, Llanvair Discoed, Chepstow, Gwent NP6 6RD. Tel: 01291 641222. Fax: 61777.

PARTS 2, 3 AND 4

All About Selling, A Williams (McGraw-Hill)
British Rate & Data (monthly)
Careers in Catering and Management (Kogan Page)
The Catering Management Handbook 1994, Judy Ridgway and Brian Ridgway (Kogan Page)
Guide to Careers in the Catering, Travel and Leisure Industries (Kogan Page)
How to Run Your Own Restaurant, B Sim and William Gleeson (Kogan Page)
Money, Health and Your Retirement, E V Eves (Paperback Choice)
The Publican's Handbook (Kogan Page)
Setting up a Workshop (Crafts Council)
Writers' & Artists' Yearbook (A & C Black)
Writing for the BBC, Norman Longmate (BBC Publications)

OTHER USEFUL BOOKS FROM KOGAN PAGE

Buying a Shop, 4th edition, A St John Price
Law for the Small Business, 8th edition, Patricia Clayton
Running Your Own Boarding Kennels, 2nd edition, Sheila Zabawa
Running Your Own Catering Company, 2nd edition, Judy Ridgway
Running Your Own Photographic Business, 2nd edition, John Rose and Linda Hankin
Running Your Own Pub, 2nd edition, Elven Money
Running Your Own Shop, 2nd edition, Roger Cox
The Small Business Action Kit, 4th edition, John Rosthorn and others
Taking up a Franchise, 11th edition, Colin Barrow and Godfrey Golzen
Understand Your Accounts, 3rd edition, A St John Price

Be Your Own Accountant, Philip McNeill and Sarah J P Howarth
Budgeting for Business, Leon Hopkins
Business Cash Books Made Easy, Max Pullen
Business Plans, Brian Finch
Controlling Costs, John F Gittus
Costing Made Easy, Graham Mott

Pricing for Profit, Gregory Lewis
Taxes on Business, Kevin Armstrong

PUBLICATIONS FOR SMALL BUSINESSES FROM KOGAN PAGE

BDO Stoy Hayward Guide to the Family Business, 3rd edition, Peter Leach
The Business Plan Workbook, 3rd Edition, Colin Barrow and Robert Brown
Cheque's in the Post: Credit Control for the Small Business, Andrea Shavick
Do Your Own Bookkeeping, Max Pullen
Do Your Own Market Research, 3rd edition, Paul Hague
Financial Management for the Small Business, 4th edition, Colin Barrow
Getting Started in Export: A Practical Guide, 2nd edition, Roger Bennett
Getting Started in Importing, 2nd edition, John Wilson
How to Prepare a Business Plan, 3rd edition, Edward Blackwell
How to Set Up and Run Your Own Business, 15th edition
Practical Marketing and PR for the Small Business, 1998, Moi Ali
Running a Home Based Business, Diane Baker
Start Your Own Business in 30 Days, Gary Grappo
Successful Marketing for Small Business, 4th Edition, Dave Patten

A SELECTION FROM THE KOGAN PAGE CAREERS SERIES

Careers in Art and Design, 8th edition, Noel Chapman
Careers in Catering, Hotel Administration and Management, 5th edition, Russell Joseph
Careers in Computing and Information Technology, David Yardley
Careers in Fashion, 5th edition, Noel Chapman
Careers using Languages, 7th edition, Edda Ostarhild
Careers in Retailing, 1997, Loulou Brown
Careers Working Outdoors, 7th edition, Allan Shepherd

To order Kogan Page books contact:
Littlehampton Book Services
PO Box 53
Littlehampton BN17 7BU
Tel: 01903 828 800
Fax: 01903 828 802
E-mail: orders@lbsltd.co.uk

Or order through the Kogan Page Web site: www.kogan-page.co.uk

Index of Advertisers

Index

References to addresses of organisations are in italics.

Hotel and Catering Training Company 282
Hotel and Management International Management Association 272
hotels 262–63, 267–68
hours of work 4, 10, 31, 148, 248, 249

illustrators 286
improvement subsidies 71
Incorporated Society of Musicians 288
Incorporated Society of Valuers and Auctioneers 284
indexer 286
Industrial Development Board for Northern Ireland 296
industrial tribunal 149
industry sectors for business starters 6
inflation 117, 169
informal equity capital 76–78
information and communication technology (ICT) xi, xii, 182, 193, 196–98, 200, 214, 225–28
Information Society Initiative (ISI) 136, 196–97, 227, 301
inheritance 168–69
Inland Revenue 32, 59, 259, 273, 293 see also tax
Institute of Agricultural Secretaries and Administrators 260
Institute of Carpenters 281
Institute of Chartered Accountants 53, 54, 299
Institute of Directors 297
Institute of Horticulture 284
Institute of Linguists 286
Institute of Management 301
Institute of Management Consultants 287, 301
Institute of Paper Conservation 282
Institute of Plumbing 289
Institute of Qualified Private Secretaries 288
Institute of Scientific and Technical Communicators 292

Institute of Translation and Interpreting 286
Institute of Travel and Tourism 291
insurance 34, 49, 57–59, 62, 80, 161, 191, 243–44, 252, 267–68
insurance brokers 57, 62, 243, 244
intellectual property 61
interest 69, 70, 76, 80, 160–61, 164
Interior Designers and Decorators Association 286
International Health and Beauty Council 280
Internet 129, 135–36, 193, 196–98, 200, 214, 225–28
Internet service providers (ISPs) 214, 228
interpreters 286
Investors in Industry (3i) 70, 298
invoices 81, 98–102, 103, 143, 144
IT consultant 281

jewellery 287
Job Centre 74
job description 156
job satisfaction 9
job titles 148
'joint-and-several' liability 70
journalists 287
just-in-time manufacturing 3

landscape architects 287
Landscape Institute 287
large companies 122–23
law x, 39, 40, 98, 100, 147–56, 229–35, 252, 266, 267–68 see also solicitors
Lawplan 59
Law Society 53
lawyers see solicitors
Lawyers for Your Business (LFYB) 53, 297
layout and display 254
leasing xi, 29, 37, 50, 189–90, 253
ledger 90
letterheads 23, 30
letting rooms 40
liability 17, 19–20, 25, 30
licensing 268, 270

Index